American
SPEAK
OUT

Advanced
Student Book

with DVD/ROM and MP3 Audio CD

Pearson

Antonia Clare • JJ Wilson

)) CONTENTS

LESSON	GRAMMAR/FUNCTION	VOCABULARY	PRONUNCIATION	READING
UNIT 1 ORIGINS page 7 ● Interviews | How has your family influenced you?				
1.1 What's in a name? page 8	the continuous aspect	phrases with *name*	unstressed auxiliary verbs	read an article about names
1.2 What are you like? page 11	describing habits	personality; idioms for people	stressed/unstressed *will/would*	read a questionnaire about language learning
1.3 Picture perfect page 14	speculating	images	connected speech: linking, elision	read about photographic portraits
1.4 Francesco's Venice page 16				
UNIT 2 OPINION page 19 ● Interviews | What is the best or worst advice you've been given?				
2.1 Words of wisdom page 20	hypothetical conditional: past	learning and experience; metaphors	double contractions	read an article about good and bad advice
2.2 Changing your mind page 23	verb patterns	collocations: opinions	word stress	read an essay about homelessness
2.3 Who do you trust? page 26	introducing opinions	idioms of opinion	intonation for emphasis	read an article about the most and least trusted professions
2.4 Chess master page 28				
UNIT 3 PLACES page 31 ● Interviews | What is your favorite place?				
3.1 Lonely planet page 32	noun phrases	landscapes	word stress: compound nouns/adjectives	read three texts about memorable vacation moments; read a city guide
3.2 Home from home page 35	relative clauses	-y adjectives; prefixes	long/short vowels	read about a famous hotel
3.3 Welcome to perfect city page 38	making a proposal	city life	shifting stress: suffixes	read an article about solutions to urban problems
3.4 London page 40				
UNIT 4 JUSTICE page 43 ● Interviews | What legal or social issues concern you?				
4.1 Fight for justice page 44	introductory *it*	crime collocations; lexical chunks	pauses and chunking	read an article about a miscarriage of justice
4.2 Social issues page 47	the perfect aspect	social issues	stress patterns	
4.3 Do the right thing page 50	expressing hypothetical preferences	decisions	intonation: adding emphasis	read about a real-life hero
4.4 The con artist page 52				
UNIT 5 SECRETS page 55 ● Interviews | Are you good at keeping secrets?				
5.1 Family secrets page 56	modal verbs and related phrases	idioms: secrets	connected speech: elision	read a true story
5.2 Truth or myth? page 59	the passive	truth or myth; multi-word verbs	stress: multi-word verbs	read about everyday myths
5.3 Tell me no lies page 62	making a point	journalism	intonation: appropriacy	read about investigative journalism
5.4 Secret Island page 64				

DVD-ROM: ● DVD CLIPS AND SCRIPTS   ● INTERVIEWS AND SCRIPTS

LISTENING/DVD	SPEAKING	WRITING
	talk about names	write a personal profile
listen to a radio program about a personality test	discuss the results of a personality test	
listen to a discussion about photographic portraits	speculate about people based on their portraits	
▶ **Francesco's Venice:** watch a documentary about Venice	describe a treasured possession	write a description of an object
	talk about words of wisdom	
listen to a radio program about a living library event	discuss controversial ideas	write a discursive essay
listen to a discussion about trustworthiness	discuss dilemmas at work	
▶ **The Young Chess Master:** watch a program about a young chess prodigy	take part in a panel discussion	write a summary
	describe a vacation memory	write a guidebook entry
listen to an account of homes around the world	talk about an "alternative" home	
listen to a proposal for a city improvement scheme	make a proposal	
▶ **One day in London:** watch a program about London	present a documentary proposal	write a proposal for a documentary
	talk about criminal justice	
listen to people describe someone they admire	discuss social issues	write a problem-solution essay
listen to a discussion about witnessing a crime	discuss moral dilemmas	
▶ **The Con Artist:** watch a program about a con artist	recount a crime story	write a short article
listen to a radio program about secrets	talk about secrets	write a narrative
	debunk a myth	
listen to a conversation about WikiLeaks	discuss freedom of information	
▶ **New York's Abandoned Island:** watch a program about a secret island	talk about secret places in your city	write a secrets guide

▶ CLASS AUDIO AND SCRIPTS

)) CONTENTS

LESSON	GRAMMAR/FUNCTION	VOCABULARY	PRONUNCIATION	READING
UNIT 6 TRENDS page 67 ▶ Interviews | Do you follow trends in music and fashion?				
6.1 Future gazing page 68	future forms	predictions	connected speech: auxiliary verbs	read about the far future
6.2 A global language? page 71	concession clauses	language	intonation: concession clauses	read about a radio program
6.3 Trendsetters page 74	describing cause and effect	trends	connected speech: swallowed sounds	read about how trends spread
6.4 Tech Trends page 76				
UNIT 7 FREEDOM page 79 ▶ Interviews | What makes you feel free?				
7.1 The great escape page 80	cleft sentences	collocations	word stress: suffixes	read an article about a man who disappeared
7.2 Switching off page 83	participle clauses	idioms: relaxing	word stress: idioms	read a promotional leaflet
7.3 Free to make mistakes page 86	exchanging opinions	risk	polite tone	read an article about safety and risk
7.4 Gandhi: The Road to Freedom page 88				
UNIT 8 TIME page 91 ▶ Interviews | What is the best time of life?				
8.1 History in a box page 92	future in the past	time expressions; proverbs	rhythm: proverbs	read about time capsules
8.2 I remember … page 95	ellipsis and substitution	memories	connected speech	read a personal story
8.3 Time savers page 98	discussing ideas	collocations with *time*	word stress: phrases	read time-saving tips
8.4 What is time? page 100				
UNIT 9 INSPIRATION page 103 ▶ Interviews | Do you do anything creative in your life?				
9.1 Icons page 104	tenses for unreal situations	adjectives: the arts	irregular spellings	read about living statues
9.2 Feeling inspired page 107	adverbials	ideas	pronunciation: "o"	
9.3 Love it or hate it page 110	ranting/raving	express yourself	positive/negative intonation	read a website extract
9.4 The Philanthropist page 112				
UNIT 10 HORIZONS page 115 ▶ Interviews | What are your goals in life?				
10.1 On the road page 116	inversion	collocations	stress/unstress	read about an epic car journey
10.2 Dreams come true? page 119	comparative structures	ambition	intonation: emphasis; rhythm	read an essay about celebrity
10.3 Making a plan page 122	negotiating	negotiation	polite intonation	read tips for negotiating
10.4 Wildest Dreams page 124				

IRREGULAR VERBS page 127   LANGUAGE BANK page 128   VOCABULARY BANK page 148

4

LISTENING/DVD	SPEAKING	WRITING
	evaluate future inventions	
listen to a program about global English	discuss trends in language learning	complete a report
listen to descriptions of how trends started	describe changes in your country	
▶ **Technology Trends:** watch an extract from a program about technology trends	decide which trends to fund	write about a trend
	talk about an escape plan	
listen to people describing how they relax	discuss ways to escape your routine	write a promotional leaflet
listen to a discussion about whether children are over-protected	talk about personal choice	
▶ **Gandhi:** Watch a documentary about Mohandas Gandhi	talk about freedom	write about what freedom means to you
	choose objects that represent you	
listen to a program about memory and smell	talk about memories	write a personal story
listen to an interview about time management	discuss ways to save time	
▶ **Wonders of the Universe:** watch an extract from a documentary about the role of time in the creation of the universe	talk about a turning point in your life	write about a major decision in your life
	choose sculptures to suit clients' needs	
listen to people talking about where they get their ideas	talk about boosting creativity	write a review
listen to rants/raves	rant or rave	
▶ **The Vegetable Seller:** watch an extract from a program about an unusual philanthropist	nominate someone for an award	write about an inspirational person
	plan your dream adventure	
listen to an author reading from his memoirs	talk about real-life success stories	write a "for and against" essay
listen to a talk about stages in a negotiation	negotiate a plan for a film festival	
▶ **Wildest Dreams:** watch a program about budding wildlife filmmakers	present ideas about a dream job	write about your dream job

COMMUNICATION BANK page 158   AUDIO SCRIPTS page 165

PARTS OF SPEECH

1 A Complete the text with the words/phrases in the box.

> according   to forget   changed
> remembering   Interestingly
> It's been suggested   the
> get hold of   might   on

Has Google made us stupid?

The rise of Google and other search engines has [1]_____ the way we remember information, [2]_____ to research. Because we now have access to all [3]_____ information we could possibly want at the touch of a button, we no longer need to store so much information in our heads. [4]_____ that this is actually changing the way our brains store and recall information. We're quite likely [5]_____ information that we believe we can find online and more likely to remember something that we [6]_____ not be able to access on the internet. We are now better at remembering where we can [7]_____ the information than we are at [8]_____ the information itself. [9]_____, the brain is a malleable organ, which changes according to our circumstances. So, it's not just Google that can change the way we remember things. We have always looked to "experts" to remember things for us. And even in more informal ways, long-term couples also learn to rely [10]_____ each other for remembering information. Now, where did I put my keys?

B Match the words in the box above with parts of speech 1—10.

1 present participle
2 past participle
3 infinitive with *to*
4 adverb
5 definite article
6 multi-word verb
7 modal verb
8 passive
9 gerund
10 dependent preposition

ERROR CORRECTION

2 A Correct the mistakes. There is one mistake in each sentence.

1 One of the most interesting of things about my job is the people I meet.
2 I haven't seen my parents since five years.
3 I studied geography in college, so I'm knowing a lot about different countries.
4 I haven't told nobody about my hobby.
5 Its difficult to find work these days.
6 I've been to Spain many times in last few years.
7 Do you think it's enough warm for me to go without a coat?
8 I adore to live by the sea.

B Find one example of each mistake in sentences 1—8 above.

a) incorrect tense
b) incorrect word order
c) incorrect pronoun
d) incorrect preposition
e) incorrect punctuation
f) incorrect verb pattern
g) missing word
h) extra word

C Rewrite three of the sentences to make them true for you. Compare your sentences in pairs.

PRONUNCIATION

3 A Work in pairs. Which underlined sound is the odd one out?

1 f<u>ie</u>rce   s<u>ee</u>k   h<u>ea</u>r
2 b<u>ou</u>ght   h<u>ou</u>se   c<u>ow</u>
3 s<u>ai</u>l   bl<u>a</u>me   <u>a</u>ware
4 c<u>al</u>m   b<u>ea</u>r   h<u>ea</u>rt

B Listen and check.

C Listen and check the words you hear. Then read the pairs of words aloud.

1 badge batch
2 thistle this'll
3 of off
4 vision fission
5 rise rice
6 pig pick

MULTI-WORD VERBS

4 A Read the definitions. Complete the multi-word verbs with the words in the box.

> look   work   get   watch
> hold   carry   make   come

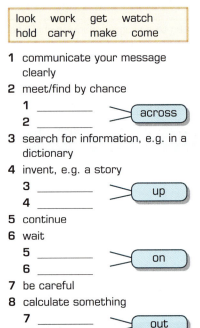

1 communicate your message clearly
2 meet/find by chance
   1 _____
   2 _____ ⟩ across
3 search for information, e.g. in a dictionary
4 invent, e.g. a story
   3 _____
   4 _____ ⟩ up
5 continue
6 wait
   5 _____
   6 _____ ⟩ on
7 be careful
8 calculate something
   7 _____
   8 _____ ⟩ out

B Work in pairs. What should you do when you hear a new multi-word verb? Write advice using some of the multi-word verbs above.

When you come across a new multi-word verb …

REGISTER

5 Read sentences a)—f). Answer questions 1—3 for each sentence.

a) All guests must be signed in by a member.
b) A bunch of people turned up at his place well after midnight.
c) The committee reached an affirmative decision with regard to termination of his contract.
d) Are you gonna be at the game on Saturday?
e) Great food, this.
f) Payment shall be subject to the fulfilment of clause 5.3.

1 Is the sentence formal or informal? How do you know?
2 Where might you see/hear it?
3 Can you rephrase the sentence to change the register?

1) Origins

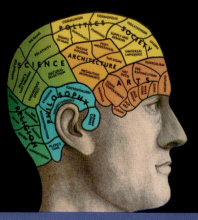

WHAT'S IN A NAME?   p8

WHAT ARE YOU LIKE?   p11

PICTURE PERFECT   p14

FRANCESCO'S VENICE   p16

SPEAKING	1.1 Talk about names
	1.2 Discuss the results of a personality test
	1.3 Speculate about people based on their portraits
	1.4 Describe a treasured possession
LISTENING	1.2 Listen to a radio program about a personality test
	1.3 Listen to a discussion about photographic portraits
	1.4 Watch a documentary about Venice
READING	1.1 Read an article about names
	1.2 Read a questionnaire about language learning
WRITING	1.1 Write a personal profile
	1.4 Write a description of an object

How has your family influenced you?

INTERVIEWS

1.1))) WHAT'S IN A NAME?

G the continuous aspect
P unstressed auxiliary verbs
V phrases with *name*

SPEAKING

1 Work in groups. Check you know everyone's name. Discuss the questions.

1 Do you think your name is difficult to pronounce for foreigners? Why/Why not? Is it an international name, or is it mainly used in your country?

2 Do you have any nicknames? How did you get them?

VOCABULARY

PHRASES WITH *NAME*

2 A Choose the correct words to complete the expressions in bold. Compare your answers with other students.

1 I was **named** *after/to* my great-grandmother. She was also **named** Linda.

2 I'm from a famous family and it's not easy to **live** *on/up* **to** my name.

3 I worked hard for twenty years and *did/made* **a name for myself** in movies.

4 He used to be **a** *household/celebrity* **name**, but he's not famous anymore.

5 I *threw/put* **my name forward** for class president.

6 Even though she was innocent, it took her years to *clear/clean* **her name**.

7 She addressed all her employees *by/for* **name**.

8 He was a king *in/through* **name only**. He had no power.

9 My **last name** is Jones, my **middle name** is Wheatley, and my *first/main* **name** is Stephen.

10 My *maiden/born* **name** is Smith, but my **married name** is Edelstein.

B Work in pairs and answer the questions. Which of the expressions:

a) are on your passport/identity document?

b) might change in your lifetime?

c) are related to reputation?

d) means "using their names"?

e) means "volunteered"?

f) means "famous"?

g) means "it's only a title"?

h) is in honor of someone else?

C Work in pairs. Think of someone who:

• is a household name.

• had to clear their name.

• has made a name for him/herself recently.

• has to live up to his/her name.

• used to be a big name.

• is so famous that they're known by their first name.

READING

3 A Work in pairs and discuss the questions.

1 What do you think are the world's most common first names?

2 What are the most common last names in your country?

3 Why do you think people change their names?

B Read the article and complete the sentence.

The main idea of the text is that ...

C Answer the questions.

1 According to the article, is it only celebrities who choose strange names for their children?

2 What do the results of Mehrabian's research show?

3 According to the study in paragraph 6, how might your name affect your chances of getting a job?

4 In Satran's opinion, what influences the way people name their children?

4 A Work in pairs and discuss the questions.

1 Do you agree with Mehrabian that "Names generate impressions"?

2 Do you agree with Satran that "Celebrity culture and ethnic diversity have made people much more eager to look for a wide range of names of their own"?

3 Why do you think certain names are associated with success?

4 The research for this article was done in the USA. Do you think the results would be the same if the research was done in your country?

B The article contains several colloquial expressions. What do you think words/phrases 1—7 mean? Use a dictionary to help you if necessary.

1 favoring (paragraph 1)

2 increasingly outlandish (paragraph 2)

3 reach the top of the tree (paragraph 5)

4 career-wise (paragraph 5)

5 cut and dried (paragraph 6)

6 call-backs (paragraph 6)

7 individuals like (paragraph 7)

named / movies / last name / first name   called / film / surname / given name

Making your name

Approximately 130 million babies are born each year, and under normal circumstances, they all get a name within days of their birth. The most common given name is thought to be Mohamed (it can be spelled in different ways). And the most unusual? Well, take your pick. British model Jordan called her daughter Princess Tiaamii; Jermaine Jackson (Michael Jackson's brother) named his son Jermajesty; and actor-director Sylvester Stallone called his son Sage Moonblood. But it isn't just celebrities who are favoring strange-sounding names.

"My students have increasingly outlandish names," says one secondary school teacher from London. She cites "poorly spelled names" such as Amba, Jordon, Charlee and Moniqua, and what she calls "absurd names" like Shaliqua and Sharday. How will such names affect her students when they go out to get a job? "I think it's a serious disadvantage," she says.

Albert Mehrabian, professor emeritus of psychology at the University of California, agrees with her. "Names generate impressions, just like a person's appearance can generate a positive or negative impression, "he says. "But names also have an impact when you're not physically present, such as when you send in a résumé."

Mehrabian researched people's instinctive reactions to hundreds of first names. It's striking how many positive associations some names carry, and how negative the connotations of others turn out to be – particularly when it comes to linking names with "success", which Mehrabian takes to include ambition, intelligence, confidence and other attributes.

So what kind of name does it take to reach the top of the tree, career-wise? Based on research in the USA, Mehrabian says that Alexander scores 100 percent for "success". William gets 99 percent and John 98 percent. For the girls, Jacqueline rates very highly, as do Diana, Danielle and Catherine, although Katherine with a k does slightly better than Catherine with a c.

But can the impact of a first name really be that cut and dried? Pamela Satran, co-author of eight baby-naming books, is less convinced that the power of a name can be quantified. "There isn't that much hard evidence that's absolutely conclusive," says Satran. She recalls one American study where researchers submitted identical résumés to a number of employers. The given name on half of the résumés was Lashanda, "seen as a stereotypical African-American name," says Satran. The name on the other half was Lauren – seen as much more white and middle class. In one study, the name Lauren got five times more call-backs than Lashanda, says Satran. But in another study the rate was similar for both names. "I've seen similarly conflicting studies," Satran adds.

Satran also believes that people's attitudes towards names are changing. She says, "Celebrity culture and ethnic diversity have made people much more eager to look for a wide range of names of their own. The thinking is: if you have a special name, that makes you a special person." Let's hope so for individuals like a certain individual born in 1990 in Java; this young man is named Batman bin Suparman, a name that went viral and spawned a Facebook fan page that now has over 11,000 followers.

GRAMMAR
THE CONTINUOUS ASPECT

5 A Check what you know. Why is the continuous form used in these sentences?

1 These days it's getting easier and easier to change your name.

2 She's always talking as if she's a household name, but she's only been on TV once!

3 I'm considering naming my dog after my hero: Che Guevara.

4 The author of the book has been trying to think of a good name for it for months.

5 My partner was reading a book about babies' names when I got home.

6 I was hoping to borrow your car, if that's OK.

B Check your answers. Match uses a)—f) with sentences 1—6 above.

a) to describe a background action that was in progress when another (shorter) action happened *5*

b) to talk about something that's incomplete, temporary, or still in progress (often emphasizing the length of time)

c) to talk about situations that are in the process of changing

d) to emphasize repeated actions (that may be annoying)

e) for plans that may not be definite

f) to sound tentative and less direct when we make proposals, inquiries, suggestions, etc.

▶ page 128 **LANGUAGE**BANK

6 A Which underlined verbs would be better in the continuous form? Why? Change them as necessary.

1 John's not in the office. He might have lunch.
   be having (The action is still in progress.)

2 I'm fed up. We've waited for an hour!

3 She owns a small house by the river.

4 Can you be quiet? I try to work.

5 The letter arrived today. She had expected the news since Monday.

6 That chicken dish tasted great.

7 Who do these keys belong to?

8 By next September, we will have lived here for twenty-five years.

9 I work on a project at the moment.

10 My partner made dinner when I got home, so I helped.

B Listen and check your answers.

C UNSTRESSED AUXILIARY VERBS Listen to some of the sentences in Exercise 6A. How are the auxiliary verbs *was, have, been*, etc. pronounced in the continuous form? Listen again and repeat the sentences.

7 Complete the sentences to make them true for you. Make the verbs negative if necessary.

1 I work …/I've been working …

2 I study …/At the moment I'm studying …

3 I usually write …/I've been writing …

spelled / students / résumé / emphasize   spelt / pupils / CV / emphasise

about us

WRITING

**A PERSONAL PROFILE;
LEARN TO PLAN YOUR WRITING**

8 A Read the personal profile. Where do you think it will appear?

Mira Kaya

About me

I'm half-Turkish, half-British. I was born in Istanbul, but I live in London. I'm the author of over a dozen children's books and several plays that have been produced in the U.K., France, Turkey, Germany and other countries.

For six years, I was a teacher at a school in North London, where I worked extensively with children with learning difficulties. This led to my first publication, a picture book named *Bobby Blue's Big Day*. The story was later made into a short movie. Other books followed, including *Night Owl* and the *Rooftop Ringleaders* series, for which I was nominated for several awards.

Besides writing, my passion is cycling. I hit the road whenever I have a spare moment (there aren't many), and can be found whizzing up hills outside London in bright yellow spandex most Saturdays. My other passion is my two wonderful children: Gulay and Baha, who are the first editors for every story I write. My second editor is my husband Martin. We've been married for ten years.

B Read the guidelines for writing a personal profile. To what extent does Mira Kaya's profile follow them?

1 Share positive things.
2 Keep it short: condense rather than use very long sentences.
3 Choose specific details and examples, not generalizations.
4 Don't lie, boast or exaggerate.
5 Keep it informal and friendly.

9 A Which information in the box would you include in a profile for:

• a blog/a social networking site?
• a networking site for professionals/a job application?

> where you're from   family information
> likes/dislikes   hobbies   talents and skills
> education/grades/qualifications   goals and plans
> favorite music/food
>
> religious or spiritual beliefs   address
> pet peeves   groups you belong to
>
> job   trips and unusual experiences
> professional achievements

B What information from the box above would you leave out?

> **American Speak TIP** Think of writing as a conversation. Always remember your audience. Who will read your writing? What do they expect (think about content, length, tone and formality)? What do they know about the topic?

10 A Look at the outline of a profile for a personal website. Is there any information that is NOT suitable?

Introduction:	name & where I'm from
Interests:	love children, music, dance
Skills:	play guitar & piano, drawing, costume-making
Qualifications:	3 "A" Levels: Geography, History, English; Bachelor's: Geography
Family:	husband & daughter

B Discuss. Which of the following things do you do when you write? What does it depend on?

1 Brainstorm ideas.
2 Write notes.
3 Write an outline.
4 Discuss your ideas with someone before writing.
5 Visualize your readers and imagine how they will react to your writing.
6 Write the first draft quickly and roughly.

11 Write a personal profile as part of a class profile. Follow stages 1—4 below.

1 Think about your audience and what you need to include. Make notes.
2 Write an outline for your profile.
3 Write your profile (150—200 words). Check it and make any corrections.
4 Share your profile with other students. What common features are there in your class, e.g. professions, hobbies, where you're from, etc.?

> "A" Levels are pre-university qualifications given for two-year programs in different subjects. There is no exact equivalent in the American school system.

generalization / favorite / visualize   generalisation / favourite / visualise

G describing habits
P stressed/unstressed will/would
V personality; idioms for people

Are you a good language learner?

1 I'm always watching videos or reading articles in English, and that helps me a lot.
Gwen_H

2 I'm quite analytical, so I have a tendency to focus on grammar and on being accurate.
grammargeek

3 I'm always looking for opportunities to use and learn the language outside class. I just need to keep practicing.
Claudio96

4 As a rule, I'm happy to take risks with language and experiment with new ways of learning.
Araksan

5 I'm inclined to be very analytical. Like a detective, I'll look for clues that will help me understand how language works.
techgirl

6 I'm prone to making mistakes with grammar, but I have a good ear for language, so nine times out of ten, I'll just know if something is wrong. I use my instincts and when I don't know, I guess.
MaxK

7 When I started, I tended to get frustrated because I kept making mistakes. Now, I've learned not to be embarrassed.
wei chen

8 At first, I would spend hours studying grammar rules, but I didn't use to have the confidence to speak. So I decided to set myself goals to improve my pronunciation and speak as much as possible.
Sveta GK

SPEAKING

1 A Read the comments on the message board. Do statements 1—8 apply to you? Mark each statement:

✓✓ strongly agree ✓ agree
✗ disagree ✗✗ strongly disagree

B Work in pairs and compare your answers. Is there anything you do that should be included on the list? Is there anything your partner does that could help you to improve?

GRAMMAR
DESCRIBING HABITS

2 A Look at the questionnaire again and underline verbs/expressions used to describe present or past habits. Add examples to complete the table.

present habit	past habit
1 *will* + infinitive **I'll look** *for clues that will help me.*	8 *used to* + infinitive _____ 9 *would* + infinitive _____
2 *is always* + *-ing* _____, _____	10 *was always* + *-ing* **I was always looking** *for new ways to*
3 *keep (on)* + *-ing* *She **keeps on** calling me.*	11 *kept (on)* + *-ing* _____
other phrases to describe a present habit	**other phrases to describe a past habit**
4 *I have an inclination to/* *I'm _____ to/* *I'm _____ to*	12 *I was forever making mistakes.*
5 *I'm prone to/I tend to/I have _____ to*	13 *I was prone to* _____
6 *As a* _____	
7 *Nine times* _____	

B Listen and write sentences 1—3. Check your answers in audio script S1.3 on page 165.

C STRESSED/UNSTRESSED *WILL/WOULD* Listen to the sentences being said in two different ways. What effect does the change in pronunciation have on the meaning?

D Listen and repeat the sentences. In which sentence does the person NOT sound annoyed?

▶ page 128 LANGUAGE**BANK**

3 A Add the words in the box to sentences 1—6.

to as would looking of a

1 I have̷ tendency to sleep in late.
       a
2 I'm not inclined be very laid-back.
3 I'm always for new things to learn.
4 A rule, I try not to work on the weekend.
5 Nine times out ten, I'll be right about my first impressions.
6 As a child, I spend hours reading.

B Make two or three of the sentences in Exercise 3A true for you. Compare your ideas in pairs.

C Think about a good/bad habit that you, or other people you know, have. Did you have this habit or other good/bad habits as a child? Tell your partner. Do/Did they share any of the same habits?

practicing / learned / on the weekend

practising / learnt / at the weekend

VOCABULARY
PERSONALITY

4 A Work in pairs. Brainstorm adjectives for describing people's personalities.

B Look at the words in the box. Give examples of how people with these qualities might behave.

> perceptive   inspirational   over-ambitious   conscientious
> obstinate   neurotic   open-minded   prejudiced   apathetic
> insensitive   solitary   rebellious   mature   inquisitive

C Find a word in the box above to describe someone who:

1 notices things quickly and understands people's feelings.
2 has an unreasonable dislike of a thing or a group of people.
3 is not interested or willing to make the effort to do anything.
4 is determined not to change their ideas, behavior or opinions.
5 deliberately disobeys people in authority or rules of behavior.
6 spends a lot of time alone because they like being alone.
7 is unreasonably anxious or afraid.
8 is willing to consider or accept other people's ideas or opinions.

D Work in pairs and write definitions for the other words in Exercise 4B. Choose three words your friends would/wouldn't use to describe you.

▶ page 148 VOCABULARYBANK

LISTENING

5 A Read the radio program listing below and answer the questions.

1 What does the Myers-Briggs Type Indicator do?
2 Who uses it?
3 Do you think this type of test can be useful? Why/Why not?

B Listen to the program and answer the questions.

1 According to the program, what causes a lot of stress at work?
2 What kinds of people does the MBTI test?
3 What kinds of questions does the interviewer ask Mariella?

How Myers-Briggs Conquered the Office

It was created by a mother and daughter team, neither of whom were trained as psychologists, yet today it is the world's most widely used personality indicator, used by leading companies like Shell, Procter & Gamble, Vodafone and the BBC. In this radio program, Mariella Frostrup tells the story of The Myers-Briggs Type Indicator (MBTI), created by Katherine Briggs and her daughter Isabel Briggs Myers. Participants are asked a series of questions intended to reveal information about their thinking, problem-solving and communication styles. At the end of the process each participant is handed one of sixteen four-letter acronyms which describes their "type". ENTPs are extrovert inventors, ISTJs are meticulous nit-pickers. Mariella finds out what type she is – will it change the way she works?

6 A What do the following expressions from the program mean?

1 sweeping generalizers
2 detail-obsessed nit-pickers
3 obsessive planners
4 last-minute deadline junkies
5 recharge your batteries
6 ready-to-assemble furniture

B Listen again. Choose the option, a), b) or c), which best describes Mariella's answer to the question.

1 How do you like to recharge your batteries at the end of the day?
   a) She goes out for a nice meal.
   b) She stays at home and reads a book.
   c) She watches TV and goes to bed.

2 If you have ever had the opportunity to put together any ready-to-assemble furniture, how did you go about it?
   a) She always follows the instructions carefully.
   b) She finds the whole process infuriating, so she doesn't buy ready-to-assemble furniture.
   c) She tends to lose the instructions and the parts.

3 If you imagine that a friend of yours gives you a call and says, "I've just been robbed," what would you do? What would your reaction be?
   a) First, she would ask her friend how she was feeling.
   b) First, she would be concerned about the practicalities, then she would ask about feelings.
   c) She would only ask about the practical details.

4 How do you go about doing the grocery shopping?
   a) She generally keeps a careful list of all the things she needs. Then she buys it all online.
   b) She hates internet shopping, so she goes to the supermarket once a week.
   c) She buys most of her groceries on the internet, but she doesn't use a list so she forgets things.

C Work in pairs. Answer the questions in Exercise 6B for you. Then compare your answers with your partner.

behavior / program / ready-to-assemble /
robbed / grocery shopping

behaviour / programme / flat pack /
burgled / food shopping

SPEAKING

7 A Read about the different types of people in the Myers-Briggs test below. Which type are you more inclined to be like? Choose a letter for each section (I or E, N or S, T or F, J or P) to work out your profile, e.g. ENTJ.

B Turn to page 158 to read more about your profile. Do you agree with the description?

C Tell other students about the result of your test, what it says about your personality and whether you agree with the result.

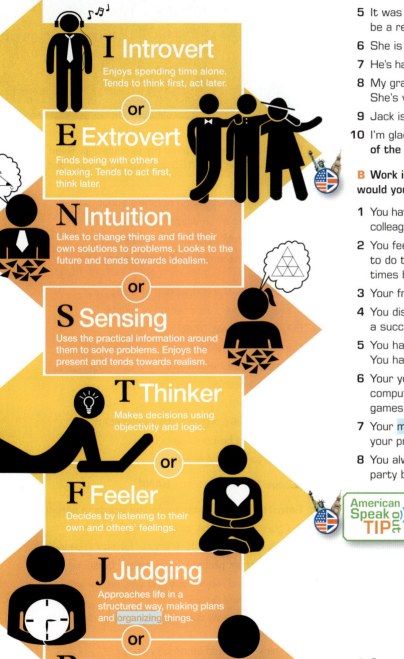

I Introvert
Enjoys spending time alone. Tends to think first, act later.

or

E Extrovert
Finds being with others relaxing. Tends to act first, think later.

N Intuition
Likes to change things and find their own solutions to problems. Looks to the future and tends towards idealism.

or

S Sensing
Uses the practical information around them to solve problems. Enjoys the present and tends towards realism.

T Thinker
Makes decisions using objectivity and logic.

or

F Feeler
Decides by listening to their own and others' feelings.

J Judging
Approaches life in a structured way, making plans and organizing things.

or

P Perceiving
Finds structure limiting, likes to keep their options open and go with the flow.

VOCABULARY *PLUS*
IDIOMS FOR PEOPLE

8 A Work out the meanings of the idioms in bold.

1 He's a bit of a **yes-man**. He agrees with anything the boss says.

2 The new engineer knows what he's doing. He's a real **whiz kid**.

3 She knows everything about everyone. She's the office **busybody**.

4 There is never a quiet moment with Kate. She's a real **chatterbox**.

5 It was very annoying of him. Sometimes Joe could be a real **pain in the neck**.

6 She is a **dark horse**. I didn't know she was rich.

7 He's had plenty of experience. He's an **old hand** at the job.

8 My grandmother has the same routine every day. She's very **set in her ways**.

9 Jack is a rebel. He's the **black sheep** of the family.

10 I'm glad we invited her. She's always the **life and soul of the party**.

B Work in pairs. Which of the idioms in Exercise 8A would you use in the following situations?

1 You have suggested a new way of working, but your colleague is reluctant to change the way he does things.

2 You feel sure that you can trust the person you asked to do this particular task because he has done it many times before.

3 Your friend loves talking.

4 You discover that your colleague is the lead singer in a successful band. She has never mentioned it.

5 You have to complete your accounts by tomorrow. You hate doing it.

6 Your young nephew shows you how to play a new computer game. He has already applied to work as a games developer.

7 Your mail carrier is always asking questions about your private life.

8 You always invite your sister when you're having a party because she makes people laugh.

> **American Speak out TIP**
> Here are four ideas to help you remember idioms.
> 1 Translation – are any of the idioms in Exercise 8A the same in your language?
> 2 Group by topic – do you know any other idioms for describing personality?
> 3 Visualize – can you think of images to help you remember the idioms in Exercise 8A?
> 4 Personalize – can you use the idioms in Exercise 8A to talk about people you know?

C Can you think of anyone from your own life, or news/film/television or politics, that could be described by the expressions in Exercise 8A?

▶ page 148 **VOCABULARY BANK**

organize / whiz kid / mail carrier / personalize

organise / whizzkid / postman / personalise

1.3)) PICTURE PERFECT

VOCABULARY
IMAGES

1 A Look at the photographic portraits. What do you think makes a good photo portrait?

B Read the text. Does it mention your ideas? What does Bailey feel is important when taking a photo portrait?

A

Getting the picture

A great photographic portrait **captures the beauty** of the human soul in a unique and inspiring way. It's so much more than just a black and white pose. It's **evocative** and has attitude, and it helps us see a person's true personality. So, what is it that can make a portrait truly **iconic**?

In *Getting the Picture*, David Bailey, world-famous photographer, whose **revealing** images are instantly recognizable and have charted decades of fashion, celebrity and notoriety, reveals how he got involved in photography and how he has produced some of the most **striking** and **provocative** images, which have defined our times.

"You've got to see things as they are, not as you think they are," says Bailey. "If someone's in a bad mood, I don't mind, because I encourage the bad mood, you know, wind them up a bit. And then you get a reaction from them. You can't be judgmental and be a photographer."

C Work in pairs. Check you understand the meaning of the words/expressions in bold. Can you use other words to explain them?

captures the beauty – shows you how beautiful something is

FUNCTION
SPECULATING

2 A Look at each portrait more carefully. Work in pairs and discuss the questions.

What can you say about the person's character from the picture?

What job do you think they do?

B Listen to people discussing the portraits and make notes. What do they say about each person's:
- character/appearance?
- possible job?

C In which portrait do they say the person:
1 has something about him/her which says (sort of) creative?
2 looks quite serene?
3 gives the impression of being very intellectual?
4 has something in his/her eyes that makes you think he's/she's about to laugh?
5 might have something to do with fashion?
6 looks pretty cool?

D Listen again to check your ideas.

F speculating
P connected speech: linking, elision
V images

3 Look at the language used for speculating. Read audio script S1.7 on page 165 and find some examples of this language.

I suppose/guess/imagine he/she's about …

I'd say he/she's …/I wouldn't say he/she's …

He/She/It could be/could have been …

He/She/It makes me think (that) maybe he/she/it …

He/She gives the impression of being …

It seems to me …/It seems like he/she …

(It) might suggest (that) …

I wonder what he/she …

I'm pretty sure he/she …

There's something … about him/her.

I'd guess (that) …

If I had to make a guess, I'd say (that) …

He/she could be/could have been …

It looks to me as if he/she …

▶ page 128 **LANGUAGE**BANK

4 Rewrite the sentences using the words in parentheses.
1 I guess she's a bit lonely. (It / seems / me)
2 It looks as though he's angry. (gives / impression)
3 I think she's probably an actress. (imagine)
4 If you asked me, I'd say she was happy with her life. (had / make / guess)
5 I'd definitely say that he's not telling us everything. (pretty)
6 I think she could be an only child. (imagine / guess)

recognizable / imagine / parentheses   recognisable / reckon / brackets

LEARN TO
USE VAGUE LANGUAGE

5 Look at the examples of vague language. Some are from the conversation in Exercise 2B. Why do the speakers use vague language? Does it sound formal or casual?

Vague nouns: *thing, stuff, bit* **There's something in her eyes.**
Quantifiers: *one or two, a few, a couple of, a lot of, plenty of, loads of, a bit (of)* **There's a bit of flour.**
Vague numbers: *around, about fifty, more or less, fifty or so* **He's about forty-ish.**
Generalizers: *sort of, kind of, you know* **He looks sort of creative.**
List completers: *and stuff, and so on, or something (like that)* **She could be a model, or something like that.**

American Speak TIP To sound fluent in English, avoid long pauses in your speech by using fillers like *uh* and *um*. Vague language (*sort of/kind of/you know*) and hedges (*I'd say/I imagine/I suppose*) are also used as fillers. Read audio script S1.7 on page 165 and find examples of fillers.

6 A Correct the mistakes in the sentences.

1 I'll be there soon. I just have a couple things to do.
2 Why don't we meet at exactly eight-ish?
3 I left a lot of stuffs at the hotel, but I can pick it up later.
4 Don't worry. We've got a plenty of time.
5 We've sort finished the accounts.
6 There'll be about forty and so people attending.

S1.8

B CONNECTED SPEECH: linking, elision Listen to the corrected sentences. Find examples of the following:

1 linking between words which end in a consonant sound and words which begin with a vowel sound.

   I just have‿a couple of things to do.

2 elision (when a sound disappears) between two consonant sounds, e.g. must‿be /mʌsbiː/.

   Why don't‿we meet at about eight-ish?

C Mark the links between words in the following examples. Try saying the phrases.

1 It looks as if he's got a lot of work to do.
2 She looks about fifty or so.
3 It's a bit dark, isn't it?
4 I've got a couple of things to ask.

S1.9

D Listen and check. Then listen and repeat.

SPEAKING

7 A Work in pairs. Look at the portraits on page 158 and follow the instructions.

B If you had a photograph portrait taken of you, where would you be? What kind of portrait would you like to have? Compare your ideas with other students.

1.4))) FRANCESCO'S VENICE

DVD PREVIEW

1 Work in groups. Look at the photo and discuss the questions.

1 What do you know about this city? Think about its geography and history.

2 Have you been there? Would you like to go?

3 What would it be like to live in Venice? How might it be different from where you live now?

2 Read the program information. Why do you think Francesco is a good person to host the program?

> ### ▶ Francesco's Venice
>
> *Francesco's Venice* is a documentary that tells the story of the great Italian city, Venice. Francesco da Mosto, a historian and writer, explains how this city – with no firm ground, no farmland and no army – acquired its power and fame. During the series, da Mosto describes the city's history and shows how his own family's fortunes have been closely related to the fortunes of Venice. In this episode, he goes to a house that his family built centuries ago and imagines his ancestors' lives as merchants.

3 Complete the sentences about Francesco's ancestors' house with the words in the box.

warehouse   bequeathed   showroom   rotting

1 The house is damp and in terrible condition, and the wood is _____.

2 Chiara da Mosto _____ the house to another family after falling out with her relatives.

3 This room was a _____. They used it to store goods before selling them.

4 It served as a _____. They used it to show goods to clients.

DVD view

4 Watch the DVD. Number the scenes in the order they appear.

a) Francesco stands on the balcony and looks across the canal.

b) He sails a small boat and looks at the house.

c) He walks through the house.

d) He imagines his ancestors and other people inside the house.

5 A Answer the questions.

1 Why does the story of his ancestors' home break Francesco's heart?

2 When did his ancestors build the house?

3 What happened to the house in 1603?

4 Apart from living there, what did his ancestors use the house for?

B Watch the DVD again to check.

6 Work in pairs and discuss the questions.

1 What did you think of Francesco's house?

2 What did you find interesting about his story?

3 Does your personal family history involve any particular countries or cities? Which ones?

American Speakout a possession

7 A Listen to someone talking about a treasured family possession. What is the object? What does she say about the points below?

- **Background:** the history of the object.
- **Physical description:** what it looks/feels/sounds/smells like.
- **Value:** why it is so important.
- **Memories:** what feelings or stories are associated with it.

B Listen again and check (✔) the key phrases you hear.

> **KEYPHRASES**
>
> (It) has been in my family for four generations.
>
> My grandmother inherited it.
>
> It has sentimental value.
>
> (It) was bequeathed to me.
>
> I should repair it.
>
> I will always treasure it.

8 A Now think about a treasured possession of your own or a place that is special to your family. Make notes on the points in Exercise 7A.

B Work in groups and take turns. Tell each other about your possession/place.

writeback a description of an object

9 A Read a description of an object. Why is the object special to the writer?

I own an antique gramophone player that belonged to my grandfather and then my father. It was made in Germany in the 1920s and has a heavy base made of pine wood and a large brass horn. In the days before cassette players, CDs and iPods, this is how people listened to music at home.

The gramophone reminds me of my childhood because when we went to my grandfather's house in Essex, near London, he used to play records on it. While his grandchildren were running and bellowing all over the house, he would be sitting there drinking tea and listening to a scratchy recording of a Bach sonata or Fauré's *Requiem*.

When he died, the gramophone was handed down to my father. It sat in the corner of the living room where a light skin of dust settled upon it. It was a piece of furniture, an heirloom that no one used or noticed but that just seemed to belong there, just as now it belongs in its own special corner of my living room. I don't know if many people nowadays would recognize a gramophone if they saw one, but I treasure the object because of the memories associated with it.

B Write about an object or a place that is important to you. Use the key phrases to help.

V PHRASES WITH NAME

1 Underline the correct alternative.

1 He was innocent, but it took him years to *live/clear/make* his name.

2 I was named *before/after/of* my grandfather.

3 My married name is Kovacs, but my *maiden/principle/single* name is Warsawski.

4 Zara made a name for *self/her/herself* as the best designer in the business.

5 He's a good actor but not a *house/household/family* name like Brad Pitt or Johnny Depp.

6 His real name is Keanu, but his *nickname/friendly name/fun name* is Nunu.

G THE CONTINUOUS ASPECT

2 A Complete the pairs of sentences using the same verb. Use one simple form and one continuous form. Some verbs are in the negative.

1 a) My friend _____ to visit next week.

 b) Harada is Japanese. He _____ from Osaka.

2 a) I _____ ten days off work – I can't seem to get rid of this flu.

 b) I _____ tennis lessons for two years.

3 a) My office _____ painted yesterday, so I stayed home.

 b) The garden _____ really beautiful when I was a child.

4 a) The children _____ homesick at all, so they love traveling.

 b) The economy _____ any better – jobs are still at risk.

5 a) They knew me already because I _____ for that company before.

 b) I was exhausted because I _____ for sixteen hours.

B Work in pairs. Discuss why we use the simple or continuous forms in the sentences above.

In 1a) it's a future plan, so this uses the present continuous.

G DESCRIBING HABITS

3 A Find and correct the mistakes in sentences 1—6. There is one mistake in each sentence.

1 I'm prone leaving things until the last minute, and then I always have to rush.

2 I don't tend needing as much sleep as I used to.

3 I keep forget her birthday.

4 My parents were always very strict, and they wouldn't to let me out late at night.

5 I'm more inclination to call people than to send them a text.

6 I'm always clean my house. I can't stand it when it's a mess.

B Work in pairs. Change information in the sentences above to write three or four sentences about your partner (guess if necessary). Then compare your sentences.

A: I guess you're prone to leaving things until the last minute.

B: Actually, I tend to be quite organized.

V PERSONALITY

4 A Complete the words in sentences 1—6.

1 We're m_____ enough to disagree but still respect each other.

2 You're right. I hadn't noticed. That's very pe_____ of you.

3 He was a very o_____ man. He refused to do what I asked.

4 She is a c_____ teacher. She prepares her lessons carefully.

5 It's important to remain o_____ -m_____ and consider all options.

6 I'd have asked more questions, but I didn't want to seem too i_____.

B Work in pairs and take turns. Choose a word from Exercise 4A and describe an occasion when you can be like this. Can your partner guess the word?

A: In the office, I work hard and make "to do" lists.

B: Conscientious?

F SPECULATING

5 A Match the sentence halves.

1 I imagine

2 If I had to make a guess,

3 I wonder

4 She gives the impression

5 I'd guess

6 There's something

7 It looks to me

8 I'm pretty

a) as if Nataly has an artistic streak.

b) guess that Felix has a tendency to be a little absent-minded.

c) Guido's probably obsessive about keeping his house clean.

d) of being a little apathetic about politics.

e) I'd say that Monika is a conscientious student.

f) if Alex has a solitary side to his nature.

g) mysterious about Martha.

h) sure that Olga is a fitness fanatic.

B Write two or three sentences speculating about things that might happen in the next year. Compare your ideas with other students.

If I had to make a guess, I'd say that the government will change within the next twelve months. I'm pretty sure this government won't get through the next elections.

traveling / clean   travelling / tidy

2)) opinion

WORDS OF WISDOM   p20

CHANGING YOUR MIND   p23

WHO DO YOU TRUST?   p26

SPEAKING
2.1 Talk about words of wisdom
2.2 Discuss controversial ideas
2.3 Discuss dilemmas at work
2.4 Take part in a panel discussion

LISTENING
2.2 Listen to a radio program about a living library event
2.3 Listen to a discussion about trustworthiness
2.4 Watch a program about a young chess master

READING
2.1 Read an article about good and bad advice
2.2 Read an essay about homelessness

WRITING
2.2 Write a discursive essay
2.4 Write a summary

What is the best or worst advice you've been given?

 INTERVIEWS

CHESS MASTER   p28

G hypothetical conditional: past
P double contractions
V learning and experience; metaphors

Words from **the wise**

Everyone needs words of wisdom. When we're trying to find our feet, we all need help. Sometimes it's the wise words of our mentors that can do the trick.

1 JANE GOODALL
PRIMATOLOGIST AND CONSERVATIONIST

When I was about ten years old and dreaming of going to Africa, living with animals and writing books about them, everyone laughed at me. Africa was far away and full of dangerous animals, and only boys could expect to do those kinds of things. But my mother said, "If you really want something, and you work hard, and you take advantage of opportunities – and you never, ever give up – you will find a way." The opportunity was a letter from a friend inviting me to Kenya. The hard work was waitressing at a hotel to earn money for the trip – and spending hours reading books about Africa and animals, so I was ready when Dr. Louis Leakey offered me the opportunity to study chimpanzees.

2 SIR RICHARD BRANSON
ENTREPRENEUR

My mother, Eve, always taught me never to look back in regret but to move on to the next thing. A setback is never a bad experience, just another one of life's lessons.

3 ROBIN PAGE
COLUMNIST

My geography master told me: "When people tell you that there are two sides to every argument, it is nonsense. There are three: your side, their side and the truth."

READING

1 A Can you remember any useful advice you have been given? Who gave it to you?

B Work in pairs. Which pieces of advice a)—h) do you agree/disagree with? Why?

a) Look on the bright side, and appreciate the good things in your life.

b) Don't be afraid to disagree with the majority. The crowd isn't always right.

c) Success isn't about the hours you work; it's about getting the job done.

d) Use every chance you get.

e) An original idea is no use unless you work to perfect it.

f) Don't be afraid to make mistakes.

g) Don't waste time wondering what might have been. Look to the future.

h) Work hard and have confidence in your abilities.

2 A Read the article. Match advice a)—h) with 8 of the people.

B Work in groups and discuss the questions below.

1 Which three pieces of advice do you like the best? Are there any that you don't like?

2 Have you ever been in a similar position to any of the people in the text? What did you do?

VOCABULARY
LEARNING AND EXPERIENCE

3 A Find expressions in the article with the following meanings.

1 become familiar with a new situation or experience (introduction)

2 use the chances you get (paragraph 1)

3 a problem that prevents or delays progress (paragraph 2)

4 in a position in which you quickly have to learn something difficult (paragraph 4)

5 finding out how something is done in a particular place or situation (paragraph 6)

6 changed a person deeply, e.g. the way they understand the world (paragraph 7)

7 believe that your feelings are correct (paragraph 9)

8 act according to your personal feelings about something (paragraph 9)

B Look at questions 1—8 and choose three or four that you are happy to answer. Compare your answers with other students.

1 When were you last on a steep learning curve? What was the most difficult thing to learn?

2 In what situations do you always trust your instincts?

3 What opportunities have you taken advantage of?

4 Can you think of a situation or place in which you had to learn the ropes?

5 Can you think of a great event or person that had a profound effect on you?

6 How long did it take you to find your feet in your current school or workplace?

7 What's the best way to deal with a setback at work?

8 Are you analytical when you make decisions, or do you usually go with your gut feeling?

Dr. Dr

4 HONG BO CHIN
FINANCIER

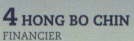

For my first year in corporate finance, I was on a steep learning curve and thought I needed to work eighteen hours a day to impress everyone. I'd get to the office exhausted, until one day an older employee told me, "You're not impressing anyone by working ridiculous hours. Just get the job done." I wish I'd spoken to him earlier. If it wasn't for his advice, I would have worked myself into the ground.

5 PETER BARRON
HEAD OF EXTERNAL RELATIONS FOR GOOGLE

All the best advice I received was from my father, and I even took some of it. My favorite is: "The man who never made a mistake never made anything."

6 STEFAN OROGOVITZ
BRAIN SURGEON

A journalist asked me, "Why do brain surgeons have such large egos?" I said, "We need them. We lose ninety-five percent of our patients." If I'd known that statistic when I was learning the ropes, I'd be selling insurance today. How can you keep working with figures like that? You do all you can, never apologize, and believe in yourself.

7 PAOLA GAVAZZI
SCREENWRITER

A movie director kept asking me to rewrite a screenplay. I kept protesting. Eventually he just said to me, "You're not paid to write. You're paid to rewrite." That had a profound effect on me.

8 SANTA SEBAG-MONTEFIORE
AUTHOR

When we were skiing in Klosters, my father would say "It's sunny at the top", before heading up the mountain in thick fog. He meant "be positive", and always be grateful for what you have.

9 NOBANTU SESEKE
PUBLISHER

Early in my career, I received some amazing manuscripts, but my colleagues weren't sure, and I ended up saying "no". I now regret rejecting some authors who went on to have good careers. What I've learned is to trust your instincts. Go with your gut feeling. Had I done this, I would have said "yes" to some great books. If only I'd known then what I know now.

10 MATTHEW WILLIAMSON
DESIGNER

My co-founder and CEO, Joseph Velosa, said to me years ago: "If you don't have passion, then you have nothing. If you don't believe in what you are doing, why would anyone else?"

GRAMMAR
HYPOTHETICAL CONDITIONAL: PAST

4 A Look at paragraphs 4, 6 and 9 in the article. Underline three conditional sentences and three phrases to describe regrets.

B Check what you know. Answer the questions.

1 How do we make past conditionals? (If + past perfect + …)

2 Instead of *if* + past perfect, two of the conditional sentences (in paragraphs 4 and 9) use alternative forms. What forms are they?

3 Are these forms more or less formal than an *if* clause?

4 Look at the conditional sentence in paragraph 6. Do both clauses refer to the past? What forms are used? Why do you think this is sometimes called a "mixed conditional"?

5 Two of the phrases to describe regrets use the same verb tense. What tense is this?

C Read the rules about hypothetical past conditionals.

> **RULES**
>
> 1 Use *if* + past perfect and *would* + present continuous/simple present to form a mixed conditional.
>
> 2 Use a mixed conditional to say that if something in the past had been different, the present would be different.

▶ page 130 **LANGUAGEBANK**

5 A Complete the sentences with one word in each gap.

1 If she had helped him back then, he would _____ helped her.

2 _____ for Ahmed's efforts, this conference would not have happened.

3 If _____ we had arrived earlier, we would have seen the sunrise.

4 _____ I known about her illness, I would have come sooner.

5 I _____ doing some things I did when I was younger. I was thoughtless then!

6 I _____ I'd known about the free food!

7 If he hadn't come, everyone would _____ died.

8 I _____ be working here if I hadn't met Layla in 2008.

B DOUBLE CONTRACTIONS In sentences 1—4, some double contractions are possible (where two consecutive words can both be contracted). Can you see where?

In sentence 1, "he would have" can be contracted: "he'd've helped her".

C Listen to the recording and focus on the contracted sounds. Listen again and repeat the phrases.

SPEAKING

6 A Complete the sentences and make them true for you.

If there's one thing I've learned …

One thing I'd never …

One thing I wish I'd known when I was …

If I had a personal motto, it would be …

My mother/father/mentor/friend always told me …

B Work in groups and take turns. Read your sentences and give some background, explaining what you wrote. Try to use contractions.

apologize apologise

VOCABULARY PLUS
METAPHORS

7 A Read the metaphor and choose the correct meaning.

I'm over the hill.

a) I can't do something well enough because I'm too old.

b) I have done the most difficult part of a task.

B Discuss the questions.

1 Can you think of other examples of metaphors?

2 Why are metaphors used?

3 How do they help to communicate an idea?

4 What can you do to remember metaphors?

> **American Speak TIP**
> Metaphors sometimes come in patterns: *your career is a journey*; *time is money*; *ideas are food*; *good is up* and *bad is down*. It is useful to write these metaphors together in your notebook. This helps you remember them.

8 Read the paragraph and underline four metaphors related to journeys. Match them with meanings 1—4. Do you have similar metaphors in your language?

> ❝ When I graduated, everyone said, "You'll go far." I joined a law firm and quickly reached the peak of my profession. But then my career started to go downhill. I argued with colleagues and lost some cases. I found myself at a crossroads: either I could continue working there, or I could take a risk and start my own firm. ❞

1 go badly

2 having to choose one thing or another

3 have a great future *(You'll) go far.*

4 become number one

9 A Work in pairs. Student A: Read the paragraph below and underline four metaphors related to ideas. Match them with meanings 1—4. Student B: Turn to page 159.

> ❝ When I was a philosophy student in college, one day my professor said, "OK, here's an idea. For some, this might be hard to swallow, but I have a proposal. Instead of making you take tests, in which you just regurgitate the book, at the end of term you all give a talk about something you found interesting in class." He paused. Silence. "It's just food for thought," he said. "You don't have to decide now." None of us had done anything like this before. But, as if to prove it wasn't just a half-baked idea, at the end of term, he made us do it. It was the best thing I did in my four years in college. ❞

1 reproduce without thinking

2 difficult to believe/accept

3 badly thought-out

4 something to think about

B Read your paragraph to your partner twice. Which metaphors did he/she notice? Explain the meaning of the four metaphors to your partner.

10 Replace the underlined phrases with metaphors and any necessary verbs.

1 My teachers said, "You have a great future ahead of you." *You'll go far.*

2 A friend told me she was related to Albert Einstein, but I find that difficult to believe.

3 You should save some time free to visit the National Gallery of Art when you're in Washington.

4 He had a badly thought-out plan to start a website selling cars.

5 I began my career by winning two tennis tournaments, but then things started to go wrong.

6 Our dog had been sick for years and was expected to die at any moment.

7 He was at the height of his career when he decided to retire.

8 Someone once said "all children are born geniuses". That's something for us to think about.

11 A Work in pairs and think of two:

- half-baked ideas that could change the world.
  Allow all schools to be run by the students.
- tips for reaching the peak of your profession.
- things you can't afford (either the money or time) to do.
- activities you would do if you put aside some time for yourself.
- reasons why famous people's careers go downhill.
- things you heard in the news that you find hard to swallow.

B Share your ideas with the class.

▶ page 149 **VOCABULARY**BANK

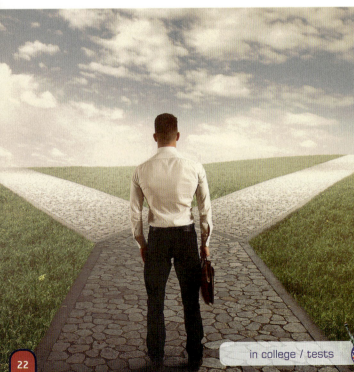

in college / tests

at university / exams

2.2)) CHANGING YOUR MIND

- **G** verb patterns
- **P** word stress
- **V** collocations: opinions

Can you change people's opinions by talking to them?

The idea of the "living library" originated in Scandinavia. "Readers" come to the library to borrow real people in the same way that they would normally borrow books. They can then take them away to a corner for a fifteen-minute chat, in the course of which they can ask any questions they like and hear real live answers. The idea is that by doing this, the "reader" will start to uncover some of the preconceptions that they may have, and the "book" is able to try to dispel a few of the typical stigmas, stereotypes and prejudices they encounter in their everyday lives.

LISTENING

1 A Have you heard of a living library? If not, what do you think a living library is?

B Read about living libraries. Were your ideas right? Do you think they are a good idea?

2 A Listen to a radio program about living libraries. Work in pairs and discuss these questions with a partner.

1 Has your opinion of living libraries changed?
2 How did the speakers feel about taking part?
3 Would you ever take part? Why/Why not?

B Listen again and answer the questions.

1 What was written in the catalogue next to "student"?
2 How did Alex feel about this?
3 What did Alex expect the man to do?
4 What actually happened?
5 What was the first thing Sarah noticed about Carrie?
6 What opinion is Carrie hoping to change?
7 How does being blind affect Carrie's life?
8 Why does Carrie feel that she is a good judge of character?

VOCABULARY
COLLOCATIONS: OPINIONS

3 A Work in pairs and complete the phrases using words from the box.

> perspective   mind   eye-opening   narrow-minded
> convincing   preconceptions   stereotypes   second

1 People tend to have various _____ about what a drug addict is.
2 The aim is to challenge the _____ that exist about immigrants.
3 I was feeling nervous and beginning to have _____ thoughts about the whole idea.
4 It's important to keep an open _____ before making a judgement.
5 His attitude is very _____ and intolerant of alternative opinions.
6 The experience of talking so directly was _____. I had never done anything like it before.
7 I saw the situation from a whole new _____ after our conversation.
8 I don't think he really knew his facts, so his argument wasn't very _____.

B WORD STRESS Listen to the words/phrases and write them in the right place according to their stress patterns. Listen again and repeat.

oOo   ooOo   Oooo

perspective

C Respond to situations 1–5 using the prompts and phrases from Exercise 3A.

1 You are supposed to get married next month, but you're feeling nervous about the decision.

   I'm having second thoughts about getting married.

2 You spend a week living in a small community with a very different lifestyle to your own. It gives you a new outlook on life.

   It was an ... experience. It has ...

3 You meet your new father-in-law, and he is a police officer. You had ideas about the kind of person he is, which you discover are wrong. *I had some ...*

4 Politicians are arguing that nuclear power is safe. You are not sure how true that is. *I don't find ...*

5 You used to think it would be great not to work, but then you lost your job. *Losing my job ...*

D Work in pairs and answer the questions.

How might a living library combat prejudice where you live? What type of book would you be?

▶ page 149 **VOCABULARY**BANK

police officer   policeman

GRAMMAR
VERB PATTERNS

4 A Check what you know. Underline the correct alternatives to complete what other people have said about living libraries.

1 It was great being able to say those things you're usually scared *to say/say/saying* and ask questions you're usually afraid to ask.

2 We were given the freedom *to ask/ask/asking* questions without having to worry about *to be/be/being* judged. I admit *to feel/feel/feeling* a little nervous about a few of the questions.

3 I wanted *to offer/offer/offering* some insights into my job. I took part in the living library event *to challenge/challenge/challenging* stereotypes and misconceptions I'd encountered.

4 I enjoyed *to talk/talk/talking* to different people. I learned more about where my arguments for *to be/be/being* a vegan fall down. I had to apologize for not always being able to answer the question properly.

5 They advised me *to be/be/being* as honest as possible.

6 *To sleep/Sleep/Sleeping* outside in the middle of winter isn't the problem. Coping with how people treat you is much harder *to deal/deal/dealing* with.

B Look at Exercise 4A again. Find examples to match the patterns 1—9 below.

1 Verb + *to* + infinitive, e.g. *I decided to explain.*

2 Verb + object + *to* + infinitive, e.g. *They encouraged me to apply.*

3 Noun + *to* + infinitive (as part of a semi-fixed phrase), e.g. *It's time to ...*

4 Adjective + *to* + infinitive, e.g. *I was happy to talk to them.*

5 *to* + infinitive used to express purpose e.g. *She left early to catch the train.*

6 verb + *-ing* e.g. *I recall feeling apprehensive.*

7 preposition + *-ing* e.g. *Are you interested in learning about the issues?*

8 *-ing* used as a noun (gerund), e.g. *Smoking is bad for you.*

9 like/love/hate etc. + *-ing*, e.g. *I hate arguing about politics.*

C Match examples 1—3 with rules a)—c).

1 They seem to have forgotten why we came here.

2 Not understanding people's reasons for why they do the things they do is a big problem.

3 He is always being stopped by police just for the way he looks.

▶ page 130 **LANGUAGEBANK**

5 A Complete the sentences with the correct form of the verb in parentheses.

1 I didn't expect _____ (feel) so embarrassed, but the questions they asked were so personal.

2 _____ (meet) Linda and _____ (have) the chance to talk about her experience was enlightening.

3 They had the opportunity _____ (ask) me anything that they wanted.

4 It's hard _____ (imagine) what it's like to live with a disability.

5 I wouldn't even contemplate _____ (leave) the country.

6 She had refused _____ (marry) the man her parents had chosen for her.

7 Somehow he seemed _____ (lose) all the money already.

8 He is fed up with _____ (be) called rude names.

B Work alone and think of:

• one thing you would never consider doing.

• something you regret doing/not doing.

• three things you find hard to tolerate.

• something you have recently been persuaded to do.

C Compare your ideas in pairs.

SPEAKING

6 A Mark the statements below with a number from 1—5 (1 = strongly agree, 5 = strongly disagree).

> Medical and technological advances will mean that in the future there will be no disabilities.

> Women should be promoted to top jobs in business and politics before men.

> Everybody in the world should have access to a library.

> Students, not the government, should pay college tuition fees.

> Individual countries do not have the right to interfere with the affairs of another country.

B Work in groups. Discuss two of the statements and modify them until everyone in the group agrees with what they say.

C Compare your new statements with the rest of the class.

Are we doing enough to help the homeless?

Homelessness is a major problem in any big city. There are regular attempts by authorities to clear the streets of the homeless, typically in cities hosting events like the Olympics. Homelessness doesn't look good, and it makes politicians feel uncomfortable. Is enough being done to resolve the problem, **however**?

Many people assume that homeless people live on the streets as a result of drug or alcohol misuse. **Consequently**, they assume we can do little to help as drugs will continue to be a problem. **Additionally**, charitable organizations already help the homeless, **so** this may be sufficient. In my opinion, this approach ignores the bigger picture.

There is no doubt that drug abuse is a major contributing factor leading to homelessness. **On the other hand**, there are increasing numbers of people who are homeless because of the lack of affordable housing. **In addition to this**, as unemployment increases, more people struggle to keep up with payments on their homes.

A frightening number of the homeless are families with children. They are, **in fact**, the fastest growing part of the homeless population. **Furthermore**, it's not only the unemployed who cannot afford housing. According to a recent survey, more than a quarter of homeless people (25–40 percent) actually work. **Nevertheless**, they still cannot afford to pay for accommodations.

In today's society, it is unacceptable that working people cannot afford to pay for a house to live in. **For this reason**, it's essential that governments ensure people are paid sufficient wages. **Likewise**, since housing prices are so high, governments should focus on providing accommodations for low-income families. **In conclusion**, the responsibility for homelessness should not just be left to charities, but as a society we need to help people before they find themselves on the streets.

WRITING
A DISCURSIVE ESSAY; LEARN TO USE LINKING DEVICES

7 A Look at the photo. What do you think are the main reasons for homelessness? What is the best way to reduce the problem?

B Read the essay. Does the writer share your ideas?

8 Look at the guidelines for writing a discursive essay. How far does the essay in Exercise 7B follow the guidelines?

1 Include an introductory paragraph.
2 Divide your essay into for and against sections.
3 Use linking words and phrases.
4 Write a concluding paragraph.

9 A Complete the table with phrases in bold from the essay.

introduce additional information (meaning "and")   what is more, another (problem/issue/point, etc.),   _____, _____, _____, _____
indicate a contrast with what has come before (meaning "but")   in contrast, on the contrary, conversely, _____,   _____, _____
follow a logical argument (meaning "therefore")   thus, hence, accordingly, as a result, _____, _____,   _____
prove your point   evidently, obviously, indeed, to conclude, _____, _____

American Speak TIP Most linking words come at the beginning of a sentence (followed by a comma), or in the middle of the sentence (usually with a comma before and after the linker). Some linkers can be used at the end of clauses. Underline an example in the essay of where the linker appears at the beginning, in the middle and at the end of a sentence.

B Delete the incorrect alternative in each sentence.

1 Most computer users have, _in conclusion/evidently/in fact_, never received any formal keyboard training. _As a result,/However,/So_ their keyboard skills are inefficient.

2 He is old and unpopular. _On the contrary/Furthermore/In addition to this_, he has at best only two more years of political life left.

3 The laws were contradictory. Measures were taken to clarify them, _accordingly/as a result/hence_.

4 What he said was true. It was, _nevertheless/thus/however_, unkind.

5 I don't mind at all. _Indeed/In fact/To conclude_, I was pleased.

6 Many employees enjoy music in the workplace. _However/Conversely/In addition to this_, some people find it distracting or, _indeed/in fact/obviously_, annoying.

10 A Work in groups. Choose a statement from Exercise 6A and discuss the arguments for and against it.

B Plan an essay about your statement. Write a few key sentences using linking words.

C Write a discursive essay (250—300 words).

organization / accommodations   organisation / accommodation

2.3)) WHO DO YOU TRUST?

F introducing opinions
P intonation for emphasis
V idioms of opinion

SPEAKING

1 A Work in groups and discuss the questions.

1 Which professions are the most/least trusted by the public? Think of the top three (most trusted) and the bottom three (least trusted). Compare your ideas with other students.

2 Do you think public trust in some professions has changed over the years? Why/Why not? What has happened to make people more/less trusting of these professions?

B Read the article about the most and least trusted professions in the U.K. Would the results be the same in your country?

In a recent U.K. poll to find the most trustworthy professions, doctors came first. Ninety-two percent of people trust them. Other highly trusted professions included teachers, judges and clergy. Near the bottom of the list were business leaders and journalists, but politicians came last. Only thirteen percent of people trust them.

Three of the most trusted professions gave us their comments.

Mary Davis, teacher

"We make every effort to get to know each individual student, and we also try very hard to be part of the community. As well as knowing the students, we get to know their families."

Dr. David Bailey, doctor

"I qualified when I was twenty-three years old. I have every intention of working until I'm sixty-five, so I've got a real vested interest in making sure that my patients think I am trustworthy. You do that by the way you behave towards people."

Professor Justin Lewis, university professor

"We don't have an axe to grind. Our business is doing research; teaching. In good faith, we try to produce things that are of value to society in general."

VOCABULARY
IDIOMS OF OPINION

2 A Work in pairs. Underline two idioms in the article and check you understand them.

B Work in pairs. Underline the idioms in sentences 1—4 and choose the best definition, a) or b).

1 I'm going to play devil's advocate. Let's imagine the company goes bankrupt. What happens to the employees?

a) give a very negative opinion about someone or something

b) take a deliberately contrary position in an argument to force people to justify their opinions

2 I'm going to speak my mind. I think this situation is absolutely terrible, and we have to find a solution.

a) change your opinion after reconsidering something

b) say what you really believe

3 If you have to make a decision, it's no use sitting on the fence. You must choose one or the other.

a) being unable to commit yourself to one opinion or one side

b) asking lots of people to help you make a difficult decision

4 Let's not beat around the bush. You have committed a serious crime and now you must pay for it.

a) give an opinion based on false evidence

b) talk a lot, but avoid directly addressing the most important point

C Which idioms in Exercise 2B can be used to introduce opinions or knowledge?

3 As far as I'm *opinionated/concern/concerned*, postal workers are the most trustworthy professionals.

4 To my *knowledge/view/opinion*, there are no professions that are "squeaky clean"; all of them have "bad apples".

5 If you *tell/inquire/ask* me, librarians are the most trustworthy people; they have no reason to lie.

6 If you want my *truest/honest/perfect* opinion, I'd say trust nobody, ever.

B Do you agree with opinions 1–6 above? Why/Why not?

LEARN TO
EXPRESS DOUBT

6 A Listen to three extracts from the debate in Exercise 3A. Check (✔) the phrases you hear for expressing doubt.

1 I don't know about that.

2 I'm really not sure about that.

3 That's debatable.

4 I find that highly unlikely.

B Which expression above shows the most doubt?

C INTONATION FOR EMPHASIS Listen to four sentences using the expressions above. Notice the intonation on the modifiers *really* and *highly*. Listen again and repeat.

SPEAKING

7 A Read about three real cases of untrustworthy behavior at work. If you were the boss in these cases, what would you do? What would it depend on? Think of some ideas and make notes.

Case 1 Your company has started using an online management system for all of its business. Your assistant sometimes refuses to use this system and sends you documents the old way (by hand or by email).

Case 2 Someone in your company uses social media to gossip about his co-workers and recently started a blog criticizing the company's practices. He doesn't mention names, but it's obvious who he is referring to.

Case 3 A co-worker has been claiming expenses for expensive meals and events. She says she was entertaining clients, but you know she was in the office on those days.

B Compare your ideas with other students. If you were the boss, what options would you have? Debate the issues.

C What do you think the bosses really did? Turn to page 159 to find out. Do you think they did the right thing?

FUNCTION
INTRODUCING OPINIONS

3 A Listen to a debate. What issue are the speakers discussing and what conclusion do they reach?

B Listen again and check (✔) the ideas that are mentioned.

1 Journalists have an axe to grind.

2 Most journalists are truly impartial.

3 Some journalists are there to sell newspapers.

4 A journalist's job is to get proof and ask for evidence.

5 Journalists want the truth.

6 Good journalists make the case for both sides.

7 There are many libel trials because people don't like what is written about them.

8 Some journalists "give others a bad name".

4 A What words do you think complete the expressions for introducing opinions? Which do you know? Which do you use?

If you want my honest 1_____, ...

Quite 2_____, ...

The reality is ... /In reality, ...

According 3_____ (the statistics/the facts/her), ...

From what I can 4_____, ...

As far as I'm 5_____, ...

To my knowledge, ...

Look at it this way.

If you 6_____ me, ...

B Read audio script S2.4 on page 167. Which of the expressions in Exercise 4A can you find?

▶ page 130 **LANGUAGE**BANK

5 A Underline the correct alternatives.

1 *In/Of/By* reality, all the recent political and business scandals have eroded people's trust in these professions.

2 From what I can *learn/gather/get*, nurses are extremely trustworthy. They were voted the most trusted professionals in the USA from 2004–2008.

check / behavior / criticizing   tick / behaviour / criticising

2.4 ◉)) CHESS MASTER

DVD PREVIEW

1 A Work in groups. Check you understand the words/phrases in bold.

1 Do you think musicians like Beethoven or artists like Picasso are born with an **innate talent**, or would you **put their success down to** a lifelong passion or intensive training?

2 Do you agree that any parent can train their child to become world-class at something, or does the child need to be born **academically/artistically/physically gifted**?

3 If you can **inherit** eye and hair color from a parent, do you think it is possible to also inherit personality **traits**?

4 How much do you think a parent is able to **shape** their child's future and success?

B Discuss the questions in Exercise 1A.

2 Read the program information and answer the questions.

1 Why is Carissa's achievement special?

2 Who was influential in helping Carissa become a chess master?

3 Why do you think chess masters are becoming younger and younger?

▶ BBC News: The young chess master

For centuries, chess has been a game for big thinkers and those with mathematical minds. However, child prodigies have become a well-known phenomenon in chess. And the age of becoming a chess master is getting younger and younger. Carissa Yip first started playing chess at age six, when her father, an IT architect, taught her. Within a year, she was beating him. At age nine, she became the youngest American to reach "expert" level. Now, she has fulfilled another dream, becoming the youngest female U.S. chess master, defeating grandmaster Alexander Ivanov during the New England Open. In this program, Jane O'Brien meets Carissa and investigates her remarkable story.

DVD VIEW

3 Watch the DVD and answer the questions.

1 What is Carissa's ambition?

2 Do you think it's possible that she will achieve it?

4 A Complete the extracts.

1 At this tournament in Philadelphia, she's taking on players _____ her age, and then some.

2 Fewer than _____ percent of chess players in America reach the level of master.

3 But Carissa is so unassuming that many others aren't even _____ she plays chess.

4 She's just a normal, everyday young _____ going about her business in a middle school.

5 Carissa: "I guess it's no big _____, really."

6 Mom picks her up from school, she hangs out with her friends, and she does _____, eventually.

7 But chess is her passion. And at her local club recently, she played _____ games simultaneously.

8 Chess can also be a lonely game when you're so _____ nobody wants to play with you at all.

B Watch the DVD again to check.

5 Work in pairs and discuss the questions.

1 Do you think it is a good idea for children to learn games like chess when they are very young? Why/Why not?

2 Are your own successes a result of your natural ability (inherited from your parents), your own hard work, or just pure luck?

3 Do you think your parents' interests and achievements have shaped your own? Have you inherited personality traits from members of your family?

at age six / Mom   aged six / Mum

American Speakout a panel discussion

6 A Listen to someone debating the role of nature versus nurture. Which side of the argument does she present? What examples does she give to justify her ideas?

B Listen again and check (✔) the key phrases you hear.

> **KEYPHRASES**
>
> I'd like to begin by stating that …
>
> As I see it …/What I think is …
>
> I would say it depends on …
>
> What you need to consider is …
>
> I think it's ridiculous to suggest …
>
> I absolutely reject the idea that …
>
> So, to conclude I would have to argue that …
>
> Does anyone have a question … ?/Are there any other questions?
>
> That's a good question because …

C Which key phrases are used to:

- introduce the argument?
- justify an opinion?
- conclude?
- invite questions?
- respond to questions?

7 A Work in groups. Think of points "for" and "against" the following statement.

Children should start school younger than they do now.

B Prepare to argue either "for" or "against" the statement. Follow the instructions.

- Choose a speaker for your group.
- Help them to prepare their argument.
- Make notes on how to introduce the argument, justify the opinion and conclude. Use the key phrases.

C The speakers take turns presenting their arguments. Listen and ask questions at the end. Which case was argued the most clearly?

writeback a summary

8 A Read the summary. What are the key points? Do you agree with the writer's opinion?

Should your child learn a musical instrument?

Anna: Music in a child's life has many benefits. Some even claim that early exposure to classical music for very young children (even before they are born) helps them to become more intelligent, the so-called "Mozart Effect". The claims are unsubstantiated, but there is no question that classical music is soothing to the soul. They may not become musical prodigies, but exposing your children to songs and nursery rhymes from a young age will give them a feel for rhythm and language and encourage them to appreciate the beauty of music as they grow.

At school, children who learn musical instruments are generally more successful and perform better on tests. It may be that learning music also helps children develop their reasoning skills and learn about problem-solving and decision-making. It can also be great for confidence-building and is a valuable experience that helps broaden their understanding and appreciation of the world around them.

Obviously, there are costs and commitments involved with teaching a child a musical instrument. But, if you ask me, it's one of the most precious gifts you can offer a child and one that he or she will appreciate for a lifetime.

B Write a summary (200—220 words) of your opinion about one of the issues in Exercises 6A or 7A .

V LEARNING AND EXPERIENCE

1 Find and correct the mistakes in sentences 1—8. There are five mistakes.

1 I've only been working here for two weeks, so I'm still learning ropes.

2 If you're not sure, go with your guts feeling.

3 The team's hopes suffered a setback last night.

4 I decided to make advantage of the opportunity.

5 David didn't need to think because he trusted on his instincts.

6 That movie had a profound effect on me at an early age.

7 I'm still trying to find my feet in my new job.

8 It's a difficult class , and Frank's on the steep learning curve.

G HYPOTHETICAL CONDITIONAL: PAST

2 A Choose one of the scenarios below. Write as many sentences as you can, using past conditionals and regrets.

• Several years ago you had a great idea for a book, but you were too busy to write it. The story involved a schoolboy wizard and his two friends who fight against evil by using magic. Then the Harry Potter books appeared.

• You have a safe, steady job, but you are totally bored. As a teenager you were a really good dancer and had the opportunity to go to the best dance school in the country. You gave it up because the profession seemed too risky.

• A few years ago you saw a wonderful house for sale. You thought about buying it, but hesitated because of the long commute to work. By the time you decided to make an offer, it was already sold. You frequently dream about living in that house.

B Compare your ideas with other students.

V COLLOCATIONS: OPINIONS

3 A Work alone. Prepare to talk about some of the following topics.

1 Describe the national stereotype for your country. Do you think it is an accurate description?

2 Name three kinds of prejudice or stereotype people are trying to challenge in your country.

3 Describe a person you had a preconception about, who turned out to be very different.

4 What do you think leads to people becoming narrow-minded/ open-minded about an issue?

5 What is the best way to change someone's perspective about a topic?

6 Talk about something you decided to do but then had second thoughts about.

7 Describe a movie/book that you would consider eye-opening. Why?

8 Can you think of any convincing/ unconvincing arguments in the media at the moment?

B Work in pairs. Talk about as many of the topics as you can in five minutes.

G VERB PATTERNS

4 A Complete the sentence stems so they are true for you.

1 I would never expect …

2 In my school, we were required …

3 I've always been interested in …

4 I'd love to have the chance …

5 Recently, I've been making plans …

6 It's impossible …

7 I don't mind …

8 I'd advise you …

B Compare your ideas in pairs.

F INTRODUCING OPINIONS

5 A Use a word from each box to complete the conversations.

according	can	if	my
~~honest~~	reality	quite	I'm

concerned	to	gather
~~opinion~~	frankly	you	is
knowledge		

1 A: If you want my *honest opinion*, she should apologize.

   B: _____ _____, I agree.

2 A: _____ _____ the statistics, we're the industry's most successful company.

   B: As far as _____ _____, statistics are worthless.

3 A: To _____ _____, the painting hasn't been sold yet.

   B: _____ _____ ask me, the price is too high.

4 A: From what I _____ _____, there's a lot of corruption in sports.

   B: The _____ _____, there's corruption everywhere, not only in sports.

B Play devil's advocate. Choose three of the topics below and write sentences using the expressions in Exercise 5A. Read your sentences to other students. Say what you think of their ideas.

• politics and politicians

  As far as I'm concerned, taxpayers should never pay for politicians to have a second home in the capital.

• sports

• technology

• a movie or TV program

• classical music

sports   sport

3 places

LONELY PLANET p32

HOME FROM HOME p35

WELCOME TO PERFECT CITY p38

LONDON p40

SPEAKING
3.1 Describe a vacation memory
3.2 Talk about an "alternative" home
3.3 Make a proposal
3.4 Present a documentary proposal

LISTENING
3.2 Listen to an account of homes around the world
3.3 Listen to a proposal for a city improvement scheme
3.4 Watch a program about London

READING
3.1 Read three texts about memorable vacation moments; Read a city guide
3.3 Read an article about solutions to urban problems

WRITING
3.1 Write a guidebook entry
3.4 Write a proposal for a documentary

What is your favorite place?

INTERVIEWS

31

3.1))) LONELY PLANET

G noun phrases
V landscapes
P word stress: compound nouns/adjectives

VOCABULARY

LANDSCAPES

1 A Work in pairs. What comes to mind when you think of the word *landscape*?

B Match the words in the box with synonyms 1–8.

> picturesque   tranquil   bustling   magnificent
> ancient   deserted   ~~run-down~~   unspoiled

1 shabby, dilapidated, in a bad state *run-down*
2 calm, quiet, peaceful
3 stunning, breathtaking
4 old, historic
5 unchanged, not altered by tourism
6 busy, full of people and noise
7 beautiful, lovely, pretty, attractive, pleasant
8 empty, uninhabited

C Complete the sentences with adjectives from Exercise 1B.

1 The flower market was _____ with shoppers.
2 The view from the tower was _____.
3 We wandered around the _____ walled city. Life there hadn't changed for centuries.
4 Tourists haven't discovered the area yet, so the beaches are completely _____.

D Look at the photos. Use the vocabulary to describe the scenes.

READING

2 A Where do you think the places in the photos are?

B Read the texts and match stories 1–3 with photos A–C.

C Read the texts again and answer the questions.

1 How did Alistair arrive at the scene?
2 What example(s) of spontaneity does he mention?
3 What is the Malecón, and what happens there?
4 Which things in the photo and the text capture the essence of Havana for Anthony?
5 What is special about the houses in Matera?
6 How did Greg feel when he left the town?

D Discuss. Have you ever been to any of these places? Would you like to visit them? Why/Why not?

SPEAKING

3 A Think of a "snapshot" moment of a special vacation. Where were you? How did you feel? Why is the memory important to you?

B Compare your "snapshot moments" with other students.

A

Every month the *Lonely Planet* magazine runs a photo competition. They ask readers to send in pictures they have taken on their travels and tell the story behind them.

1 Taking the plunge: Sangkhlaburi, Thailand

"We were in a long-tail boat crossing the Khao Laem reservoir in Sangkhlaburi, close to the Burmese border in Western Thailand, when our driver took us on a detour to Thailand's underlined{longest wooden bridge}. As he cut the engine and we idled up to the bridge for a closer look, some local boys were enjoying a bombing (diving) competition. When they saw us, they seized the moment to showcase some of their diving and one after the other plunged into the water. We were only there for a few minutes, but this impromptu performance remains one of the highlights of my time in Thailand. This shot embodies the spontaneity of the country and its people's vibrancy."

Alistair McDonald was on a two-week vacation in Thailand.

2 Seeing the light: Havana, Cuba

"The Malecón is a five-mile-long, six-lane sea road, laid out by U.S. Marines from 1901 and fronted by nineteenth-century buildings in various states of disrepair. It is where Habaneros* hang out and party on the weekends and is the unique fingerprint of Havana. When I got there, the sun was starting to set. There was a warm breeze blowing and a strong sea swell, with waves crashing against the sea wall. The sun was barely peeping through the clouds when I noticed a 1950s Pontiac approaching in the distance. I waited until it drew closer before pressing the shutter. For me, this photo captures the essence of Havana: a uniquely photogenic city frozen in time for fifty years."

Anthony McEvoy was in Cuba for work and a short vacation.

*Habaneros – people born in Havana, Cuba

3 Time stands still: Matera, Southern Italy

"Nothing could have prepared me for my first sight of the Sassi di Matera. I wasn't sure what to expect from a cave town where the locals live in the same houses as their ancestors did 9,000 years ago. I felt like I'd wandered onto a film set. The jumble of stacked cave houses appeared to tumble down a ravine. Adding to the magic of the place was the fact that I was the only person there and it felt like a ghost town. I left feeling slightly humbled – maybe it was knowing that my hotel room was once a cave dwelling for a family of ten and their livestock!"

Greg Jackson spent his summer vacation last year in Italy.

unspoiled   unspoilt

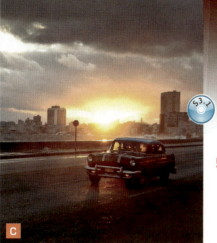

B | **C**

GRAMMAR
NOUN PHRASES

4 **A** Look at the ways in which noun phrases can be modified. Add the underlined sections in the texts to the appropriate category below.

RULES

A noun phrase is a group of words which functions as a unit to describe the noun. Information can be added before or after the noun in different ways.

1 Compound nouns

A noun can be used to modify a noun. Sometimes these are written as two words, sometimes as one word, and sometimes they are hyphenated.

cave houses, fingerprint, candy-floss, ¹_____

2 Compound adjectives

Adjectives can be used to modify the noun, using hyphens.

long-tail boat (a boat with a long tail)

When the noun part is plural, it becomes singular in a compound.

nine-year-old girl (the girl is nine **years** old), ² _____

3 Adverb + adjective combinations

refreshingly cool breeze, ³ _____

4 Adjectives

When several adjectives come before the noun, they need to be in a specific order.

Value adjectives (which give your opinion) come first, followed by size, age, shape, color, origin and material.

delicious slice of homemade apple pie, ⁴_____

5 Prepositional phrases and participle clauses

These occur after the noun.

Prepositional phrases:

a camera for filming short video clips, ⁵_____

Participle clauses:

waves crashing against the sea wall, ⁶_____

▶ page 132 **LANGUAGEBANK**

B WORD STRESS: compound nouns/adjectives Is the main stress on the first or the second word of a compound noun/adjective? Listen and repeat.

5 Put the words/phrases in the correct order to make sentences.

1 homemade / a slice of / chocolate / delicious / on top / cherries / with / cake

2 a / mountain bike / bright red / with fifteen gears / heavy-duty / brand new

3 Greek / seafood / it's a / of the best / fresh / restaurant / some / small / in the area / which serves

4 with / a / soup / traditional / freshly baked / bean / Tuscan / bread

5 a / medieval / castle / ancient / steep / on top of a very / hill / fascinating

6 **A** Look at the extra detail added to the noun phrases below. What parts of speech in Exercise 4 have been added each time?

The shop serves **tarts** and **coffee**.

1 The **shop** serves **custard tarts** and **good coffee**.

custard tarts = compound noun;
good coffee = adjective + noun

2 The **shop** serves **delicious hand-made custard tarts** and **extraordinarily good strong black espresso coffee**.

3 The **shop** serves **delicious hand-made custard tarts with a sprinkle of cinnamon on top** and **tiny cups of extraordinarily good strong black espresso coffee**.

4 The **old pastry shop in central Lisbon** serves **delicious hand-made custard tarts with a sprinkle of cinnamon on top** and **tiny cups of extraordinarily good strong black espresso coffee**.

B Work in pairs. Add more detail to the following noun phrases.

1 The man lives in a house.

2 There was a piece of cheese on the table.

3 The store sells furniture.

4 The boy enjoyed the cake.

5 The streets were empty.

6 The bus was crowded.

C Write three complex noun phrases describing:

1 a place you have visited.

2 something you have enjoyed eating/cooking.

3 something you bought recently.

D Read your sentences to other students. Can they picture the scene you describe? Ask each other questions to find out more information. Who wrote the most interesting descriptions?

WRITING

A DESCRIPTION OF A PLACE; LEARN TO ADD DETAIL

7 A Read the *Lonely Planet* guidebook entry for Lisbon. Make notes about the city under the following headings.

- Location
- Nearby sights
- Things to see/do
- History
- Architecture
- Food and drink

LISBON

Situated on the southwestern coast of Portugal and overlooking the Rio Tejo, Lisbon offers all the delights you'd expect of Portugal's star attraction. Gothic cathedrals, majestic monasteries and quaint museums are all part of the colorful cityscape, but the real delights of discovery lie in wandering the narrow lanes of Lisbon's lovely backstreets.

As bright yellow trams wind their way through curvy tree-lined streets, Lisboêtas stroll through the old quarters, much as they've done for centuries. Village-life gossip in old Alfama is exchanged at the public baths or over fresh bread and wine at tiny patio restaurants, as fadistas (proponents of fado, Portugal's traditional melancholic singing) perform in the background.

Meanwhile, in other parts of town, visitors and locals chase the ghosts of Pessoa (a Portuguese poet) in warmly lit 1930s-era cafés. Yet, while history is very much alive in ancient Lisbon, its spirit is undeniably youthful.

In the hilltop district of Bairro Alto, dozens of restaurants and bars line the narrow streets, with jazz, reggae, electronica and fado filling the air and revelers partying until dawn. Nightclubs scattered all over town make fine use of old spaces, whether on riverside docks or tucked away in eighteenth-century mansions.

The Lisbon experience encompasses so many things, from enjoying a fresh pastry and bica (espresso) on a petite leafy plaza to window-shopping in elegant Chiado or watching the sunset from the old Moorish* castle.

Just outside Lisbon, there's more to explore: the magical setting of Sintra, glorious beaches and traditional fishing villages.

*Moorish – relating to the Moors (Muslim people from Northern Africa)

B Work in pairs and discuss the questions.

1 What tense(s) does the writer use to describe Lisbon? Why?

2 Do you think the language in the article sounds formal or informal? Why?

3 Do you think the writer likes the place? Why/Why not?

8 A What kinds of details did the writer add to improve the sentences below?

1 Trams travel along the streets of the old town, where many locals walk.

2 In Alfama, people gossip in the public baths, or in restaurants where they enjoy bread, wine and traditional Portuguese music.

3 In Bairro Alto, you can find many restaurants and bars that play live music.

4 Nightclubs around the town can be found in all kinds of interesting places, near the docks and in old mansions.

5 In Lisbon you can do many things, like enjoy a coffee at a pavement café, go window shopping or visit the castle.

6 Outside Lisbon, it is worth visiting the town of Sintra, and also beaches and fishing villages along the coast.

> **American Speak out TIP**
> Add color. Details help to make your writing more colorful and interesting for the reader. Try to use a rich range of vocabulary and add details (colors, shapes, sounds, smells, tastes, feelings) to help the reader experience your description. Underline the sections in the article which add colorful detail to the description.

B Read the description below. Underline phrases which refer to the senses and identify each sense.

Approaching the central square, you can hear the voices of the market sellers, advertising their wares. The sweet smell of fruit ripened in the hot sun lingers in the air, mixing with the aroma of strong, fresh coffee and gas fumes from the small, three-wheeled motorized vans the local farmers, or "contadini", use to bring their produce to market. Each stall has mountains of different colored fruits and vegetables, firm red peppers, purple beans, tomatoes of all shapes and sizes. There's a liveliness in the air, as the old ladies haggle over the price of the cherries and wave their arms in rebuke at the younger workers.

9 A Plan a guidebook entry. Choose a place you know well. Make some notes using the headings in Exercise 7A. Think about how you can add some interesting detail.

B Write your guidebook entry (200–250 words).

reveler / gas / motorized   reveller / petrol / motorised

3.2)) HOME FROM HOME

G relative clauses
P long/short vowels
V -y adjectives; prefixes

LISTENING

1 Work with other students. Look at the photos and discuss the questions.

1 Why do you think houses are designed and built like this? What are the advantages?

2 Do you think they look comfortable? What problems might there be?

2 A Listen to an interview with an expert on homes around the world. What is the man's answer to question 1 above?

B Listen again and look at the words/expressions in the box. What do they mean and what does the speaker say about them?

> ~~a refuge from wild animals~~   spirits are earthbound
> wooden stilts   acts as an insulator
> so-called primitive dwellings
> adorned them with figurines   nomads in Central Asia

A refuge is a place where you can hide from something. He describes tree houses as a refuge from wild animals.

3 Read the extracts from the recording and discuss the questions.

1 "I had a real awakening when I traveled in Africa."

What does *have an awakening* mean? Can you think of a time when you had an awakening?

2 "I saw these enormous tree houses … and it just took my breath away."

What does *take your breath away* mean? What does it mean when something is *breathtaking*?

3 "These houses are built in accordance with the habitat."

What does this mean? What kind of habitat do you live in?

4 "Houses can be beautiful, but in most cultures they're built to be purely functional."

Think of three objects that are *purely functional*.

VOCABULARY

-Y ADJECTIVES

4 A Read descriptions 1–5. Are they from a lecture, an ad, or a piece of fiction? How do you know?

1 In hotter climates, people are forced to take refuge in shady dwellings.

2 The gloomy room suited her dejected mood. She stared at the dreary, gray carpet and waited.

3 Roomy cottage, spacious, good views, airy kitchen with large windows, sleeps eight.

4 Native peoples would use animal skins to insulate the house from chilly weather in winter.

5 He saw the poky interior — tiny, cramped — was adorned only by a cabinet repainted in gaudy colors: bright red, purple and yellow.

B Underline the adjectives in Exercise 4A. Are they positive, negative or neutral? Think of more examples to describe a place or room.

> **American Speak out TIP**
> Many adjectives end in -y. Some come from the root word, e.g. *dirty, noisy, smelly*. Others do not have a root word, e.g. *happy, pretty, silly*. If we don't know the meaning, we need to guess from the context. Do the adjectives in Exercise 4B have a root word?

5 A LONG/SHORT VOWELS Are the bold vowel sounds long or short? Underline the odd one out in each set.

1 dreary/city/really
2 gaudy/body/naughty
3 gloomy/footie/roomy
4 hockey/jokey/poky
5 shady/ready/daily
6 bury/airy/ferry

B Listen and check. Then listen again and repeat.

▶ page 150 VOCABULARYBANK

GRAMMAR
RELATIVE CLAUSES

6 Read what six people say about homes. Which sentences are true for you?

1 Most people who work at home need peace and quiet, but I need noise and chaos. **Salih Moustafa, inventor**

2 My first home was by the sea. It was dreary and poky and chilly in the winter, none of which mattered because the location was perfect, and location is everything. **Pablo Anaya, nurse**

3 A home for me is anywhere I can put my feet up and let my hair down. **Hannah Obi, maintenance worker**

4 You have to separate home from work. I started a company in my garage. A year later, six colleagues were pretty much living there 24/7, at which point I knew we needed an office. **Kath Scheidel, entrepreneur**

5 A home is only a home because of your memories in it. The door on which I drew marks to show my children getting taller is just a piece of wood, but it is priceless to me. **Paul Hartfeld, sanitation worker**

6 The best homes are those whose major characteristic is brightness. Good light can compensate for almost anything. **Jiao Cheung, architect**

7 A Check what you know. Look at comments 1 and 2 in Exercise 6 and underline the relative clauses. Which relative clause is defining (gives essential information)? Which is non-defining (adds extra information)? Which uses a comma?

B Underline the relative clauses in comments 3–6. Are they defining or non-defining?

C Match descriptions a)–f) with the relative clauses in Exercise 6.

a) a sentence in which a preposition comes before the relative pronoun (*which/who/when*, etc.) *5*

b) the possessive *whose* (used only before nouns)

c) a fixed phrase (usually three words) with *which*. It usually starts with a preposition, e.g. *by which time*.

d) a relative pronoun after *some of, all of, none of,* etc.

e) a defining relative clause with no relative pronoun

f) a defining relative clause in which the relative pronoun (*who, which*, etc.) can be replaced by *that*

D Work in pairs and answer the questions.

1 In what kinds of clauses (defining or non-defining) can you sometimes use *that* instead of *who, where, when,* etc.?

2 If a relative pronoun (*which, who,* etc.) refers to the object of the sentence, we can sometimes omit it. Which relative pronoun has been omitted from sentence 3?

3 Which sentence, a), b), or c) is incorrect?

a) I have the thing that you want.

b) I have the thing what you want.

c) I have what you want.

▶ page 132 **LANGUAGE**BANK

8 Cross out the incorrect option in each sentence.

1 My aunt and uncle, _____ cook well, spend most of their time in the kitchen.

   a) both **b)** both of whom **c)** who both

2 That's the run-down little bar _____ we first met.

   a) in which **b)** where **c)** which

3 The hill _____ overlooks a secluded hotel off the beaten track.

   a) on where the castle was built
   b) on which the castle was built
   c) which the castle was built on

4 The group of friends, _____ I've known for ages, went on a yearly vacation together.

   a) who **b)** whose **c)** a few of whom

5 We decided to go home in 2014, _____ we had traveled to thirty-five countries.

   a) at which point **b)** since when
   c) by which time

6 The food _____ they served was wonderful.

   a) – **b)** that **c)** what

7 We watched the election, _____ was never in doubt.

   a) the result of which **b)** that result
   c) whose result

8 She was the person _____ for our information.

   a) on whom we relied **b)** whom we relied
   c) who we relied on

SPEAKING

9 A Work in pairs. You're going to design a dream "alternative home". Where will it be and what will it look like? Think about the following topics and make notes. Design your ideal alternative home.

- shape/type/design of home
- special features
- decoration
- objects/furniture
- size
- view

B Work in groups. Take turns describing the home.

CHELSEA HOTEL

To say that the Chelsea Hotel has an interesting history would be an understatement.

Since the early twentieth century, the hotel has been home to dozens of celebrities. The fame of the building itself pre-dates its fame as a hotel; when it was constructed in 1883 as an apartment building, it was New York's tallest building. It became a hotel in 1905. Although prosperous at first, during a period of maladministration the hotel began to degenerate. It went bankrupt and changed hands in 1939. Its proactive new managers soon got it up and running again, and in the post-war era, its fame grew.

As a part of the New York artistic scene, the hotel is irreplaceable. Its famous residents have included actors, artists, singers, writers and numerous anti-establishment figures. Frida Kahlo, Jean-Paul Sartre, Jackson Pollock, Marilyn Monroe, Bob Dylan, Jimi Hendrix, Madonna and Uma Thurman all lived there for a while, and the hotel has been immortalized (and some would say overexposed) in dozens of songs, books and films (*9½ Weeks*, *The Interpreter*). Always a place of non-conformity, the hotel's management sometimes allowed penniless residents to pay for their rooms with artworks, some of which still hang in its lobby today. Its famous residents have found the hotel conducive to creativity. Arthur C. Clarke and Jack Kerouac wrote, respectively, *2001: A Space Odyssey* and *On the Road* while living in the hotel, and Madonna used it for a photo shoot for one of her books. Unfortunately, the hotel is also associated with artistic misbehavior and tragedy. One of numerous examples of wild adventures behind its closed doors, the poet Dylan Thomas allegedly collapsed in room 205 of the hotel after partying too hard. He died four days later.

VOCABULARY *PLUS*
PREFIXES

10 Read about a hotel. Why is it famous?

11 **A** Read the text again. Find and underline an example of a word beginning with each prefix in the table.

prefix	meaning	example
de- ir- im- non- un-	*negatives/ opposites/reverse*	*degenerate*
under- over-		
mal- mis-		
pre- post-		
pro- anti-		

B Complete the second column of the table with the meanings in the box.

> ~~negatives/opposites/reverse~~   size or degree
> time (before or after)   wrong or bad
> attitude or opinion (for or against)

C What parts of speech do we use the prefixes with?

D Work in groups. Add your own examples to the third column of the table.

12 One statement about prefixes is true. Correct the false statements.

1 When we add a prefix to the root word, the spelling of the root word usually changes.

2 We cannot add more than one prefix at a time to root words.

3 Learning to recognize prefixes helps us build our vocabulary and guess unknown words.

4 There are rules that tell us which prefixes we can add to each root word.

13 **A** Complete the words by adding prefixes.

1 a place that is _____known to most tourists because it's _____exposed in the media

2 a hotel, restaurant, bar or café that looks _____descript but is _____rated

3 a hotel, restaurant, bar or café that you think is _____attractive and a bit _____rated

4 a building that is _____inhabitable because it was _____managed in the past

5 a threatened habitat that is _____replaceable, but _____possible to save

B Work in pairs. How many examples of places in Exercise 13A can you think of? Compare your ideas with other students.

A place that is unknown to most tourists is Regent's Canal in London. You can walk nine miles along it from Camden Market to Little Venice, and it's great!

▶ page 150 **VOCABULARYBANK**

immortalized / misbehavior   *immortalised / misbehaviour*

3.3)) WELCOME TO PERFECT CITY

F making a proposal
P shifting stress: suffixes
V city life

Dubai

VOCABULARY
CITY LIFE

1 A Work in groups and discuss the questions.

1 Have you been to any of the cities in the photos?

2 What do you think might be good about living in them? What problems might there be?

3 What is good and bad about the city or town where you live?

4 What other problems connected with urban living can you think of?

B Read the article. Does it mention any of the issues you discussed in Exercise 1A?

Welcome to **Perfect City**

Environmental psychology looks at the ways in which we are affected by our surroundings. Almost every aspect of the built environment, from the color of hospital walls to the type of grass used in parks, can have a dramatic impact on crime, health, education, commerce and happiness. *BBC Focus* magazine reports on how psychologists are teaming up with designers to build safer and healthier spaces.

Classic trick
In the mid-nineties in Montreal, it was discovered that playing classical music through the public address system would drive away crowds of loitering teenagers and cut crime. The idea soon caught on. Now, classical music is played in over 60 London subway stations.

Stop signs
Sometimes less is more – towns such as Bohmte in Germany have found that the best way to slow traffic is to remove all road signs and markings. Without these guides, drivers have to slow down and negotiate rights of way with other drivers, cyclists and pedestrians.

Dipping distractions
Researchers in Manchester found that pickpockets took advantage of pedestrians distracted by confusing environments. With visual clutter removed and spaces made easier to navigate, pedestrians are more aware of their surroundings and less likely to become crime victims.

Delays stress
A study of rail commuters found the highest levels of the stress hormone cortisol among those who perceived their journey as unpredictable. Real-time transportation updates, such as a text message letting you know exactly when the next bus will arrive, have been found to reduce stress.

2 A Look at the words connected to city life. Which do you know? Work with other students to complete sentences 1–4.

> amenities   infrastructure   congestion
> abandonment   tolls   renewal

1 The best thing to do with loitering teenagers is to give them _____ such as sports facilities.

2 The city can't host a major international event because it doesn't have the _____. The transportation is poor.

3 The _____ of run-down old buildings used to be a real problem where I live, but the area has undergone urban _____, so now it's full of nice stores and houses.

4 There's always traffic _____. We should have _____ so people pay to drive in the city.

B Which three words in the box contain suffixes that turn them into nouns? What are the nouns' root words?

C **SHIFTING STRESS:** suffixes Listen to the pronunciation of some words with and without suffixes. Notice how a different syllable is stressed when a suffix is added to the root word. Listen again and repeat.

FUNCTION
MAKING A PROPOSAL

3 A Listen to someone proposing an idea to improve an area of their city. What is the idea? What is the speaker proposing to do now?

B Complete the notes. Then listen again to check.

> • *Harrogate Council to set up cycle hubs in the next* ¹_____ *years.*
>
> • *Idea: to increase* ²_____ *use.*
>
> • *Hubs to go in the city* ³_____, *where many cyclists go.*
>
> • *Will make the* ⁴_____ *safer for cyclists.*
>
> • *Benefits of cycling: fast, good for environment,* ⁵_____ *and good for fitness.*

subway / transportation / renewal   underground / transport / regeneration

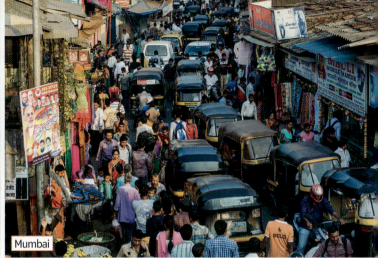

Paris

Mumbai

4 A Put phrases a)—g) under the correct headings below.

a) The main goal/objective of our proposal is to …

b) The short-term/long-term benefits include …

c) To sum up, we're proposing …

d) Is there anything that needs clarification?

e) This idea is feasible because …

f) To start with, I'm going to talk briefly about …

g) We're going to build/develop/come up with …

Introducing your proposal

Just to give a bit of background information, …

1 _____

Stating the purpose

The aim of the project is to …

2 _____

Describing your idea

What we plan to do is …

3 _____

Justifying your idea

This solution will help us to …

4 _____

Listing the benefits

In the first instance, this would mean …

5 _____

Summarizing your proposal

So, basically, what we're proposing (to do) is to …

6 _____

Soliciting questions

Does anyone have any questions?

7 _____

B Which expressions were used by the speaker in Exercise 3A? Read audio script S3.5 on page 168 and check.

▶ page 132 LANGUAGEBANK

5 Some of the sentences below contain extra words. Cross out the extra words and check the correct sentences.

1 To start up with, I'm going to talk briefly about Manor Studios.

2 The main goals objective is to renovate the building.

3 The aim of the project is to use the building as a film museum.

4 What we plan to do is but renovate and paint the main studio.

5 This idea is too feasible because the buildings have potential.

6 In the first of instance, our plan requires a $1 million investment.

7 The long-term benefits include bringing jobs to the area.

8 So that's our plan. Is there anything that needs the clarification?

LEARN TO
SUGGEST MODIFICATIONS

6 Look at phrases a)—f) which are used to suggest modifications or changes to a proposal. Answer questions 1—4.

a) I'd like to propose a compromise.

b) Let's try to come up with a solution.

c) Let's look at it another way.

d) How about if we combine our ideas?

e) Is there any way we can reduce the costs?

f) Is there any leeway regarding the schedule?

1 Which two expressions mean we should put separate ideas together?

2 Which two expressions ask if there is flexibility to change a plan?

3 Which expression means we should think of an answer to a problem?

4 Which expression asks to rethink a problem?

SPEAKING

7 A Work in groups. Think of an area you know, for example part of your city, and make notes on the questions below.

1 What problems does the area have? Think about:

- buildings
- facilities
- appearance
- user-friendliness
- safety
- noise levels

2 How could the area be improved?

3 What would be the benefits for the community?

B Your group is applying for a $1 million grant to improve the area. Plan a proposal using the structure in Exercise 4A. Decide who will say which part and practice the proposal.

C Present your proposal to the class. Which idea do you think should win the grant?

summarize   summarise

3.4 LONDON

DVD PREVIEW

1 Work in pairs and discuss the questions.

1 What do you think of when you think about London?
2 What would you expect to see/hear about in a video promoting London?

2 Read the program information. What do you think the writer means by "London is a world in a city"?

One day in London

By 2050 it is expected that more than three-quarters of the world's population will live in cities. With more than 8.6 million inhabitants, London is a world in a city; a world-class city to live and study in; a city where over 300 languages are spoken. But what drives its success? And how can it take the best from its past and turn it into a dynamic future? In *One day in London*, we meet the man who's revolutionized the iconic red double-decker bus; take a trip to the annual Wimbledon championships; and learn about what inspires London fashion designers of the future.

DVD VIEW

3 Watch the DVD and complete the information.

1 London is the U.K.'s financial _____.
2 SW19 is one of the most _____ zip codes on the planet.
3 Over _____ million people visit London every year.
4 The _____ industry contributes over $30 billion dollars a year to the U.K. economy.

4 A Answer the questions.

1 What do we learn about London's financial sector?
2 What can you find in London's Savile Row?
3 What does Paul Frearson, the tailor, like about London?
4 Why does Roger Federer think that Wimbledon is unique?
5 What was special about the 1950s Routemaster?
6 What inspires London's fashion designers?

B Watch the DVD again to check.

5 Work in pairs. Discuss the questions.

1 What impressions do you get of London?
2 How is London similar to/different from your capital city?
3 Do you think capital cities are representative of the rest of the country, or do they have a distinct character/culture/economy? Can you give examples?

revolutionize / zip codes   revolutionise / postcodes

American Speakout your country

6 A Listen to two people from Canada and Argentina. Make notes on what they say about their countries.

B Compare your notes in pairs. What do they say in answer to the questions below? Which questions don't they answer?

1 What is special about your country?

2 What are the highs and lows of living in your country?

3 How would you describe your country geographically? What features would you focus on in a documentary about your country?

4 Is your country experiencing any particular changes at the moment? Do you feel strongly about any of them?

5 Does your country have any interesting customs or events? What are they?

6 What are the similarities and differences between your country and your neighboring countries?

C Listen again. How do the speakers complete the key phrases? Check your answers in audio script S3.6 on page 168.

> **KEYPHRASES**
>
> (Canada) has one of the highest ... in the world.
>
> On the downside, I suppose, you have to deal with ...
>
> I would describe (Canada) as geographically ...
>
> We're very, very lucky in (Canada) to have ...
>
> Undoubtedly one of the best things about (Argentina) is the ...
>
> People are very warm, ..., and we've got a great sense of ...
>
> (Argentinians), we've got a sense of longing for ...

7 A Work in pairs. Ask and answer the questions in Exercise 6B. Do you have similar answers?

B Work in groups. Read the instructions for developing a documentary proposal. Decide what you would include in a program about your country and make notes.

> ### Lights, camera, action!
>
> You need to pitch a plan for a short documentary about your country. Think about your audience – who is the documentary for? Think about your purpose – what issue would you like to focus on? What do you want people to learn from your video? What attitude do you want them to leave with? Think about your plan – how will you make your information engaging and appealing? Who/Where will you film? Will you include interviews? What will you call the documentary?

C Present your ideas to the class.

writeback a proposal

8 A Read the sample proposal. Do you think this pitch would receive funding? Why/Why not?

> ### The music of our heritage
>
> This documentary would examine the importance of the National Folkloric Festival (Festival Nacional de la Mejorana) in Panama. The *mejorana* is a small guitar, and the music and dance associated with it form an important part of Panama's cultural heritage. Nowadays though, fewer people know how to make the instrument or how to play it.
>
> The aim of the documentary would be to film the four-day festival in order to raise awareness of the *mejorana* and the consequences of losing this tradition in favor of more modern music.
>
> During the festival, groups from all around the country gather to enjoy Panamanian folklore. There are musical performances, dances, singing, bullfights, traditional contests and an ox-cart parade. It is a colorful and spectacular occasion. The documentary would highlight the atmosphere at the festival, filming music and dance performances, and interview young and old visitors to gather opinions about the importance of the *mejorana* and of protecting the traditional customs that are an integral part of Panamanian life.

B Write a short proposal (200–250 words) for your documentary idea. Use the instructions in Exercise 7B.

favor favour

V LANDSCAPES

1 A Match the sentence halves.

1 It was a shabby little restaurant,
2 In the summer the normally calm,
3 Hong Kong is a
4 Loreto is an ancient
5 With its largely unspoiled
6 The beach was completely

a) hillside town with cobbled streets.
b) deserted and not safe for swimming.
c) tranquil streets fill with tourists.
d) but the food was exquisite.
e) natural beauty, Vietnam is a top tourist destination.
f) bustling, fascinating city.

B Choose three adjectives from Exercise 1A. Use them to describe places you know to your partner.

shabby –The tapas bar near where I live has been run by the same couple for thirty years. It's a bit shabby now and needs to be redecorated.

G NOUN PHRASES

2 A Add detail to sentences 1–4 using words/phrases in the box.

> cups of   old   Japanese green
> steaming hot   cross-country
> top-of-the-range   in the rain
> laptop   five-mile-long   farm
> on top of the hill   brand-new
> to keep me awake
> with all the latest graphic
> technology

1 I drink tea.
2 They bought the house.
3 I bought a computer.
4 She went for a run.

B Work in pairs and take turns. Extend the descriptions of the nouns in the box by adding one extra piece of information each time.

> a book   coffee   a cake
> cigars   the house   a day

A: an old book
B: an old book with torn-out pages

V -Y ADJECTIVES

3 A Read about three places. Complete the descriptive adjectives.

1 The Pear Tree is a g_____, dark bar. It's quite p_____ with uncomfortable wooden chairs, but it has live music every night.

2 Jackie Brown's is a large café with a r_____ interior. Set in a picturesque part of the city, it is very a_____, with huge windows that look out onto a big park.

3 Bangles II is a bright, loud hangout. It has a g_____, multicolored decor and a DJ who plays hip hop. It gets c_____ in winter.

B Work in pairs and discuss which places in Exercise 3A you would most like to visit regularly/work in.

G RELATIVE CLAUSES

4 A Underline the correct alternatives to complete the riddles.

1 I am taken from a mine and shut in a wooden case *of which/from which/which* I am never released, but almost everyone uses me. What am I?

2 I have a little house *which I live alone/that I live alone/in which I live alone*. It has no doors or windows, and if I want to go out, I have to break through the wall. What am I?

3 What is one question *to which you can never answer "yes"/ at which you can never answer "yes"/that you can never answer "yes" for*?

4 A barrel of water weighed ten pounds. Someone added something to it, *to which point/ by when/at which point* it weighed four pounds. What did they add?

B Try to solve the riddles and then check your answers on page 161.

F MAKING A PROPOSAL

5 Work in pairs and complete the proposal. You may need to add more than one word in each blank.

1 Just _____ give _____ background information, I have ten years' experience in marine research.

2 _____ main objective _____ proposal _____ get funds for marine research in Australia.

3 _____ aim _____ project _____ document the gradual destruction of Australia's Barrier Reef.

4 _____ plan _____ is measure the coral every week for a year.

5 Then _____ come up ____ a plan to minimize the damage.

6 _____ idea _____ feasible _____ it follows previous research on the reef.

7 I hope _____ solution _____ help _____ slow down the destruction of the reef.

8 _____ first instance, _____ mean talking to the Australian authorities about the problem.

9 _____ long-term benefits _____ preserving the reef with all its diversity of marine life.

10 _____ basically, _____ proposing is _____ carry out the study in a year and find solutions after that.

11 _____ anyone _____ questions?

minimize   minimise

4)))justice

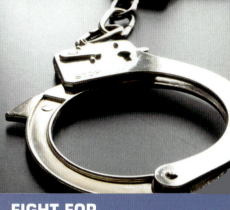

FIGHT FOR JUSTICE   p44

SOCIAL ISSUES   p47

DO THE RIGHT THING   p50

THE CON ARTIST   p52

SPEAKING
4.1 Talk about criminal justice
4.2 Discuss social issues
4.3 Discuss moral dilemmas
4.4 Recount a crime story

LISTENING
4.2 Listen to people describe someone they admire
4.3 Listen to a discussion about witnessing a crime
4.4 Watch a program about a con artist

READING
4.1 Read an article about a miscarriage of justice

WRITING
4.2 Write a problem-solution essay
4.4 Write a short article

What legal or social issues concern you?

INTERVIEWS

4.1)) FIGHT FOR JUSTICE

G introductory it
V crime collocations; lexical chunks
P pauses and chunking

READING

1 A Work in pairs. Discuss the questions.

1 Imagine you were arrested for a crime you didn't commit (e.g. murder). What would you do?

2 Imagine you are offered a choice: admit a lesser charge and go to prison for a shorter time (even though you are innocent) or fight to protect your freedom. What would you choose?

B Read an article about a young waitress. Why was she arrested?

2 Work in pairs and answer the questions.

1 What crime was Dee Roberts charged with?

2 Did the police have any strong evidence against her?

3 What was the difficult choice that she was offered?

4 Who pressured Dee Roberts to plead guilty? Why?

5 Why do you think she chose not to plead guilty?

6 According to the article, what are the faults of the criminal justice system?

3 Discuss.

1 Do you think Dee Roberts was right to do what she did? Was it worth the risk?

2 Do you think similar problems exist within the criminal justice system in your country?

VOCABULARY
CRIME COLLOCATIONS

4 A Choose the correct words from the box to complete collocations 1–8.

drugs   prove   dawn   carry out   driving   report
previous   appeal

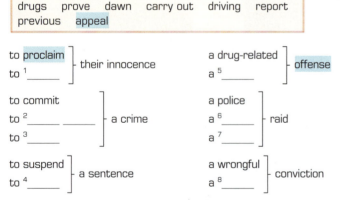

to proclaim
to ¹_____ } their innocence

a drug-related
a ⁵_____ } offense

to commit
to ²_____ _____ } a crime
to ³_____

a police
a ⁶_____ } raid
a ⁷_____

to suspend
to ⁴_____ } a sentence

a wrongful
a ⁸_____ } conviction

B Choose the correct collocation to complete sentences 1–6.

1 She refused to plead guilty and was determined to *protest/commit* her innocence in court.

2 Weapons were seized during a *driving/dawn* raid by the police.

3 Both men had *previous/report* convictions for violent crimes.

4 They used specialist tools to help them *protest/carry out* the crime.

5 Her lawyer advised her to *suspend/appeal* the sentence.

6 You could lose your license if you commit another *driving/raid* offense.

▶ page 151 **VOCABULARYBANK**

SPEAKING

5 A Work in groups. Each group choose one of the topics below to discuss.

1 Why do you think the wrong people are sometimes sent to prison?

2 Is prison an effective deterrent against crime?
Why/Why not?

3 Can the public do anything to help reduce crime?
What can governments do to improve the situation?

4 Why do young people turn to crime?
What is the best way to stop them?
Who do you think should be responsible for this?

B Summarize your ideas and report back to the class.

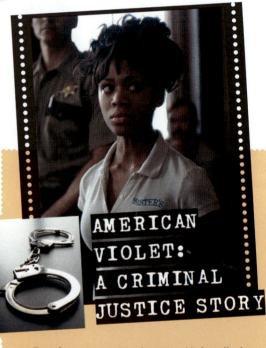

AMERICAN VIOLET: A CRIMINAL JUSTICE STORY

Based on true events, *American Violet* tells the astonishing story of Dee Roberts, a courageous young waitress who is prepared to risk everything in a battle for justice that will ultimately change
5 her life forever.
It is the last thing she expects to happen. Dee Roberts, a single twenty-four-year-old mother of four children, is working her shift in the local diner of a small Texas town, when police storm into
10 the café and drag Dee out in handcuffs. Arrested for suspected drug offences, Dee is left in the county prison, where she learns that police have raided the housing project where she lives, and arrested a number of people. Dee soon discovers
15 she is being charged as a drug dealer, based on evidence provided by a single, unreliable police informant, who is facing his own drug charges.

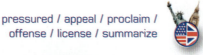

pressured / appeal / proclaim /
offense / license / summarize

pressurized / appeal against / protest /
offence / licence / summarise

GRAMMAR
INTRODUCTORY *IT*

6 A Look at the sentences from the text. What does *it* refer to?

1 *It* is the last thing she expects to happen. (line 6)

2 *It* is regular practice for these types of raids to take place. (line 32)

3 *It* seems that the more guilty plea agreements that are signed … (line 37)

B Check what you know. Add *it* in the correct place(s) in sentences 1–10.

1 I could hardly believe when the police officer told me what had happened.

2 Has been reported that a number of people in the area were affected.

3 Is no use! I've looked everywhere for my wallet, but I can't find anywhere.

4 We would appreciate if you didn't tell anyone about this.

5 Is surprising how quickly I was able to master the skill.

6 Is no wonder you couldn't find your bag. You left in the café.

7 **A:** How much further is? **B:** Is not far now.

8 Is a shame that you won't be able to make to the lunch.

9 Was a warm day for the time of year.

10 Appears that someone has made a mistake.

Although she has no previous convictions, and no drugs are found on her at the time of her arrest, or in any other subsequent searches,
20 Dee is offered an impossible choice: plead guilty to the charges and be allowed home as a convicted criminal, with a ten-year suspended sentence; or stay in prison to fight the charges and risk a much longer prison sentence if she loses her case. Everybody, from her mother, who is looking after her children, to her lawyer, who offers little hope of
25 winning the case, urges Dee to accept the deal, and plead guilty to a crime she hasn't committed. But Dee's sense of justice prevails, and she decides to risk her own freedom and the custody of her children to stand up for what she believes is right. She chooses to fight the district attorney who ordered the racially motivated drugs raid and
30 refuses to confess to something she did not do.

   Working together with a lawyer from the civil liberties union and a previous narcotics officer, Dee discovers that it is regular practice for these types of raids to take place and that the war on drugs in the USA means that local police forces get more money
35 according to the number of convictions they make. This situation leads to arrests being made based on little or no evidence and pressure being put on those arrested to sign plea agreements. It seems that the more guilty plea agreements that are signed, the easier it is for the district attorney to build a record as a crime
40 fighter, even though in reality it is really he who is committing the crime. Those who are arrested often have little choice but to agree to the guilty plea and accept the conviction. They simply don't have the courage and the resources to be able to fight the system and prove their innocence.
45   The film *American Violet*, which is based on the true story of Regina Kelly, who fought her case against the criminal justice system and won, highlights dysfunctions within the system and shows how difficult it can be for poorer people to defend themselves.

---

7 Look at Exercises 6A and 6B again. Find examples of *it* used for the following purposes.

RULES

Use *it* at the beginning of a sentence:

a) to talk about the weather, a situation, dates, times, distances, etc.

(*it* + verb)
It rains a lot in September.

b) to express opinion or emotion.

(*it* + adjective/noun phrase)
It's extraordinary how often we have the same ideas.

c) to talk about what you understand from the evidence.

(*it* + verb + clause)
It appears that someone broke into the office.

d) to report what someone else thinks or says.

(*it* + *be* + past participle + clause)
It has been reported that the police decided not to pursue the case.

Use *it* in the middle of a sentence:

e) as a substitute object for transitive verbs, to be expanded on later in the sentence.
I'd appreciate it if you would help with our enquiries.

f) as part of a set phrase.
I can't help it.
We made it! (succeeded)

▶ page 134 **LANGUAGEBANK**

8 A Complete the sentences with the words in the box.

difficult	help	fault	funny	shame
appears	important	wonder		

1 It's to believe he would have left the money here.

2 It's no you were scared. That car nearly hit you.

3 It's not my we didn't finish on time.

4 I can't it if I keep making mistakes. Nobody's perfect.

5 It's that we clear up any misunderstandings.

6 It was a that we didn't see the beginning.

7 It to have been a mistake.

8 It's how things always turn out OK in the end.

B Complete the sentences so they are true for you.

• It's no wonder that …

• I couldn't believe it when …

• I think it's important to …

• It's pointless …

• It's amazing that …

• I'd appreciate it if …

• It's hard to know if …

C Work in pairs and take turns. Compare your sentences and ask questions.

A: I think it's important to find time to keep in touch with friends.

B: Why do you think that?

---

shame   pity

VOCABULARY *PLUS*

LEXICAL CHUNKS

9 A Work in groups. Think of words that often collocate with *justice*.

a sense of justice, to demand justice

B Read sentences 1–6 and add any more phrases with *justice* to your list.

1 Families of the victims demanded that the killers be found and brought to justice as soon as possible.

2 Mr. Jobe is an experienced lawyer who specializes in this particular area of criminal justice.

3 It is imperative that young people on the streets who are committing crimes should not be allowed to escape justice.

4 It's up to the courts to uphold justice – you can't take the law into your own hands.

5 A surprising number of people came to him demanding justice for how they had been treated.

6 Gangs in the vicinity have been known to practice a kind of rough justice on their members.

C Why do you think the other phrases in sentences 1–6 have been underlined?

D Which underlined phrases in Exercise 9B could be replaced with the following?

1 a sort of
2 it's the responsibility of
3 try to implement the law yourself
4 it is extremely important
5 in the area

> **American Speak TIP** A lexical chunk is a group of words commonly found together. They include collocations, but while collocations tend to consist of content words only, lexical chunks are more phrasal and may include grammatical words like prepositions and articles, e.g. *miscarriage of justice*. Lexical chunks may act as discourse markers or adverbials, e.g. *at that time, in her own way*. Find a lexical chunk in Exercise 9B that acts as a time adverbial.

10 A Work in pairs. Look at the movie posters and read the synopses. What do the movies have in common? Which would you prefer to watch? Why?

B PAUSES AND CHUNKING Listen to someone reading the first synopsis. Notice how they chunk the language, pausing between the chunks (marked 'I'). When we speak, we group words into meaningful chunks of language.

C Mark possible chunks in the second synopsis.

D Listen to check. Listen again and shadow read the story.

The movie | is based on the true story | of Manny Balestrero, | an honest, hard working musician | who is unjustly accused | of armed robbery | when he goes to an insurance firm | to borrow some money, | and employees mistake him | for the armed robber | who had robbed them | the year before. | In classic Hitchcock form, | Balestrero vehemently proclaims his innocence, | but unfortunately | he acts guiltily, | leading a host of policemen | and witnesses | to identify him | as the thief. | The trial goes badly for Manny, | but things are even worse for his wife, | Rose, | who struggles to cope | with the strain of his ordeal.

Dr. Richard Kimble, a well-known Chicago surgeon, returns home one night to find that his wife has been viciously murdered in their own home. When police find Kimble at the scene of the crime, he is arrested, and later charged and convicted of his wife's brutal murder. However, on the way to the prison, a failed escape attempt by other prisoners gives Kimble his chance of freedom. While on the run from U.S. Marshall Samuel Gerard, Kimble's only hope of proving his innocence and clearing his name is to find out for himself who was responsible for his wife's death and to lead the team of detectives on his trail to the real perpetrator.

specialize / practice / movie / hardworking

specialise / practise / film / hard-working

4.2)) SOCIAL ISSUES

G the perfect aspect
V social issues
P stress patterns

SPEAKING

1 Work in groups. Look at the photos and discuss the questions.

1 What are the three most important social issues in your country and in the world at the moment?

2 What is being done about them? Do you know of anyone who is involved in tackling these issues?

VOCABULARY

SOCIAL ISSUES

2 A Work in two groups. Group A: look at the expressions in box A. Group B: look at the expressions in box B. Discuss what they mean and think of an example sentence for each.

> **A** human rights   intellectual property
> child labor   economic development
> capital punishment   religious freedom

> **B** environmental awareness   gun control
> illegal immigration   civil liberties
> free trade   freedom of speech

B Work in pairs with a student from the other group. Explain the meaning of your expressions, using your example sentence if necessary.

3 A STRESS PATTERNS What stress patterns do the expressions in Exercise 2A have? Match them with the patterns below.

1 Oo Ooo   *civil liberties*   7 ooOo Ooo

2 Oo O   8 O oo

3 O O   9 oOooo oOo

4 Oo o O   10 Ooo Ooo

5 oOo Oo   11 Oooo oOoo

6 oOo ooOo   12 O Oo

B Listen and check. Repeat the collocations slowly and tap your fingers at the same time (use both hands). Now say the collocations at full speed.

> **American Speak out TIP**)) The more ways you interact with new words, the better you will learn them. Research suggests that we need to use, see or hear new words six times (minimum) before we "know" them. Use different methods: write sentences including the new word, teach the new word to someone else, pronounce the word many times and try to use the word in conversation. Which of these do you usually do?

▶ page 151 **VOCABULARY**BANK

labor labour

Cornel West

Rigoberta Menchu

Malala Yousafzai

LISTENING

4 Work in pairs and discuss the questions.

1 Do you know of any celebrities who campaign about social issues? Are they effective?

2 What are the best ways to fight for social justice?

5 A Listen to three speakers talking about the people below. What issues is each involved in? Why do the speakers admire them?

B Compare your ideas with a partner. Then listen again to check.

C Discuss the questions below with other students.

1 The "heroes" are described as *a beacon*, *a tower of strength*, *a stellar figure* and *one in a million*. What do these expressions mean? Do you have similar metaphors/expressions in your language?

2 The speakers say their heroes *advocate for* (*something*), *campaign against* ..., and *shed light on* ... . What do these expressions mean?

3 The recording mentions *struggles*, *human rights violations* and *atrocities*. What do these mean? Can you give any examples?

GRAMMAR

THE PERFECT ASPECT

6 Read 1–7 and match the verbs used in these sentences to tenses a)–g).

1 For over forty years, Menchu has been advocating for women's rights.

2 West's ability to perform in public seems to have helped him attract followers.

3 Before leaving high school, West had already participated in civil rights demonstrations.

4 Menchu's work has helped to shed light on the situation confronting indigenous people.

5 If she continues, by 2050, Yousafzai will have been fighting for human rights for over 50 years.

6 Yousafzai had been campaigning for children's rights before she was attacked.

7 Some people think that by 2040, Yousafzai will have become Pakistan's president.

a) present perfect *4*   e) future perfect

b) present perfect continuous   f) future perfect continuous

c) past perfect   g) perfect infinitive

d) past perfect continuous

7 Read the description of perfect tenses. Look at the sentences in Exercise 6A and answer the questions.

We use perfect tenses to create a link between two times: to look back from one moment in time to a time before that.

1 Which three sentences link the past and the present? *1,*

2 Which two sentences link the past to a time before that?

3 Which two sentences link a time in the future with a time before that?

4 Which three sentences focus on the action's duration?

▶ page 134 **LANGUAGEBANK**

8 Work in pairs. Decide if there is a difference in meaning between the pairs of sentences. If so, what is the difference?

1 a) I've read that book about free trade.

b) I've been reading that book about free trade.

Sentence a) focuses on the completed action. The speaker finished the book. Sentence b) focuses on the action of reading, but the speaker has not finished the book.

2 a) I hope to have become an intellectual property lawyer by the time I'm thirty.

b) I hope I will have become an intellectual property lawyer by the time I'm thirty.

3 a) How long have you worked in economic development?

b) How long have you been working in economic development?

4 a) Had you heard of Malala Yousafzai before?

b) Have you heard of Malala Yousafzai before?

5 a) I've reported a crime.

b) I've been reporting a crime.

6 a) The judge said he'd been wrongfully convicted.

b) The judge said he's been wrongfully convicted.

7 a) By 2030, we will have helped more than 100,000 immigrants during a twenty-year period.

b) By 2030, we will have been helping immigrants — more than 100,000 of them — for twenty years.

8 a) By 2025 they expect to have ended capital punishment forever.

b) By 2025 they will have ended capital punishment forever.

WRITING

A PROBLEM-SOLUTION ESSAY; LEARN TO USE PARALLELISM

9 A Which items in the box would you expect to find in a problem-solution essay?

> personal information   dialogue   anecdotes
> reference to research   facts and figures
> a description of a problem   a conclusion
> rhetorical questions   a plan of action

B Read the example essay and answer the questions.

1 What issue does it deal with?

2 What do you think of the writer's idea?

3 Which features in Exercise 9A does it contain?

Could New Technology Be the Solution?

1 How many people are killed with guns every year? Let's take a round number – one million – and look at the figures for gunshot deaths. In Japan, 0.7 people per one million inhabitants are killed by gunfire in a year. In South Korea it's 1.3; in England it's 4.6; in the Netherlands it's 7; in Spain it's 9; in Kuwait it's 12.5. In the United States, it's 152.2. That's not a misprint. The figure illustrates one of today's most important issues: gun control.

2 One of the causes of this figure in the U.S.A. is the citizens' "right to bear arms" (carry weapons) written into the U.S. constitution. The country has an extremely violent past, and this has resulted in an ingrained sense of the need to protect oneself and one's family. Another reason is the rate of gun ownership. Around forty-six percent of families in the U.S.A. have a gun in the house.

3 How can countries – the United States in particular – reduce the number of gun deaths? A complete ban on guns is barely imaginable in the U.S.A. However, there are a number of other options. These include developing better systems for registering guns and ammunition, instigating background checks for prospective gun owners and introducing tougher prison sentences for people who own guns illegally. The problem is that these solutions have already been proposed, passed into law and denounced as failures.

4 One possible solution that hasn't been tried yet is "ID tagging" on guns. Each gun would be registered to one person's fingerprint, and only that person would be able to fire the gun. If someone else attempted to fire it, the gun wouldn't work. This would mean that stolen guns would be useless. Also, the police would have fewer problems identifying the killers.

5 In conclusion, the solution proposed here is one for the future. The idea would not bring an end to gun deaths. Until guns are completely banned, it is unlikely that anything could reduce that number to the magic zero. But the idea of using new technology (ID tags) to defeat the ills brought about by old technology (guns) is not just a shot in the dark. It could become reality sooner than you think.

10 Look at the expressions below for different parts of a problem-solution essay. Check the expressions used in the model essay.

Introducing the problem

(This) illustrates one of today's most important issues …

This represents a growing problem.

Describing causes of the problem

One of the causes is … This is largely due to …

Describing consequences of the problem

This has led to/resulted in/brought about …

One of the consequences of this is …

Suggesting solutions

One possible solution …

There are a number of (other) options. These include …

Concluding

In conclusion, …   To sum up, …

The purpose/aim of this essay was to …

11 A Read two examples of parallelism from the essay in Exercise 9B. Find another example in paragraph 3.

> In South Korea it's 1.3; in England it's 4.6; in the Netherlands it's 7 …

> These include developing better systems for registering guns and ammunition, instigating background checks for prospective gun owners and introducing tougher prison sentences …

B Why do you think writers use parallelism? Which idea below is <u>not</u> a good answer?

1 It gives symmetry and consistency to the writing.

2 It gives ideas equal weight.

3 It uses balance and rhythm to deliver the message.

4 It helps us write better introductions.

C Complete the sentences with the option that uses parallelism.

1 The protest against gun laws was led by a number of civil rights groups, social justice campaigners and _____.

   a) other people

   b) human rights activists

   c) those people who believe in fighting for human rights

2 In a few years, the powers-that-be may know everything about gun owners: the movies they watch, the food they eat, _____.

   a) the air they are breathing

   b) and the air they breathe as they walk around

   c) the air they breathe

12 Work in groups and choose a topic. Use your own idea or a topic in Exercise 2A. Follow stages 1–5 below.

1 What exactly is the problem? Write it in one sentence.

2 Brainstorm possible solutions and make notes.

3 Discuss which solutions are the best.

4 Make an outline for your essay. Use the expressions in Exercise 10.

5 Write your problem-solution essay (300–350 words).

4.3)) DO THE RIGHT THING

expressing hypothetical preferences
decisions
intonation: adding emphasis

VOCABULARY
DECISIONS

1 A Match the phrases 1–4 with phrases a)–d) which have similar meanings.

1 to take all these things into consideration

2 spent some time thinking it through

3 (be) faced with a dilemma

4 weighed the pros and cons

a) (be) in a predicament

b) considered the benefits and drawbacks

c) to bear these points in mind

d) assessed the situation

B Use phrases a–d from Exercise 1A to complete the text below.

You are ¹_____. Four friends buy you a lottery ticket for your birthday. The following week, you win $100,000 with the ticket. Your friends think you should share the winnings with them. You have ²_____. You have tried ³_____: how long you've been friends, how much your friends need the money, whether you should share the winnings equally and whether you think your friendships will survive if you keep all the money. Now you have ⁴_____, you need to make your decision.

C What would you do in this situation? Tell other students.

D Discuss. What difficult decisions/ dilemmas might the people below face?

• scientist   • teacher

• financial investor   • doctor

• soldier   • parent

A scientist would have to consider the pros and cons of his or her research.

2 A Think of a real/imaginary dilemma you have faced. Describe it using some of the expressions in Exercise 1A.

B Work in pairs and compare your stories.

FUNCTION
EXPRESSING HYPOTHETICAL PREFERENCES

3 Read a true story and discuss questions 1–3.

1 What decision did Ann Timson have to make?

2 Do you think she was a hero?

3 What would you have done in her situation?

SUPERGRAN BASHES BURGLARS

A seventy-year-old grandmother became a hero when, armed with just a shopping bag, she defied six hammer-wielding jewelry thieves on motorcycles. Ann Timson was talking to a woman on the street when she heard a commotion. She looked across the road and saw six men smashing the windows of a jewelry store in broad daylight. Seeing that other bystanders were doing nothing, Ms. Timson decided to act. She dashed across the road and started to hit one of the robbers with her shopping bag. He fell off his motorcycle and was pinned down by several members of the public before the police arrived. Amazingly, all of this was captured on film by a freelance cameraman who happened to be nearby. The footage became a YouTube sensation. Asked later if she saw herself as a hero, Ms. Timson said no, but "somebody had to do something". It turns out that Ms. Timson has been "doing something" for years. She has confronted drug dealers and other criminals before, putting her own safety at risk in order to aid the community. Although she does not generally believe that the public should take on robbers – "it's dangerous" she says – her actions have inspired others, and made at least a few would-be thieves think again.

4 A Listen to two people discussing the story. Would the speakers do what Ann Timson did?

B Listen again and try to work out what the expressions below mean.

1 an ordinary hero

2 [if/when] push comes to shove

3 jumped on the bandwagon

4 I take my hat off to her

5 I'd probably run away

6 I'd do my bit

5 A What words do you think complete the expressions for expressing hypothetical preferences?

If it was ¹_____ to me, I'd …

I'd rather …

I'd just as soon … as …

Given the ²_____, I'd …

If I ever ³_____ myself in that situation, I'd …

Far better to … than …

This would be by ⁴_____ the best option.

My preference ⁵_____ be to …

Without a shadow of a ⁶_____, I'd …

No way would I …

B Read audio script S4.5 on page 169. Which of the expressions above can you find?

▶ page 134 **LANGUAGEBANK**

jewelry / motorcycles / an ordinary / run away   jewellery / motorbikes / a have a go / leg it

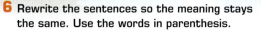

6 Rewrite the sentences so the meaning stays the same. Use the words in parenthesis.

1 You should weigh up the pros and cons rather than deciding now. (far better)

2 Which of the two candidates would you choose? (up to)

3 I definitely think we can come up with some better ideas than these. (shadow/doubt)

4 If you had the choice, would you ban all web advertising? (given)

5 I would ask my boss for advice if I faced this kind of dilemma. (found myself/situation)

6 Instead of acting rashly, I'd prefer to put important decisions on hold. (sooner)

7 I'd rather buy a house now than wait until the economy gets better. (preference)

8 She'd quit her job rather than do something unethical. (just/soon)

LEARN TO
ADD EMPHASIS

7 A Look at expressions a)—e) from the recording in Exercise 4A. Put them under the correct headings below.

a) It was totally wrong.

b) The fact is …

c) The thing is …

d) To be absolutely honest …

e) It was completely stupid …

Adverbs for emphasis

1 _____

2 _____

3 _____

Fronting: expressions before the main verb

What you have to remember is …

4 _____

5 _____

Other expressions

That's out of the question.

No chance.

Not on your life.

B INTONATION: adding emphasis Listen to the intonation of the phrases above. Repeat them using the same intonation.

> **American Speak TIP**
> When we write, we can emphasize words by using *italics* or underlining. When we speak, we use intonation to emphasize the same words. The pitch is higher and we sometimes make the vowel sounds longer. When you hear people arguing, persuading or getting excited, listen to the way they pronounce key words.

SPEAKING

8 A Read the dilemmas below. Think about what you would do and complete the notes for each situation. Use phrases from Exercises 5A and 7A to help express your ideas.

My first reaction is …

On the other hand, …

It depends on …

The best option …

1 Your friend's husband is supposed to be working late, but you see him in a bar talking in a friendly manner with another woman. You do not know the other woman. She could be a work colleague. Do you tell your friend what you saw?

2 You are in a hurry. You need to send a package urgently, but the post office will close in two minutes. There are no parking spaces except in the Disabled section of the parking lot. You are not disabled. You think you will only be there five minutes. Do you park in the Disabled section?

3 A friend of yours stole something. You promise never to reveal this. Soon afterwards, an innocent person is accused of the crime. You tell your friend that she has to own up. She refuses and reminds you of your promise. It is possible that an innocent person will go to jail. Do you reveal the truth?

B Work in groups and compare your ideas.

parking lot car park

DVD PREVIEW

1 A Work with other students. What do the words in bold mean?

1 He was a criminal **mastermind**.
2 He **conned** people out of their money.
3 The diamonds she'd inherited were **fake**.
4 They had to prove the painting's **provenance**, so they pretended it belonged to a rich family.
5 He was an expert at making **forgeries**.

B How might the words in bold in Exercise 1A be related to the pictures on this page?

2 Read the program information. What is the play on words in the title?

▶ News: The Con Artist

This news program tells the story of a painter who used his talent to commit a series of crimes in the art world. Wolfgang Beltracchi and his wife Helene embarked on a criminal scheme that resulted in prison sentences for both of them. In this program, a journalist interviews the couple, as well as one of the people responsible for catching them. She attempts to find out what lay behind the Beltracchis' scheme, how they were caught, and what they now think of their crimes.

DVD VIEW

3 Watch the DVD and answer the questions.

1 What type of crime did Beltracchi commit?
2 What mistake did Beltracchi make?
3 What does the artist do now?

4 A What do the people in the clip say about these things? Match 1–5 with a)–e).

1 The only thing the artist did wrong.
2 "My special talent".
3 Why he did it.
4 A certain pigment (type of paint).
5 What he would do differently.

a) Not use titanium white.
b) It wasn't available in 1915.
c) The signature.
d) Being a good actress.
e) The thrill, not the money.

B Watch the DVD again to check.

5 Work with other students and discuss the questions.

1 What type of people do you think Wolfgang Beltracchi and his wife are? Do you think they regret their crimes?
2 Would you describe them as serious criminals? Why/Why not?
3 Do you know of any other stories about forgers or con artists?

American Speakout recount a crime story

writeback a short article

6 **A** Read the notes about a forger and his family. How do you think they might have been caught? What do you think happened in the end?

Where: U.K.

When: between 1989 and 2006

The crime: a forging industry that made hundreds of thousands of dollars

Who: the Greenhalgh family: (1) Shaun Greenhalgh: artistic genius - created paintings, drawings, sculpture and ceramics from different centuries and different parts of the world; (2) Shaun's brother, George Junior - managed finances; (3) Shaun's elderly parents, George and Olive - sold artworks to clients - Olive's father had owned an art gallery, which allowed the family to establish genuine-sounding provenance for the artworks

Victims: numerous, including The British Museum and Tate Modern, and the auction houses Sotheby's and Christie's.

B Listen to two people talking about the case and check your ideas from Exercise 6A.

C Listen again and check the key phrases you hear. Which phrases are idioms? What do they mean?

KEYPHRASES

It's usually human error.

Could it be something to do with ...?

Maybe they let something slip.

... said something that gave the game away.

You're on the right track.

So it's connected to ...

The interesting thing is ...

In the end ...

7 Work in pairs. Follow instructions 1–4.

1 Student A, turn to page 163. Student B, turn to page 161.

2 Tell your partner the basics of your story: Who committed the forgery? What did they do? How were they caught?

3 Discuss: Do you think each man was found guilty? What do you think happened to the forgers next and to the value of their works?

4 Read the notes on pages 164 and 162 to find out.

8 **A** Read a short article based on the fact file in Exercise 6A.

The Garden Shed Gang

Shaun Greenhalgh left school at 16 with no qualifications. He wasn't from a wealthy family and had no useful connections in the art world, but within little more than ten years he was producing forgeries of paintings, ceramics and sculptures that fooled experts at some of the U.K.'s foremost institutions. His range was astonishing. He could produce anything from ancient Roman coins to 17th-century paintings to 20th-century sculptures.

He made these works in a garden shed in the family home which he shared with his parents. When the police eventually inspected the home they were shocked first at the number of artefacts littering the house – old coins, paintings, a bust of George Washington – and second at the fact that a family making hundreds of thousands of dollars lived in relative squalor.

Shaun's father, George, was a major part of the scam. A World War II veteran, he went to museums and auction houses in a wheelchair, playing the role of an innocent old man. The family cleverly provided documents to prove the provenance of the artworks they tried to sell, and George usually pretended not to know the true value of the artefacts.

Eventually they were caught when Shaun attempted to create an Assyrian relief from 600 BC. He made several mistakes, the most glaring of which was a horse's reins in the wrong style and a spelling mistake on an inscription. At first the family proclaimed their innocence, but when the scale and variety of their forgery began to become apparent, Shaun came clean. While his parents were considered too elderly and infirm to endure prison sentences, Shaun served over four years in jail. Like many ex-forgers he is now trying to make an honest living selling his own art.

B Write a short article (200–250 words) about one of the court cases you discussed in Exercise 7. Use the fact files on pages 161 and 163 and invent any additional details necessary.

first 🗽 firstly

V CRIME COLLOCATIONS

1 A Complete the sentences with an appropriate word.

1 She was offered a s_____ sentence and allowed to return home.

2 He has always p_____ his innocence, claiming he was not involved.

3 Disabling the alarm system enabled them to c_____ o_____ the crime without being discovered.

4 Several students were held for d_____ -r_____ offenses.

5 It made the news headlines when it was discovered that he'd been w_____ convicted.

6 She was given a light sentence due to the fact that she had no p_____ convictions.

B Work in pairs. Test your partner.

A: This means you take an active part in some illegal activity.

B: You carry out a crime.

G INTRODUCTORY *IT*

2 Use the prompts to make statements about yourself or people you know.

1 … would love it if …

I would love it if my husband surprised me by cooking dinner tonight.

2 … adore(s) it when …

3 … can't stand it when …

4 … find(s) it easy to …

5 It's pointless …

6 It's essential to …

V SOCIAL ISSUES

3 A What issues do the definitions describe?

1 _____: the employment of children (especially in manual jobs) who are under the legal or generally recognized age

2 _____: the movement of people across international borders in a way that breaks the immigration laws of the destination country

3 _____: the notion of being free to practice and teach any religion you choose

4 _____: basic freedoms that everyone should enjoy, e.g. freedom of thought and expression, the right to be free

5 _____: when a country grows richer because of activity relating to business and money

6 _____: something which someone has invented or has the right to make or sell, especially something that cannot legally be copied by other people

B Work in pairs. Complete the definitions.

1 freedom of speech: the right to …

2 free trade: a system of trade in which …

3 civil liberties: freedoms that protect …

4 gun control: efforts to regulate …

5 environmental awareness: an understanding of how …

G THE PERFECT ASPECT

4 Complete the jokes with the phrases in the box.

> it will have been   have you been feeling
> I've broken   have turned   to have been ignoring

1 "Doctor, doctor, I keep thinking I'm a cat." "How long _____ like this?" "Since I was a kitten."

2 "Doctor, doctor, I appear to _____ into a dog." "Sit on the chair and we'll talk about it.' 'I can't. I'm not allowed on the chair."

3 "Doctor, doctor, I'm in agony! _____ my arm in three places!" "Well, don't go to those places anymore."

4 "Doctor, doctor, tomorrow _____ ten years since I last had my eyes tested. I think I need glasses." "You certainly do. You've just walked into a gas station."

5 "Doctor, doctor, people seem _____ me for years." "Next please!"

F HYPOTHETICAL PREFERENCES

5 A Correct the word order in speaker B's responses.

1 A: I could have had a vacation on a beach or gone on a cruise.

B: If it was to up me, I'd have taken the cruise.

2 A: I don't know whether to read the book or watch the movie.

B: I rather would watch the movie than read the book.

3 A: We can either go to a fancy international restaurant or eat at the street market.

B: I'd rather eat local food than dine in a fancy restaurant.

4 A: So I was lost with a broken-down car in the middle of nowhere.

B: If I myself found in that situation, I'd go to the nearest house and beg for help.

5 A: We decided not to give Christmas presents because there are thirty people in the family now.

B: Better far to do that than buy presents for everybody!

6 A: We're thinking of taking trains around Europe rather than flying.

B: That would be by the far best option if you want to see places along the way.

7 A: I hated my job so I quit, even though I needed the money.

B: I'd have done the same a without shadow of a doubt.

8 A: I got rid of my cell phone. It was too expensive.

B: Way no would I do that unless I really had to.

B Decide if you agree with speaker B. If not, change the response. Practice the conversations in pairs.

gas station / rather / than / fancy

petrol station / sooner / as / posh

5))) secrets

FAMILY SECRETS　p56

TRUTH OR MYTH?　p59

TELL ME NO LIES　p62

SPEAKING
5.1 Talk about secrets
5.2 Debunk a myth
5.3 Discuss freedom of information
5.4 Talk about secret places in your city

LISTENING
5.1 Listen to a radio program about secrets
5.3 Listen to a conversation about WikiLeaks
5.4 Watch a program about a secret island

READING
5.1 Read a true story
5.2 Read about everyday myths
5.3 Read about investigative journalism

WRITING
5.1 Write a narrative
5.4 Write a secrets guide

Are you good
at keeping secrets?

INTERVIEWS

SECRET ISLAND　p64

5.1)) FAMILY SECRETS

- **G** modal verbs and related phrases
- **P** connected speech: elision
- **V** idioms: secrets

LISTENING

1 Work in groups and discuss the questions.

1 Why do people keep secrets? If someone tells you something in confidence, are you likely to keep their secret or to tell someone else?

2 Who would you talk to if you wanted to tell someone your innermost thoughts? Who would you definitely not talk to?

2 A Read the radio program listing. It says that society has become more "confessional". What do you think this means? Do you agree with the statement?

Everyone has a secret at some point in their lives and most of us will be told a secret and asked to keep it quiet. As society allegedly becomes more "confessional", are we far too willing to talk about matters that should be kept hidden? Are we losing the ability to keep secrets? When is it appropriate to divulge a secret, and how should it be done? Are there types of secrets that should never be revealed?

This radio program asks members of the public about their secrets, and Jenni Murray takes up the discussion with Eva Rice, whose new novel is called *The Lost Art of Keeping Secrets*.

B Listen to the program. How many secrets do they mention? What are they?

C Listen to the interview again and answer the questions for each section.

1 What would have made the presenter's father furious?

2 A girl revealed her friend's secret. Was she forgiven?

3 What secret did the wife want to know from her husband?

4 Is the woman who had another relationship still married?

5 What kind of secret would the author keep?

D Discuss. How would you react if someone revealed a secret you'd asked them to keep? Would you like to read the book? Why/Why not?

VOCABULARY
IDIOMS: SECRETS

3 A Complete the sentences below with the words in the box.

cat	stay	game	beans	let	themselves	doors

1 We were raised in an atmosphere where families **kept to** _____ and you told nobody your business.

2 We became more knowledgeable about the kind of dangerous secrets that might be held **behind closed** _____ and the damage they could do.

3 He almost _____ **it slip** where he was.

4 So when should you **spill the** _____ and be honest?

5 When is it better **to keep/**_____ **mum**?

6 It's a secret, so try not to **let the** _____ **out of the bag**.

7 We pretended we didn't know it was her birthday, but Sam **gave the** _____ **away**.

B Match the expressions in bold above with meanings a)–e). Some expressions have the same meaning.

a) deliberately disclose a secret (1 expression)

b) when something happens in private and the public are not allowed to know about it (1 expression)

c) tell something (possibly by mistake) that someone else wanted you to keep a secret (3 expressions)

d) remain silent, or say nothing (1 expression)

e) live a quiet private life, not doing things involving other people (1 expression)

▶ page 152 **VOCABULARY**BANK

SPEAKING

4 Work in groups and discuss the questions.

1 When would it be important to keep a secret?

2 When might you have to reveal someone's secret? Explain why.

3 When is it important for people to speak openly rather than keep secrets?

4 When is it better for the public not to know a secret?

keep to themselves / mum keep oneself to oneself / schtum

GRAMMAR
MODAL VERBS AND RELATED PHRASES

5 A Check what you know. Match the underlined forms in sentences 1–8 with the meanings in the box.

> it's possible   it's expected   I was obliged (strong)
> I was obliged (weak)   it isn't a good idea
> you did it, but it was unnecessary
> it wasn't possible/I wasn't able
> ~~I did it, but it wasn't a good idea~~

1 I <u>never should have</u> told her. It was my fault.

   I did it, but it wasn't a good idea.

2 I <u>couldn't</u> live with this secret.

3 I <u>had to</u> tell him.

4 Keeping a secret <u>can</u> be something that can bring about a more positive outcome.

5 You're <u>supposed to</u> tell everyone the way you feel twenty-four hours a day.

6 We'd <u>better not</u> start until everyone is here.

7 I felt that I <u>ought to</u> let her know.

8 You <u>didn't need</u> to tell him.

B Match each sentence with the correct meaning, a) or b).

1 We're supposed to catch the 8:30 train.

2 We have to catch the 8:30 train.

   a) It's very important that we catch the 8:30 train as there are no more trains after that.

   b) Ideally, we would catch the 8:30 train, but if we need more time, we can catch a later one.

3 You shouldn't tell him about the relationship.

4 You don't have to tell him about the relationship.

   a) It's definitely not a good idea to tell him.

   b) Nobody is forcing you to tell him about it. It's up to you.

5 You shouldn't have called the hotel first.

6 You'd better call the hotel first.

   a) It would have been better to call the airport first.

   b) I think you should call the hotel before the airport.

C Find pairs of words/phrases in sentences 1–10 which have similar meanings.

   1 allowed = 5 permissible

1 Dictionaries are **allowed** in the test.

2 Alcohol is strictly **forbidden** in some countries.

3 It's **obligatory** for companies to provide details of their industrial processes.

4 She **had the courage to** tell him what had happened.

5 They reached the maximum **permissible** level of radiation.

6 She felt **compelled to** resign because of the scandal.

7 Cars have been **banned** from downtown.

8 Only a few journalists **dared to** cover the story.

9 Math and English are **compulsory** for all students.

10 Many companies have been **forced to** close.

▶ page 136 **LANGUAGEBANK**

downtown / math

6 A CONNECTED SPEECH: elision Listen to some of the sentences from Exercise 5C. Notice how some sounds disappear or change in connected speech (elision).

1 A syllable containing an unstressed vowel is often lost.

   diction(a)ry   obligat(o)ry

2 /t/ and /d/ are often lost when combined with other consonants.

   compelle(d)_to   dare(d)_to

3 The sound /h/ is often omitted.

   tell him what (h)ad happened
   cars (h)ave been banned

B Listen and repeat the sentences.

7 Choose the best alternatives to complete the texts.

FAMILY SECRETS

Shary: "My grandmother disapproved terribly of smoking, so people [1]*were never allowed to/weren't supposed* smoke in the house. She didn't even realize that her own daughter, my mother, aged sixty, was a smoker. We all [2]*ought to/had to* go outside and smoke on the balcony, and my grandmother never realized what we were doing. She [3]*was supposed to/used to* think we were hanging out the washing and things like that. I suppose we [4]*should have/ought have* told her."

Emma: "My uncle thought he [5]*d better not/d not better* tell anyone when he decided to get married for the first time at the age of sixty-five. He kept it a secret which nobody [6]*should have known/was supposed to know* about. He [7]*would have/could have* told us – everyone [8]*should have/would have* been delighted for him. It wasn't as if he was marrying an eighteen-year-old. His bride was seventy-eight and was also marrying for the first time."

8 Choose two or three of the topics below. Work in pairs and take turns talking about them.

Talk about something:

• you would never dare to do.

• you should have done this week, but you haven't.

• you weren't supposed to do as a child, but you did anyway.

• which is obligatory in your country, but not in other countries.

• you should never have done.

• you weren't allowed to do as a child, which you enjoy doing now.

• you'd better not forget to do.

the city centre / maths

WRITING
A NARRATIVE; LEARN TO USE TIME PHRASES

9 A Read the true story below. What do you think was in the box? Turn to page 159 to find out.

1 As a child, my grandmother would often tell me stories. Stories of times gone by. And I would listen with eager fascination, especially to the stories of her childhood. One story I will always remember was of my "Auntie Madge", my great-aunt. She was a quiet, unassuming woman, who I once met as a child. My grandmother told me how Auntie Madge had been a dazzling young lady, and how all the boys in the neighborhood had wanted to take her out. But Auntie Madge only had eyes for one very nice young man, who she had fallen in love with.

2 Although the young couple planned to spend the rest of their lives together, there was a problem: my great-great-aunt Ada, Auntie Madge's mother. Ada had a reputation for being a bit of a dragon and wanting to control everything. Ada didn't approve of the young man in question, and she wasn't at all happy to let her daughter marry him.

3 After some persuasion, however, she reluctantly made a deal with Auntie Madge, saying, "OK. If the two of you are determined to marry, then all I ask is that you stay away from each other for one year. During that time, you can't see each other, speak to each other or write each other letters. And if, after a year, he writes to you and still wants to marry you, then I will accept. I'll consent."

4 It was a long year, but the couple kept their promise. But, after a year, Auntie Madge never heard from the young man and had to assume that he'd found someone else. She subsequently married another man, but the marriage was very unhappy and eventually ended in divorce. From then on, Auntie Madge lived alone, and never had children.

5 Years later, when her mother died, Madge found a box belonging to her mother …

B Work in pairs and discuss. What do you think of Ada's behavior? Can you think of a good title for the story?

10 A Which features 1–10 are often found in narrative writing?

1 an introduction to set the scene

2 detailed descriptions of people, places or objects

3 detailed statistics and evidence

4 descriptions of feelings/actions to suggest mood

5 direct speech and adjectives/adverbs for impact

6 a summary of the main events

7 narrative tenses and time phrases to show the sequence of events

8 an unexpected end to the story

B Read the story in Exercise 9A again. Which features in Exercise 10A does it contain?

11 A Look at the extract from the story. Underline the time phrase.

During that time, you shouldn't see each other, speak to each other or write each other letters.

B Underline the time phrases in paragraphs 4 and 5 of the story in Exercise 9A.

C Complete sentences 1–8 with the time phrases in the box. There may be more than one possible answer and you don't have to use all of the phrases.

> after   as soon as   the moment   afterwards
> meanwhile   ever since   originally   while
> instantly   previously   subsequently   eventually
> immediately   in the meantime   from then on

1 _____ she entered the room, she knew there was something wrong.

2 The experience haunted me for years _____.

3 Cromwell, _____, picked up his hat and dusted it off.

4 They recognized him _____.

5 She knew she could never trust her boss again, and _____ she left the job.

6 He _____ escaped and made his way back to France.

7 She has been terrified of the sound of aircraft _____ the crash.

8 They met in 1998, and _____ they were firm friends.

D Complete the sentences in any way you choose. Use the time phrases in Exercise 11C.

1 It was love at first sight. The moment …

2 He recognized her immediately. Previously, …

3 She arrived on a boat from Costa Rica. As soon as …

4 It was a long and tedious journey. Eventually, …

12 A Follow stages 1–4 to draft a narrative of your own (200–250 words).

1 Identify an experience to write about (e.g. a childhood experience, a challenge, achieving a goal) and think about why it is significant.

2 Make notes about the experience, including details (sounds, colors, etc.).

3 Create an outline of the story.

4 Use the outline to write a first draft.

> **American Speak out TIP** After drafting your narrative, spend some time away from it. Then try reading it out loud. This helps highlight any missing or repeated words or missing punctuation. Can you add any more detail to improve it? Are there any details you can remove because they distract from the main story?

B Check your draft. How many correct features from Exercise 10A did you use? Try to make some improvements and redraft your story.

5.2)) TRUTH OR MYTH?

G the passive
P stress: multi-word verbs
V truth or myth; multi-word verbs

READING

1 A Read the introduction to the article below. Can you think of any commonly held beliefs that are actually myths?

B Work in pairs. Student A: read the myths below and answer the questions. Student B: turn to page 160.

1 What is the myth?
2 Which myths were disproved by experiments?
3 What is the truth about the myth?

C Tell your partner what you learned. Then read your partner's section of the article quickly.

VOCABULARY
TRUTH OR MYTH

2 A Find the expressions below in the articles on this page and on page 160 and answer the questions.

> conventional wisdom   a commonly held perception
> a fallacy   verify   uncover the truth   intuitively true
> debunk a myth   disprove a myth

1 Which expression means "many people think it's true, but it isn't"?
2 Which three expressions mean "people think it's true, but there's no scientific evidence"?
3 Which verb means "reveal"?
4 Which two verbs mean "prove something isn't true"?
5 Which verb means "prove something is true"?

B Add the missing word in each sentence.

1 It is a held perception that no one can survive a plane crash.
2 Wisdom says you shouldn't swim soon after eating.
3 Scientists in Panama recently disproved myth that sloths are lazy.
4 The myth that you lose most of your body heat through your head has been.
5 It seems intuitively that long-distance running is bad for your knees, but recent research suggests otherwise.

C Do you think the sentences in Exercise 2B are myths or the truth? Tell a partner.

Is it true?

Does sugar make kids hyperactive, and does cold weather really give you a cold? Conventional wisdom says "yes", but what does science say? Are these commonly held perceptions of the world we live in really true, or are they fallacies? We've spoken to experts to verify the rumors and uncover the truth.

1 Sugar makes kids hyperactive

Not one study has conclusively shown that children with a sugar-laden diet behave differently from those with a sugar-free diet. Most of the studies come from the USA with titles such as *Hyperactivity: is candy causal*?, but time after time, no link has been found. Despite the evidence, parents simply can't believe this is a myth. In an experiment where they were told their children had been given a sugar-loaded drink, parents rated the children as "significantly more hyperactive" than parents whose children had received a sugar-free drink. In reality, the children had been given the same sugar-free drink. The difference in behavior was all in the parents' minds.

2 Get cold and you get ill

One professor uncovered the truth by studying volunteers who were asked to dunk their feet in cold water. He discovered that being chilled does make a cold more likely. But it's not quite as simple as that. The crucial requirement is that your body is harboring a cold virus in the first place. No virus, no cold.

3 Turning your PC off without shutting it down damages it

According to tests in the USA, as long as your PC isn't in the middle of an epic video editing project or full of unsaved documents, bypassing the full shutdown rigamarole shouldn't cause any major harm. After you've hit the power button, Word and Excel easily recover your previous spreadsheets and musings.

4 Reading in the dark ruins your eyesight

Reading in the dark can make your eyes tired, but won't damage them as it causes no permanent changes to your eyes' structure. You might get eye strain, but this goes away when you turn on the lights.

rumor / harbor / rigamarole / turn on   rumour / harbour / rigmarole / tun up

GRAMMAR
THE PASSIVE

3 A Read the statements. Are any of them true?

1 The Great Wall of China is the only man-made object visible from space.

2 Caesar Salad is named after Julius Caesar.

3 Eskimos have over one hundred words for snow.

4 Chewing gum takes seven years to pass through the digestive system.

5 A sudden shock or great stress can suddenly turn your hair white.

B Check your answers below.

1 False. The Great Wall of China cannot be seen from space with the naked eye, but cities can be made out, especially at night.

2 False. Caesar Cardini, a restaurateur, invented the recipe in Tijuana, Mexico, in 1924. He had the dish named after him.

3 False. It is claimed by linguists that Eskimos actually have about as many words for snow as we have in English (sleet, blizzard, slush, powder, etc.) — nothing like one hundred.

4 False. Chewing gum is processed through the body like any other food.

5 False. Hair isn't expected to change color suddenly, but some people's hair turns white quickly even in a stress-free situation.

C Check what you know. Underline examples of passive forms in Exercise 3B. Why do we use passive forms?

D Which sentences contain examples of:

a) a passive used when the important information in the sentence is the object of the verb?   *4*

b) a passive used to show that we are not certain about a statement?

c) a pattern that uses *have/get* + object + past participle to describe something that is done to the subject?

d) a passive used because we do not know who performs the action (or it is not important), and we are interested in the action itself?

e) a passive infinitive (*to be* + past participle + *to* + verb)?

▶ page 136 **LANGUAGE**BANK

4 Work in pairs. Which phrases in italics would be better in the passive? Change them as appropriate.

One piece of conventional wisdom that [1]*people have passed on* throughout the generations is that Friday 13th is unlucky. [2]*No one knows* where this superstition came from, though [3]*some people have attributed* it to the fact that on Friday, October 13th, 1306, King Philip of France arrested the Knights Templar and [4]*began torturing them.*

[5]*People know the fear of the number thirteen* as triskaidekaphobia, and [6]*people consider thirteen* unlucky in many cultures. [7]*We can see this superstition* in different contexts: in the United States, many skyscrapers don't have a thirteenth floor, and several airports don't have a thirteenth gate. Hospitals and hotels regularly have no room number thirteen. In Italy, [8]*the organizers omit the number thirteen* from the national lottery, while on streets in Florence [9]*people give the house between number 12 and 14 the number 12½.* Other countries have different "unlucky numbers". In Japan, [10]*people often omit the unlucky number four* from hotels, hospitals and apartment buildings.

SPEAKING

5 A Prepare to debunk a myth of your choice. It can be about a person, a profession, a country or a belief. For ideas, turn to page 160. Complete the notes below.

> ### The secret is out about ...
> - Many people think ...
> - They believe this because ...
> - The idea may have originated ...
> - They say ... but it's a fallacy inasmuch as ...
> - The truth is that .../In fact ...
> - In order to really understand ... people would have to ...
> - This would happen if ...

B Work in groups. Take turns debunking your myths. Share your ideas with the class.

apartment building   apartment block

VOCABULARY PLUS
MULTI-WORD VERBS

6 A Discuss. Which of the activities below have you done in the last twenty-four hours? Which do you do at least once every twenty-four hours?

> send a text message   play a video game   eat fast food
> go on a social networking website   hang out in a shopping mall
> talk on a cell phone   listen to music on a mobile device

B Read the book review and answer the questions.

1 What is the message in Steven Johnson's book?

2 Do you agree with this idea?

> The media is full of warnings about teens and modern life: too much technology and video games and fast food. Journalists and social theorists have looked back to the golden age before kids stood around texting and have decided enough is enough! Take away their iPods! Switch off their cell phones! But writer Steven Johnson has thought it over and come to a different conclusion. His book, *Everything Bad is Good for You: How Today's Popular Culture is Actually Making us Smarter*, boils down to one message: kids can carry on gaming and texting because as the world speeds up, these skills are turning them into quick-thinking, multi-tasking 21st-century citizens. Who's right? Could the doom-mongers be wrong? Read the book and find out for yourself.

7 A Read the review again and underline multi-word verbs with *back, around, away, off, over, down, on, up* and *out*.

B Look at some common meanings of particles in multi-word verbs. Complete the table with the meanings in the box.

> removal or disposal   think or talk about   ~~continue~~   remove,
> cancel or end something   with no direction or aim   ~~increase or improve~~
> return (to the past)   be in the open   decrease or reduce

preposition	meaning	examples
up	*increase or improve*	speed up, brighten up, jazz up
on	*continue*	go on, carry on, keep on
off		lay off, cry off, call off, switch off
out		find out, speak out, stand out, call out
down		slow down, narrow down, crack down
away		put away, blow away, take away
back		bring back, think back, look back, cast (your mind) back
around		mess around, stand around, hang around
over		mull over, pore over, look over, think over

C Which examples in the third column are new to you? Look them up in a dictionary and make a sentence with them.

8 A Complete the sentences with the correct particles.

1 The government cracked _____ on illegal immigration because the situation couldn't go _____.

2 I bought some new curtains for my bedroom to jazz it _____.

3 We mulled _____ the candidates and narrowed them _____ to a shortlist of three.

4 I've thought it _____, and I'm not going to accept the job.

5 I don't think the weather's going to brighten _____ before the game starts. Perhaps we should call it _____.

B **STRESS: multi-word verbs** Listen to the answers to Exercise 8A. Where is the stress on the multi-word verbs: on the verb or the particle? Is there a pattern? Practice saying the sentences quietly to yourself and then aloud.

9 A Underline the correct alternatives.

1 *Cast your mind back/Narrow down/Talk over* to your childhood. Who taught you your most important lessons?

2 How do you *carry on/think back/find out* if a journalist or other writer is telling the truth?

3 When faced with many possible truths, how can we *call out/narrow down/speed up* our options to one?

4 Is it always useful to *mull over/mess around/speak out* difficult issues with other people?

B Choose two questions in Exercise 9A. Work in pairs and discuss your answers.

▶ page 152 **VOCABULARYBANK**

5.3)) TELL ME NO LIES

F making a point
P intonation: appropriacy
V journalism

VOCABULARY
JOURNALISM

1 A Work in pairs. What do you know about the website WikiLeaks? Answer the questions.

1 What kind of information is published on the website?
2 Who sends the information?
3 What effect does it have on governments and large organizations?

B Read the article to check your ideas.

IN SEARCH OF THE TRUTH ...

The problem with **investigative journalism** is that scoops are increasingly hard to come by. Big companies, celebrities and governments frequently **take out injunctions** to protect information that they want to be kept secret, to prevent it from being published. But that doesn't stop websites like WikiLeaks.

The **whistle-blowing** website WikiLeaks has at times dominated the news with its steady drip feed of secret documents. WikiLeaks was responsible for the release of thousands of documents containing **sensitive information** from governments and other high-profile organizations, including classified military records. In just three years, WikiLeaks **published more scoops** than the *Washington Post* managed in thirty years.

However, the site has divided opinion. For some it is seen as the future of investigative journalism; described as the world's first stateless news organization. But for others – particularly the governments and corporations whose secrets it exposes – it poses a huge risk.

WikiLeaks allows anyone to submit documents anonymously. A team of reviewers, journalists and WikiLeaks staff decide what is published. The site then uses advanced cryptographic and legal techniques to **protect its sources** by using a network of servers around the world.

The more people who use the network, the harder it becomes to pick apart. However hard the authorities may try to stop websites like WikiLeaks, it seems that one of the new powers of the internet is that, one way or another, the truth will come out.

2 Match the words/phrases in bold in Exercise 1B to the definitions below.

1 When a journalist made a news story public before anyone else had heard about it.
2 If someone doesn't want you to publish information about them, they might use this legal procedure.
3 When a journalist thoroughly investigates a single topic of interest, often involving criminal practice by an organization.
4 Exposing unethical or illegal actions by an organization.
5 Keeping the identities of the people who provide information to journalists secret.
6 Information which, if disclosed by unauthorized people, could cause problems for a company or government, etc.

FUNCTION
MAKING A POINT

3 A Listen to a conversation about WikiLeaks. Number the points in the order they are mentioned.

a) Whistleblowers always existed, but the medium has changed now.
b) WikiLeaks seems to have no regard for the ethics of its actions.
c) Freedom of information can only be a good thing.
d) Organizations have to be able to keep some information private.
e) WikiLeaks is responsible for leaking a lot of private information.
f) Governments and companies can no longer hide behind secrets.

B Listen again and complete what the speakers say.

1 The _____ why I say that is because they are responsible ...
2 Can you be _____ about that? Is there any _____ to prove that?
3 But that's not the _____.
4 Let me _____ it this way.
5 But that doesn't take _____ of the fact that ...
6 I think you'll _____ that actually information has always ...
7 The point I'm trying to _____ is that if the chances ...

unauthorized   unauthorised

C Add the phrases in bold in Exercise 3B under the correct headings below.

Making a point

There are several reasons why I think that ...

1 _____

The facts suggest ... /The evidence shows ...

After all, ...

The point is ...

If you think about it ...

Clarifying a point

2 _____

What I'm basically saying is ...

3 _____

Actually, ... /In fact, ...

4 _____

Challenging a point

Do you think that's always the case?

5 _____

Is there any way/evidence to prove that?

6 _____

I don't see how you can say that.

7 _____

▶ page 136 **LANGUAGE**BANK

4 A Complete the responses using the prompts in parentheses.

1 A: Would you ever disclose company secrets?

   B: Let me _____, it would depend on the secret. (put)

2 A: People who download music for free should be sent to prison.

   B: I _____ say that. (see)

3 A: The public should have open access to any information they want.

   B: But that _____ that the information might be sensitive. (account)

4 A: I'm not sure that I follow what you mean.

   B: What _____ is that I don't mind. (basically)

5 A: You should never give away your intellectual property for free.

   B: I think _____ it depends on the situation. (find)

B Work in pairs. Discuss statements 1–5 in Exercise 4A using your own responses.

LEARN TO
MANAGE A CONVERSATION

5 A Work in groups. Do any of the following things happen to you when you are discussing an issue in English?

1 You struggle to find the right words in time.

2 People keep going off the topic, so you find it hard to follow.

3 Some people are reluctant to contribute to the conversation.

4 One or two people tend to dominate the conversation.

5 You pause to collect your thoughts, and someone interrupts so you can't finish what you wanted to say.

B Look at the different ways to manage a conversation. Put the phrases in the box under the correct headings below.

> Sorry, and another thing ...
> Getting back to the point, which is ...
> Where do you stand on this?
> I suppose, if you think about it ...

Encouraging someone else to contribute

So, what do you think about ... ?/But, don't you think ... ?

How do you feel about this?

1 _____

Keeping your turn

Hold on a minute. I wanted to say that ...

There are a couple of things I'd like to say about ...

2 _____

Giving you thinking time

That's an interesting question to consider.

That's something which we should consider carefully.

It's not something I've thought much about before.

3 _____

Staying on (original) topic

Going back to what you were saying about ...

I'm not sure what that's got to do with ...

4 _____

C INTONATION: appropriacy Listen to the phrases. Does the speaker sound aggressive (A) or polite (P)? Repeat the phrases copying both types of intonation.

SPEAKING

6 A Write down your answers to two or three of the questions below. Think of ideas to justify your position.

B Work in groups and discuss the questions. Try to use the phrases from Exercise 5B. Then report back to the class.

> Has the internet changed the nature of journalism for the better or the worse?

> Is it justifiable to obtain information by phone or email tapping?

> Does the public have a right to know about the private lives of people in positions of power?

> Should governments/the police/big organizations be allowed to keep information secret?

5.4)) SECRET ISLAND

DVD PREVIEW

1 A Work in pairs. Check you understand the words in bold.

1 Would you be happy to spend time on a **deserted** island? Why/Why not?

2 Why might an area become **abandoned** or **uninhabited**?

3 What kinds of people might need **rehabilitation**?

4 For what kinds of illnesses might someone require **quarantine**?

B Answer the questions.

2 Read the program information. What has the island previously been used for?

▶ New York's Abandoned Island

Imagine a place within easy reach of busy New York where there are no people, and very little noise. Located in New York City's East River, North Brother Island was once the site of a quarantine hospital, treating patients with infectious diseases such as tuberculosis. Later, it housed returning war veterans and their families, and then it was used as a rehabilitation center for drug addicts.

However, now the island is abandoned and has been uninhabited for more than fifty years. It's one of New York's best-kept secrets. A dense forest of thick vegetation conceals the disintegrating hospital buildings, and birds nest among the abandoned rubble. The island is designated as a bird sanctuary and is off limits to the general public.

The photographer Christopher Payne was granted rare permission to visit the island to take photographs. His images can be seen in the book, *North Brother Island. The Last Unknown Place in New York City*.

DVD VIEW

3 Watch the DVD. What does the photographer think is so special about the island? Is it somewhere you would choose to visit? Why/Why not?

4 A Complete the extracts.

1 It is a secret _____ in plain sight.

2 From the 1880s all the way up to the 1960s, it was _____ to thousands of people.

3 All of a sudden, you're in the middle of the city, and yet you're completely _____.

4 It's like you're walking back into _____, into another world, and yet you still hear the sounds of the city.

5 Being on the island is full of _____.

6 The most interesting building on North Brother Island by far is the _____ Pavilion.

7 You can get a sense of what happened before but also how quickly things _____.

8 It alludes to the conundrum that we face of living in a natural world which we try to _____, but always reasserts itself in the end.

B Watch the DVD again to check.

5 Work in pairs and discuss the questions.

1 "It is the most unexpected of places in a city like New York." Why do you think he says this?

2 "One time I even heard the Mr. Softy truck, which is an ice cream truck, and … it was bizarre …"Why was it "bizarre" for the photographer to hear the ice cream truck?

3 What do you think the photographer is trying to achieve with his photographs? Does he succeed? Why/Why not?

B Listen to someone talking about three secret places in their city. Make notes about the three places she mentions.

• Japanese Kyoto Friendship Gardens

• 2 Wellington Place, Leith

• Rooftop Terrace, National Museum of Scotland

C Listen again. Which key phrases does the speaker use?

American Speakout city secrets

6 A Read an extract from a website. What kind of information is available on the website?

City Secrets Guide

All cities have interesting and unusual attractions that are still well-kept secrets. Tourists won't find them and many of the locals won't know about them either. Whether it's a hidden park that makes a good place to eat lunch, or a little-known musical event, the City Secrets Guide gives you everything you need to know to discover the hidden gems of the city you're visiting, with insider information from people in the know.

B Listen to someone talking about three secret places in their city. Make notes about the three places she mentions.

- Japanese Kyoto Friendship Gardens
- 2 Wellington Place, Leith
- Rooftop Terrace, National Museum of Scotland

C Listen again. Which key phrases does the speaker use?

> **KEYPHRASES**
>
> Secluded/Hidden away …
>
> You would never believe it's there …
>
> Most people have never heard about …
>
> It's a well-kept secret …
>
> It's not what you'd call a big secret, but …

7 A Think about somewhere in your city (or a city you know well) that is secret or abandoned. It could be a park, a restaurant, somewhere you like to visit. You are going to describe why the place is special. Do you know anything about its history?

B Work in groups. Take turns describing your secret places and ask follow-up questions.

writeback secrets guide

8 A Read the secrets guide. Which of these places would you choose to visit, and why?

Edinburgh's best-kept secrets

Edinburgh is Scotland's city of secrets. Here is our guide for discovering the magic and mystery of this beautiful place.

1 Did you know Edinburgh has a river? The green, leafy footpaths and bicycle paths along the Water of Leith offer a peaceful escape from the buzz of the city.

2 Edinburgh is a city of villages and Grassmarket is a wonderful neighborhood to explore. Historically, this is where poets like Robert Burns and Wordsworth would meet in public houses. Now, with its pedestrian streets lined with fashionable boutiques, bars and restaurants it's a great place to breathe in the city's history.

3 Take a trip to Cramond Island. At low tide on a sunny day, you can walk out to this small island, about a mile out to sea. The island is abandoned but hidden amongst the woods you can still find a ruined farmhouse and some old buildings from World War II. Be careful to get back before the tide rises though!

4 Secluded off bustling South Bridge is Dovecote Studios. The building used to be a Victorian swimming pool, but is now home to a tapestry studio. You can watch the talented weavers at work, peruse art in the gallery, or just enjoy an excellent cup of coffee.

5 Feeling a little hungry? Why not pop in to I. J. Mellis Cheesemonger's in Stockbridge Market? You'll feel like you're walking back through time as you enter, but this is a great place to pick up some local farmhouse cheeses and freshly baked bread. It's one of my favorite morning stops.

B Write your own secrets guide (250 words) for a city you know well/the area where you live. Try to include five secrets about the place. You can use your own ideas and information gained from listening to other students.

bicycle paths / hungry   cycle ways / peckish

V IDIOMS: SECRETS

1 A Underline the correct alternatives.

1 **A:** What do you think of David, the new website designer?

   B: He seems really nice and *keeps/stays* himself to himself.

2 **A:** Do you know what they decided during the meeting?

   B: No. That kind of information is kept firmly behind closed *gates/doors*.

3 **A:** I don't know if I should say anything.

   B: Go on. *Spill/Drop* the beans!

4 **A:** Do you think we should tell?

   B: No. I think it's best if we keep *mum/shut*.

5 **A:** Why is your sister so angry?

   B: I let it *slip/lip* that she wasn't at Jo's house yesterday.

B Work in pairs. Write a short conversation using two phrases from Exercise 1A. Perform your conversation for other students.

G MODAL VERBS AND RELATED PHRASES

2 A Complete the second sentence. Use between two and four words.

1 I wish I hadn't gone to bed so late.

   I should _____ earlier.

2 We are expected to finish by Tuesday.

   We're _____ by Tuesday.

3 They didn't have the courage to argue.

   They _____ argue.

4 The restaurant was empty.

   We _____ booked.

5 We're not allowed to take cell phones into class.

   Cell phones _____ in class.

6 If you park here, you'll get a ticket.

   You'd _____ park here.

B Complete the sentences in any way you choose. Compare your ideas in pairs.

1 I was supposed to ..., but ...

2 As a child, I was always/never allowed to ...

3 I think we ought to ...

V TRUTH OR MYTH

3 A Find and underline the incorrect word in each sentence. Then put the underlined words in the correct sentences.

1 Perception wisdom says you have to know grammar rules to learn a language.

2 People think it's possible to learn a language in a few weeks. This myth needs to be conventional.

3 It's believed that people have a "language gene", but this is difficult to intuitively.

4 The truth has been debunked about translation: sometimes it can be useful to learners!

5 The idea that it's easier to learn foreign languages when you are young is verify true.

6 A commonly held uncovered is that bilingual children get confused learning two languages.

B Do you agree with the statements in Exercise 3A? Compare your ideas in pairs.

G THE PASSIVE

4 A Complete the text with the correct active or passive form of the verbs in parentheses.

The story of maybe

It ¹_____ (believe) that this story comes from an ancient civilization in the Americas. A farmer had a champion horse. One day, the horse ²_____ (disappear). Everyone thought the horse ³_____ (steal) and all the farmer's neighbors visited him. "What terrible news," they said.

"Maybe," said the farmer. A few days later, the horse ⁴_____ (come) back with two magnificent wild horses. The neighbors visited again to offer their congratulations.

The next day, the wild horses ⁵_____ (be) tamed by the farmer's son, when he ⁶_____ (throw) off one of them and broke his leg. Again the farmer's neighbors visited. "We are so sorry. This is awful news."

"Maybe," said the farmer. The next day, an army captain came to recruit men for a war, but because the farmer's son had broken his leg, he ⁷_____ (not recruit). He stayed at home and ⁸_____ (help) tame the wild horses, which became champions. The farmer's neighbors said, "What wonderful news that your horses ⁹_____ (recognize) as the best in the country!"

"Maybe," said the farmer. And the next day the now famous horses were gone.

B What do you think the moral of the story is? Compare your ideas with other students.

F MAKING A POINT

5 A Add the missing words to the conversations.

1 **A:** If we continue like this, there will be no fish left in the river.

   B: Is there any evidence to that?

2 **A:** Sorry, I've lost you.

   B: What basically saying is we can't afford to waste any more time.

3 **A:** If think about it, we'd be stupid to let this opportunity escape us.

   B: Yes, I think you're right.

4 **A:** I don't how you can argue that economics doesn't have an influence on the situation.

   B: I really don't see what that has got to do with the issue.

5 **A:** People aren't interested in buying organic food if it's too expensive.

   B: Can we sure about that?

B Practice the conversations in pairs. Try to extend them

civilization   civilisation

6)) trends

FUTURE GAZING p68

A GLOBAL LANGUAGE? p71

TRENDSETTERS p74

SPEAKING	6.1 Evaluate future inventions
	6.2 Discuss trends in language learning
	6.3 Describe changes in your country
	6.4 Decide which trends to fund
LISTENING	6.2 Listen to a program about global English
	6.3 Listen to descriptions of how trends started
	6.4 Watch a program about technology trends
READING	6.1 Read about the far future
WRITING	6.2 Write a report
	6.4 Write about a trend

Do you follow trends in music and fashion?

INTERVIEWS

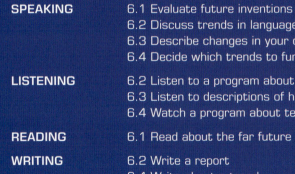

TECH TRENDS p76

P connected speech: auxiliary verbs
V predictions

Years from now	Future predictions
3,000	If civilization collapses, most buildings, bridges and dams are going to be **a distant memory**. **The signs are** that most words commonly used today will become extinct due to the rapid evolution of language.
4,000	**The days of living on islands will be over**. The ice in Greenland will have melted because of extreme global warming, and sea levels are going to be six meters higher than today.
10,000	According to some estimates, we'll be living out our final days. With overpopulation, disease and global warming, people may not survive beyond the year 10,000.
20,000	Chernobyl, the place in which a nuclear accident occurred in 1986, will finally be safe.
50,000	The KEO Time Capsule, which will have been floating in space for 50,000 years, will re-enter the Earth's atmosphere. Niagara Falls will have **become a thing of the past**. The remaining 20 miles to Lake Erie will erode and the waterfall will cease to exist.
100,000	The titanium in your laptop will begin to corrode. A global disaster **may well** have happened: either a super-volcano or a large climate-altering asteroid may have affected Earth.
500,000	A new Ice Age will probably be occurring.
1,000,000	Monuments like the Pyramids of Giza and Mount Rushmore might still exist, but all other man-made objects will be gone. All glass created up until now will have decomposed.
10,000,000	The Red Sea will have flooded the Rift Valley, dividing Africa, and a new ocean **is likely to** have formed. The planet will be bathed in gamma radiation from a supernova, triggering mass extinctions.
50,000,000	The Mediterranean will be gone. Africa will have collided with Eurasia, sealing off the Mediterranean and creating a mountain range similar to the Himalayas. The ice will have melted in the Antarctic, raising the sea level by 75 meters.
150,000,000	America and Africa will start moving back together.
250,000,000	All continents will be fused together as one land mass.
600,000,000	One of three types of photosynthesis will no longer be possible. As a result, 99 percent of species will die out.
100 quintillion	Earth will die, consumed by the sun.

READING

1 A You are going to read a text that predicts the Earth's future 1,000 years or more from now. What do you think it might say about the following?

> buildings   language   global disasters   monuments like the Pyramids of Giza   the Earth's temperature

B Read the text to see if you were correct.

2 A Work in pairs and answer the questions.

1 The text says gamma radiation will trigger mass extinctions. What is a trigger? What does the verb mean here?

2 The text says "Africa will have collided with Eurasia" and "all continents will be fused together". What is the difference between "collide" and "fuse together"? Which is the more violent action?

3 The text says an area of land will "erode", titanium will "corrode" and glass will "decompose". What is the difference between these verbs?

4 One synonym for "cease to exist" is "die out". Find two other synonyms in the text with the same meaning. They both use the verb become.

B Discuss with other students.

1 Do you think the text is optimistic, pessimistic or realistic? Explain your opinion.

2 Which of the predictions do you think are based on things that have happened before?

Most words that were used 1,000 years ago are no longer used.

VOCABULARY
PREDICTIONS

3 A Look at the expressions in bold in the text. Which refer to:

1 predictions with a link to the past? (2 expressions)
   a distant memory

2 predictions that are highly possible? (2 expressions)

3 the evidence for a prediction? (1 expression)

4 a situation that will stop because of changing conditions? (1 expression)

B Look at the expressions below. They are similar to two of the expressions in Exercise 3A. Which two?

1 The facts suggest/The figures point to

2 is bound to/is destined to

SPEAKING

4 Work in pairs. Tell your partner about:

- a prediction in the text that may well come true.
- something good that you think is likely to happen to your country or town/city.
- something that people used frequently, but which is now a thing of the past.

GRAMMAR
FUTURE FORMS

5 Check what you know. Match sentences 1–5 with rules a)–e).

1 Earth **will die**.
2 The time capsule **will have been floating** for 50,000 years.
3 Sea levels **are going to be** higher than today.
4 The ice in Greenland **will have melted**.
5 We'**ll be living out** our final days.

RULES

> **a)** Use *be going to* + infinitive to make a prediction based on current evidence.
> **b)** Use *will* + infinitive to make a prediction.
> **c)** Use the future continuous to describe an activity that will be in progress at some time in the future.
> **d)** Use the future perfect to describe something that happens before a time in the future.
> **e)** Use the future perfect continuous to describe something in progress for a period up to a specified time in the future.

6 Read about three other ways to talk about the future. Look at sentences 6–8 and choose the correct option to complete rules f)–h).

6 Time travel **could be** a reality by 2075.
7 Robot intelligence **is due to surpass** human intelligence by 2100.
8 The government **is to introduce** a new law.

RULES

> **f)** Use *could/might/may* + infinitive to describe a prediction that is *not certain/certain*.
> **g)** Use *be due to* + infinitive to describe something that is *expected to happen or arrive at a particular time/unlikely to happen soon*.
> **h)** Use *be + to* + infinitive to describe *an informal plan/an official arrangement or order*.

7 A CONNECTED SPEECH: auxiliary verbs Check (✔) the sentences you hear.

1 She'll be running. / She'll have been running.
2 I'll see him later. / I'll be seeing him later.
3 I'll be there. / I'll have been there.
4 We're going to be there at 1:00. / We're to be there at 1:00.

B Notice how some grammar words (e.g. auxiliary verbs) are pronounced in connected speech. Listen again and repeat.

She'll have been running. /ʃɪləvbɪn/

▶ page 138 LANGUAGE**BANK**

8 A Are both alternatives in sentences 1–8 possible? If so, is the meaning different?

1 By 2020, eighty percent of city dwellers *will be working/are to work* from home.
   Both are possible. We use "will be working" to make a prediction. We use "are to work" to describe an order from an authority.

2 Europe *might/will* become a united state in the next ten years.
3 Families *will be/will be being* racially very mixed.
4 By 2030, scientists *are finding/will have found* cures for most illnesses.
5 Cars *will/are due to* be banned from downtowns.
6 In fifty years' time, most rich people *will live/will have been living* until they are over 100.
7 By 2030, English *is going to be/will have become* the world's third language.
8 By 2050, it's possible that governments *will censor/will have been censoring* the web for years.

B Say the correct sentences out loud, using shortened forms of auxiliary verbs.

C Do you agree with statements 1–8? Discuss with other students.

SPEAKING

9 Read about some ideas of the future below. Discuss the questions.

1 Which ideas do you like?

2 Which do you think will come true?

3 What problems would the inventions solve?

4 What would the consequences be if these ideas became reality?

MACHINES OF THE FUTURE

Driverless car

A car that drives itself safely everywhere, navigating the roads by using artificial intelligence and information provided by satellites.

A recycler that makes drinks

A machine that recycles all food waste by blending it with proteins and chemicals to produce a nutritious drink. The drink can be used as a supplement for undernourished populations.

Body parts regenerator

A machine that grows human tissue to replace damaged body parts. It can be used to treat soldiers, accident victims and anyone with a major injury.

"Experience" implant

An implant that records everything you do, see and hear every day. It allows you to watch, hear and feel any sensation from any time in your past.

VOCABULARY *PLUS*
PREPOSITIONAL PHRASES

10 **A** Work in pairs. Read some predictions about global developments. Complete the paragraphs with suitable prepositions (one or two words). Use one preposition for each paragraph, once in every sentence.

India is [1] _____*on*_____ track to surpass China as the most populated country by 2035. In India, 48,000 babies are born every day [2] _____*on*_____ average. In the future, India's resources such as schools and hospitals will be permanently [3] ____ *on* ____ trial as they try to keep up with rising demands.

Millions of children are [4] _____ risk of contracting diseases from dirty water. Only sixty percent of the world's population has easy access to drinking water [5] ___ present. In the future, it is hoped that [6] _____ least ninety-five percent of people will have running water in their homes, but there are no guarantees of this.

As humanity's need for resources has grown, it is clear that man is [7] _____ far the most destructive animal on Earth. We are, [8] _____ nature, and prolific polluters of the planet. Soon, everyone will have to monitor pollution [9] _____ law.

The number of wild animals such as lions has been [10] _____ decline for decades, so, we are preserving the genetic codes of animals [11] _____ danger of extinction. In the future, we hope to, [12] _____ effect, "recreate" these animals.

In the early twenty-first century, corruption in business has started getting [13] _____ control. Corporations have tried to keep a number of scandals [14] ___ sight. In future, [15] _____ necessity, stricter anti-corruption laws will be passed.

B Look at all the prepositional phrases you completed in Exercise 10A and try to work out what they mean.

> **American Speak TIP**
> Prepositional phrases are short, fixed phrases (usually two or three words) that begin with a preposition. They are often followed by a noun, e.g. *at war*, *by accident*. When you notice prepositional phrases, write them down in a complete sentence. This will help you to remember them.

11 **A** Replace the underlined words below with prepositional phrases from Exercise 10A. Then use your own ideas to complete as many of the predictions as you can.

1 In the future, people will be <u>vulnerable to</u> catching a new disease called … *at risk of*

2 Birth rates are <u>falling fast</u>, so soon …

3 Inflation will get <u>completely crazy</u>, which will lead to …

4 By 2040, there will be <u>a minimum of</u> ten billion people alive, and this will cause …

5 In the future, <u>legally</u> people will have to register their …

6 To protect animals that are <u>close to becoming extinct</u>, we will …

7 People will, <u>generally</u>, have only one …

8 <u>Right now</u>, robots aren't very intelligent, but by 2040, …

B Choose a topic you are interested in (e.g. the environment, sports, technology, etc.) and do stages 1–4.

1 Write down three predictions about this topic.

2 Note some consequences of these predictions (problems or benefits).

3 Explain your ideas to other students.

4 Say which predictions you agree/disagree with and why.

▶ page 153 **VOCABULARY**BANK

6.2)) A GLOBAL LANGUAGE?

G concession clauses
P intonation: concession clauses
V language

VOCABULARY
LANGUAGE

1 A Complete the questions using the words in the box. Can you explain the meaning of the phrases in bold?

> command   mind   dead   offensive   everyday
> global   barrier   official

1 Why do you think English has become a "lingua franca", used by people around the world to communicate? What factors contributed to its rise as a _____ **language**?

2 Think of three ways to improve your _____ **of a language** and one situation where you need to _____ **your language**.

3 What happens when you experience a **language** _____? Do you think these will still exist in the future? Why/Why not?

4 Can you name an ancient or _____ **language**? Can you name a country where the _____ **language** used for legal purposes is different from the _____ **language** spoken on the street? Do you think this is a problem?

5 Would you ever use _____ **language**? In what kinds of situations?

B Discuss the questions above.

▶ page 153 **VOCABULARYBANK**

LISTENING

2 Work in pairs. Read about the radio program and answer the questions.

1 What do Stephen Fry and David Crystal discuss in the program?

2 What are the two main reasons given for why English is changing?

3 What kinds of changes are mentioned?

3 A Listen to part of the program. Check the topics that are mentioned.

- new Englishes
- culture and identity
- the type of English spoken by computers
- local languages/brands of English
- changing pronunciation
- English as a mother tongue
- English as a foreign language

B What do they say about each point?

Language is linked to your culture and identity because everything that makes up your identity (plants, animals, history, etc.) has to be expressed with language.

4 A Two of the sentences below are incorrect. Listen to the program again and correct them.

1 The way English continues to move across the globe gives us a whole range of Englishes.

2 In the beginning, there was just British English and American English, and then came Australian English, South African English, Indian English, and so on.

3 When a country adopts a new language, it changes it to suit its local needs.

4 English has been adopted by more than sixty countries around the world.

5 There are about 400 million first language speakers of English.

6 Around the world, one fifth of the population speaks English as a second or foreign language.

B Discuss. How do you think English will change in the next 200 years? Do you think it will continue to be a global language? Do you think other languages will become more important?

Stephen Fry's English Delight

As the use of English as a lingua franca continues to grow and spread around the world, the language itself is changing – adapting to how its speakers use it. The number of people who speak English as a second language has now grown to far outweigh the number of native speakers. Professor David Crystal, a world authority in language change, thinks sounds which some speakers find difficult to pronounce might disappear. And the vocabulary will certainly change, too.

The other huge influence on the way English will change relates to technology. With computers that "read" text and automatic person-to-person translators, will computers soon be joining the swelling billions who use and change English? In this radio program, Stephen Fry and Professor David Crystal discuss the evolution of English.

1 145 000+ artículos

Deutsch

Die freie Enzyklopädie

1 789 000+ Artikel

938 000+ 記事

Français

L'encyclopédie libr

1 573 000+ articles

GRAMMAR
CONCESSION CLAUSES

5 A Check what you know. Read the predictions about the future of English. Underline the correct alternatives.

1 *While/Despite* English is still the dominant language on the internet, other languages (like Mandarin, Russian, Spanish and Portuguese) will become increasingly important.

2 *In spite of/Although* 27.3 percent of internet users are English speakers, this number is closely followed by Chinese speakers (22.6 percent). *Though/Despite* we may find it hard to believe, the global language of the future might be Chinese or Arabic.

3 *Difficult though it may be/Strange as it seemed* for students, in the future many school and college subjects are likely to be taught in English, using English materials.

4 *However/Whichever* way you look at it, children need to start learning English when they are as young as possible.

5 *Even though/In spite of* increasing numbers of English speakers, the global predominance of English is likely to change.

6 *Even if/Despite* being able to use simultaneous translation on their phones to speak to each other, people will still want to learn another language.

7 *While/Whichever* people continue to use English to communicate on the internet, the language itself will continue to change.

B Work in pairs. Do you agree or disagree with the statements above? Why?

6 A Use the rule below to help you identify the main clauses and concession clauses in sentences 1–7 above.

> **RULES**
>
> Concession clauses are used to introduce information which contrasts with information in the main clause.

B Answer the questions.

1 What punctuation separates the clauses?

2 Do the linkers in italics introduce the main clause or the concession clause?

3 Most of the linkers in italics are followed by a verb clause. Which two are followed by a noun/-*ing* form?

C INTONATION: concession clauses Listen to the sentences. Which part of the sentence uses the higher intonation: the concession clause or the main clause? Listen again and repeat the intonation patterns.

▶ page 138 LANGUAGE**BANK**

7 A Write one sentence to connect each pair of ideas. Use the words in parenthesis. Think carefully about the punctuation.

1 I always try to speak to people in their local language / I don't speak it very well (even if)

I always try to speak to people in their local language, even if I don't speak it very well.

2 I spend a lot of time studying grammar / I still make mistakes (though)

3 It is difficult / I always try to believe what people tell me (difficult though)

4 It doesn't matter which way you look at it / technology is changing education (however)

5 I agree that English is important / I think students need to learn several languages (while)

6 It may seem strange / I find it hard to remember facts and figures (strange as)

7 It is a fact that I enjoy traveling / I don't get the opportunity very often (despite)

8 Learning a language is difficult / it doesn't matter which method you choose (whichever)

B Choose three of the linkers in italics from Exercise 5A (*even if*, *while*, *although*, etc.) and write sentences which are true for you (your language, your family, your job/studies etc.). Compare your ideas in pairs. Are any of your sentences similar?

SPEAKING

8 A Work in groups of three and read about three ideas for language learning. Student A: read the text below. Student B: turn to page 159. Student C: turn to page 162. Take turns to explain the ideas you read about.

Robot teachers

English-teaching robots, called "Engbots", have been introduced in schools in Korea. It is expected that in the future these robots should be able to teach on their own so that there will be no need for English teachers in the classroom.

B Discuss the pros and cons of each idea. Which language learning ideas do you think are likely to be popular in the future?

While the robot teacher would work for free, it would take away jobs from humans. Despite the appeal of the robots for children, I don't think this idea will be very popular.

WRITING
A REPORT; LEARN TO DESCRIBE TRENDS

9 A Look at the graph. What does it tell you about which languages will be important in the future? Can you make any predictions based on the evidence provided?

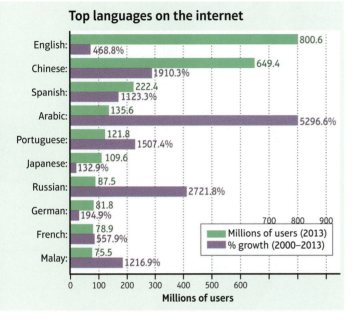

Top languages on the internet

English: 800.6 / 468.8%
Chinese: 649.4 / 1910.3%
Spanish: 222.4 / 1123.3%
Arabic: 135.6 / 5296.6%
Portuguese: 121.8 / 1507.4%
Japanese: 109.6 / 132.9%
Russian: 87.5 / 2721.8%
German: 81.8 / 194.9%
French: 78.9 / 557.9%
Malay: 75.5 / 1216.9%

■ Millions of users (2013)
■ % growth (2000–2013)

Millions of users

B Read the first part of a report about languages on the internet. Answer the questions.

1 Which language does the writer think may become the dominant internet language of the future? Why?

2 Which other languages do you think are important to mention in the report? Why?

This report will look at the changing importance of various languages on the internet and draw conclusions about the implications for language learners around the world. The graphic shows the top ten languages used on the internet and gives information about the rate of growth of each language and the total number of users.

It is quite clear from the data that languages other than English are becoming increasingly important on the internet. There has been a huge surge in demand for Chinese, for example, which has increased by 1910.3 percent in the last thirteen years and is now not far behind the use of English in terms of total numbers of users. While there are 800.6 million users of English on the internet, Chinese is fast catching up, with 649.4 million users. If the current trend continues, Chinese will soon become the most dominant language on the internet.

Another popular language currently on the internet is Spanish, with 222.4 million users, making it the third most dominant language. Spanish users have also shown a steady increase in growth (1123.3 percent) over thirteen years, indicating the continued importance of Spanish as an internet language.

However, there are other languages which show an increasing influence. In particular, …

10 Read the guidelines for writing a formal report. Which guidelines 1–6 are followed in the report in Exercise 9B? What would you expect to find in the remaining part of the report?

1 Introduce the report so that its purpose is clearly demonstrated.

2 Organize your report into paragraphs or sections under different headings/subheadings.

3 Refer to statistics, graphs and other data.

4 Give recommendations or draw conclusions about the information in your report.

5 Use formal language (objective structures like the passive, full forms rather than contractions, formal vocabulary and register).

6 Use linking words and phrases to help support your ideas.

11 A Look at sentences 1–6. Which alternative is **not** possible according to the graph in Exercise 9A? Cross out the incorrect alternative.

1 The importance of Chinese as a global language has *increased dramatically/risen sharply/dropped alarmingly*.

2 There has been *a surge/a drop/an increase* in the use of Chinese on the internet.

3 Numbers of people using Arabic on the internet have *plummeted/soared/grown* in recent years.

4 There has been a relative *surge/decline/drop* in the percentage of people using English online, as numbers of people using languages such as Chinese, Russian and Arabic have *declined/increased/grown*.

5 Numbers of Chinese speakers with access to the internet have *rocketed/exploded/collapsed*.

6 There has been a *steady/sharp/gradual* increase in the use of Spanish online.

B Use the prompts to write sentences describing trends in education. Use the present perfect tense.

1 explosion / demand for / mobile technology / language learning

2 number / people / communicating regularly / social networks / increase / dramatically

3 number / students / attend / private language schools / study English / plummet

4 sharp increase / ability / learners / access / learning materials / internet

5 gradual decline / appeal / traditional teaching methods

12 Complete the report in Exercise 9B by continuing the last paragraph and adding a conclusion (150 words). Use the language in Exercise 11A to help.

6.3)) TRENDSETTERS

VOCABULARY
TRENDS

1 A Discuss the questions.

1 How would you describe the people and things in the photos?

2 Do any of the images look out-of-date?

3 How do trends start and spread?

B Read the text about how trends spread. What is the main idea of the text? What is your answer to the question at the end of the text?

The best way to understand how trends take off might be to think of them as epidemics. How is it that unknown books suddenly become bestsellers, TV programs become instant classics, toys that were adored by generations suddenly lose their appeal? The answer is that trends spread like viruses. Somehow they capture the imagination and strike a chord with the public. Take the rise of the shoe brand Hush Puppies. Sales of Hush Puppies had stagnated to just 30,000 pairs a year. Suddenly, the shoes became the latest thing in Manhattan clubs, and stylists began to use them as accessories in fashion photo shoots. It turned out to be more than just a passing trend. In 1995, Hush Puppies sold 430,000 pairs, and in 1996, 1,700,000 pairs. Or, look at the technology revolution led by Apple Inc. The number of Apple users has risen dramatically in the last ten years. How do these changes happen? Some say it's a combination of word of mouth and pure luck, while marketers think it's something we can control. Who is right?

2 A Read the text again and find the words that complete the phrases in bold.

1 When trends suddenly become popular, they **take** ...

2 When a product goes out of fashion, it **has lost its** ...

3 One way that fashions spread is they **capture the** ...

4 When people identify with something, it **strikes a** ...

5 When a product or trend is suddenly popular, we say it **becomes the latest** ...

6 When something is popular for just a short time, we say **it's just a passing** ...

7 When there is more of something now than before, we say **the number has** ...

8 When something becomes trendy because people tell each other about it, it spreads **by word of** ...

B Work in pairs. Think of examples of:

• something that was a passing trend.

• something that has captured the public imagination.

• something that has taken off recently.

FUNCTION
DESCRIBING CAUSE AND EFFECT

3 A Listen to people describing how two trends started and answer the questions.

1 What trends do they talk about?

2 How did the trends start?

3 How/Why did the trends spread?

B Read the expressions below for describing cause and effect. Can you remember which expressions the speakers in Exercise 3A used?

	informal and neutral	formal
cause	It all started ... It originated in/from ... It's because of ...	It has its origins/ roots in ... It can be traced back/attributed to ... It stems from ...
effect	It led to ... It has caused ... Because of this, ...	It resulted in ... It gave rise to ... It brought about ...

C Listen again to check.

▶ page 138 LANGUAGE BANK

4 Rewrite the sentences using the words in parentheses. Change the verb tenses as necessary.

1 Reggae comes from Jamaica. (have/roots)

2 The Mohican haircut, in the U.K., was originally from the punk era. (have/origins)

3 Technology has led to new types of crime, such as hacking. (give rise)

4 Some say soccer started in China. (can/trace)

5 Global warming is the reason for many recent environmental disasters. (cause)

6 Better healthcare and diet, plus fewer babies per family, mean the population is aging. (because of)

7 The rising number of female world leaders can be attributed to the women's liberation movement. (stem)

8 The growth in online publishing has necessitated new laws. (lead to)

9 It's thought that chess began in India over a thousand years ago. (originate)

10 Medical procedures for disfigured soldiers led to the development of cosmetic surgery. (resulted)

LEARN TO
SUMMARIZE YOUR VIEWS

5 A Look at the expressions in the box. When do you think we usually use these expressions? What is their purpose?

> So overall, …   To sum up, …   All in all, …   Basically, …
> In conclusion, …   So what I'm really saying is, …

B Which expressions did the speakers in Exercise 3A use? Check your answers in audio script S6.4 on page 171.

6 A Complete the sentences in any way you choose.

> **American Speak TIP** When summarizing, we use different expressions depending on how formal the situation is. *To sum up* is formal. Which other expression in Exercise 5A do you think is formal?

1 People now expect to download music for free, and CD sales are at their lowest ebb. Basically, …

2 We saw some great presentations at the conference. The hotel was wonderful, and we loved the food. So, overall, …

3 Bloggers take news from reporters and write comments. They don't do much reporting. So, what I'm really saying is …

4 Sales of the game soared in May, jumped again in July and rose dramatically in December. To sum up, …

5 The report says young people believe in openness. They like sharing their private lives online. In conclusion, …

6 We had developed a great product, so logically it should have been a success. However, we had technical problems. Then a competitor stole the idea. All in all, …

B Compare your answers in pairs.

7 A Listen to completed sentences 1–6 in Exercise 6A. Are any of the endings similar to yours?

B How many vowels (including the *y* sound) do the words in the box have? When we say these words in connected speech, one vowel sound disappears. Which one?

> basically   dramatically   logically

C CONNECTED SPEECH: swallowed sounds Listen to check. Cross out the swallowed sounds.

D Practice saying the words, omitting the swallowed sounds.

SPEAKING

8 A Prepare a two-minute presentation: What has changed in your lifetime in your country? Think about trends in fashion, cost of living, free time, etc. Choose one issue. Note the causes and effects of the changes.

B Work in groups and give your presentation. Did any of you have similar ideas?

soccer / aging   football / ageing

DVD PREVIEW

1 Discuss with other students.

1 Are you a big fan of technology? Do you keep up with the latest technological developments? If so, in what fields?

2 Overall, do you think technology is a force for good in the world? Give examples.

2 Work in pairs. What do you think the words/phrases in bold mean in these contexts?

a) The pundits say this trend will never **take off**.

b) It's this year's **breakout** gadget.

c) The company really **pushed the boat out** on this product.

d) What's your **take** on these new smart watches?

e) Wearable tech has been **to the fore** this year.

3 Read the program information. What kinds of technology do you think will be discussed in the program?

▶ BBC News: Technology Trends

In this news program, journalist Rory Cellan-Jones visits the Information Age Gallery at the Science Museum. Famous for its exhibits of over 200 years of technological innovation, this is the venue where Queen Elizabeth II sent her first "tweet". Here, Cellan-Jones talks to technology experts Olivia Solon and Ingrid Lunden about the year's biggest trends in technology.

DVD VIEW

4 Watch the program. Which of the things below are mentioned? What do they say about them?

> smart watch   interactive television
> smart thermostat   driverless cars   drones
> brain imaging   genetic data

5 A Complete the extracts.

It was the year when ¹_____ technology began to take off with all sorts of devices to give you information on the ²_____.

They [Apple] were, after all, the company that really pushed the ³_____ [out] on smartphones, and with their iPhones, so you wonder if their take on the smart watch will be the watch that actually finally breaks ⁴_____ from gadget geeks.

The magic of the interconnected world is that everything's going to be ⁵_____, so you may be somebody who's driving home from work one day and using the dashboard in your car to turn on your ⁶_____ at home.

There are getting to be far more savvy and malicious ⁷_____ out there who are looking to tap into your information to exploit the fact that we have a lot of our ⁸_____ in the cloud.

B Watch the DVD again to check.

6 Work in pairs and discuss the questions.

1 The program is from 2014. Which of the objects discussed are now already out of date? Which predictions have/have not come true?

2 Can you think of any other recent technology trends?

American Speakout crowdfund a tech trend

7 A Read a description of crowdfunding from a wiki. Have you ever been involved in crowdfunding?

Crowdfunding

Crowdfunding democratizes the growth of innovations. Here's how it works. First, you need a great idea. It could be a creative project or a task. Then you reach out over the internet, explaining your idea through an online presentation, perhaps using video. Then friends, family, acquaintances and complete strangers can decide if they want to fund you. Their donation can be anything from one dollar to thousands, and they can donate anonymously if they wish. Big donors usually, but not always, get something in return.

B Listen to two people discussing whether to invest in an innovation. What is the gadget and what do they think of it?

C Listen again. Which key phrases do they use?

> **KEYPHRASES**
>
> One of the biggest benefits is …
>
> It'll go on the market for two dollars/a hundred dollars/ten euros.
>
> Can we see any drawbacks?
>
> I don't think it'll catch on.
>
> I can't really see any negatives.
>
> It seems like a great investment.
>
> It's a start-up.
>
> My initial reaction is …
>
> It has a lot of potential.
>
> It's a money-spinner.

8 You are going to decide which tech trends to fund. Work in two groups. Group A, turn to page 164. Group B, turn to page 162. Read the information and then follow instructions a)–c) below.

a) Describe the trends to a member of the other group.

b) With your new partner, discuss which trends will take off and which will not. You have $1,000 to donate. Together, decide on how you will divide the funding. You may choose to fund all, a few, or just one idea.

c) Tell other students what you decided and why.

writeback describe a trend

9 A Read an online article about a trend. How might it help the whole world?

THE MAKER MOVEMENT

People have always created their own objects, but today the practice is growing and it even has a name: The Maker Movement.

The movement uses a DIY (Do-It-Yourself) ethic and is notable for people sharing their creations and getting together in Fab Labs (Fabrication Laboratories) or Maker Spaces to collaborate on their designs. The people involved are a curious mix of computer hackers, skilled artisans with an eye for good design, and tinkerers – the type of people who used to spend their Sundays building toy railway sets.

Most of the objects they create are simple. Schoolchildren might make toys from recycled cardboard and plastic or model bridges from dry spaghetti. But in some areas – notably San Francisco – the Maker Movement is using advanced technology to create things that may benefit all of humanity. Recent products include prosthetic arms for war victims, 3D models of wild habitats that allow us to predict climate change and robots to help the disabled in the home. Many such products can be seen in the Maker Fairs held around the world.

Traditionally, innovators made things in their garage. This is where so many start-ups and famous businesses began. But the Maker Movement is increasingly being recognized and practiced in schools. Teachers have noted that Maker projects combine elements of math, science, and art, as well as creativity and critical thinking – essential skills in the twenty-first century.

B Write about one of the trends you discussed in Exercise 8. Invent any details necessary (200–250 words).

democratize democratise

V PREDICTIONS

1 Complete the text by adding one word in each gap.

The idea of resurrecting extinct species used to be science fiction, but this development ¹_____ well come true. The science already exists. The recent explosion ²_____ genome research tells us that the recipe for making a creature lies in its DNA. Creating animals from a genome sequence is impossible now, but the ³_____ are it will happen soon. When an animal dies in a dry cave or in ice, we can find intact genome sequences. We then need a surrogate species to give birth to the animal. If we wanted to bring back a mammoth, the surrogate would be an elephant. As a result of this development, fears about the extinction of some species could become a ⁴_____ memory. As the science gathers pace, conservationists are getting ready; they have begun freezing tissue samples of these animals. The days of campaigns to save the whale and so many other species could ⁵_____ over, as extinction becomes a ⁶_____ of the past!

G FUTURE FORMS

2 A Work in pairs. Student A: you are an optimist. Student B: you are a pessimist. Complete the sentences according to your role.

1 By the time I'm old, I hope I will have done many things, such as …

2 Tomorrow, I'm going to …

3 By 2020, I will have been …

4 If everything goes to plan, I will …

5 If my plan falls through, I might …

6 I'm due to …

7 I will be visiting …

8 Apparently, I am to …

B Compare your sentences. Now compare with another pair. Who was the most optimistic and who was the most pessimistic?

V LANGUAGE

3 A The phrases in italics are in the wrong sentences. Put them in the correct place.

1 It's useful to study Latin, even though it is a *command of the language*.

2 Increasing your exposure to media in the language you're studying is likely to increase your *language barrier*.

3 A simplified version of English, sometimes called "Globish", will become the dominant *dead language*.

4 I wish teenagers would *global language*. I hate to hear them swearing.

5 It's important for global economics that people can communicate without a *mind their language*.

B Work in pairs. Do you agree with the rewritten statements above? Compare your ideas.

G CONCESSION CLAUSES

4 A Match the sentence halves.

1 I'm planning to join a gym,

2 I love traveling. I always enjoy meeting people

3 However hard I try to be organized,

4 I get tempted to buy things

5 In a relationship, you need to be able to forgive people

6 No matter how early you get up in the morning,

a) whatever they do.

b) wherever I go.

c) I still forget things all the time.

d) there are never enough hours in the day.

e) although finding the time to go is difficult.

f) even though I can't really afford them.

B Use the prompts to write your own sentences. Compare your ideas in pairs.

I'm good at … even though …

I'd like to … whatever …

As hard as I try, …

No matter what happens, …

Despite feeling … I …

F DESCRIBING CAUSE AND EFFECT

5 A Correct the mistakes in sentences 1–7. What trends do they describe?

1 These can be tracing back to the 1700s, when a Dutchman attached tiny wheels to strips of wood and nailed them to his shoes.

2 This fashion item is often attributed by British designer Mary Quant in the 1960s, but ancient Roman soldiers wore a similar garment!

3 This musical style was popularized in New York in the 1970s, but it has the origins in the "talking" style of West African musician-poets.

4 These have their rooting in ancient China, though they were popularized in the USA in the early 1900s when actors wore them to avoid being recognized in public.

5 When an American engineer, Sherman Poppen, invented a toy for his daughter by fastening two skis together and attaching a rope to one end in 1965, it lead to a new sport.

6 The first type was produced in the 1960s for the University of Florida's American football team, nicknamed "the Gators" (short for alligators). This resulted on the brand name Gatorade.

7 "Weblog" was first used in 1997, but Peter Merholz divided this word into two, which gave rise of the term that describes a popular form of electronic writing.

B Check your ideas. Match the trends below with 1–7.

roller skates   blog
sunglasses   mini-skirt
hip-hop   snowboarding
energy drinks

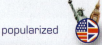

popularized   popularised

7)) freedom

THE GREAT ESCAPE p80

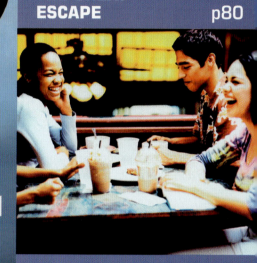

SWITCHING OFF p83

FREE TO MAKE MISTAKES p86

GANDHI p88

SPEAKING
7.1 Talk about an escape plan
7.2 Discuss ways to escape your routine
7.3 Talk about personal choice
7.4 Talk about freedom

LISTENING
7.2 Listen to people describing how they relax
7.3 Listen to a discussion about whether children are over-protected
7.4 Watch a documentary about Gandhi

READING
7.1 Read an article about a man who disappeared
7.2 Read a promotional leaflet
7.3 Read about freedom in childhood

WRITING
7.2 Write a promotional leaflet
7.4 Write about what freedom means to you

What makes
you feel free?

INTERVIEWS

G cleft sentences
P word stress: suffixes
V collocations

THE CASE OF THE DISAPPEARING MAN

When a man walked into a police station in London, claiming to be suffering from amnesia, he told officers, "I think I am a missing person." He apparently had no recollection of his whereabouts or events over the previous five years. What police didn't initially realize was that the man in front of them was in fact John Darwin, "the missing canoe man".

When John Darwin, a married father of two, initially went missing five years previously, a massive search and rescue mission was launched along the northeast coast of the U.K., near to where he was last seen. Prison officer John Darwin had been spotted paddling out to sea with his kayak early in the morning on 21st March, but it was only when he failed to arrive at work for a night shift that evening that the alarm was raised. The rescue teams searched extensively, but to no avail.

Several weeks later, when the shattered remains of John's kayak were found washed up on the beach, John Darwin was presumed dead. More than a year later, his wife threw flowers into the sea to mark the anniversary of her husband's disappearance. At an inquest, the coroner recorded an open verdict, which allowed the family to "move on". However, no trace of Mr. Darwin's body was ever found.

On his reappearance in London, his family were informed. His two sons, Mark and Anthony, were thrilled to be reunited with their father. And his wife Anne – who had sold up her properties in England and moved to Panama three months before his reappearance – expressed surprise, joy and elation at the return of her missing husband.

However, nobody could have predicted what would come to light over the following days. When John Darwin appeared at the police station, he claimed memory loss, but otherwise he appeared both fit and well, and he was also suntanned (a little unusual for December in the U.K.). An investigation was immediately launched into his disappearance.

READING

1 A Look at the photos and the title of the story. What do you think might have happened?

B Read the text to find out.

C Answer the questions.

1 Why do you think John Darwin was tanned?

2 What might have happened to his canoe?

3 Where do you think Mr. Darwin had been during those five years?

4 What do you think happened next?

D Turn to page 161. Read part two of the story and check your ideas.

2 A Work in pairs. Complete the sentences using information from part two of the story.

1 The circumstances that led John Darwin to consider faking his own death were …

2 John Darwin managed to live secretly at home by …

3 In Panama, the Darwins had hoped to …

4 The deception was uncovered by …

5 As a punishment for their crime of fraud and deception, the Darwins …

B Work in pairs and discuss the questions.

1 What do you think of what John Darwin did?

2 What do you think was the most difficult part of the deception for the Darwins?

3 Do you think it was right for the Darwins to go to prison?

4 What do you think Anne Darwin should/shouldn't have done?

GRAMMAR
CLEFT SENTENCES

3 A Sentences 1–4 express ideas in the story, but are phrased slightly differently. Rewrite them using the prompts in italics.

1 Police didn't initially realize that the man in front of them was John Darwin, "the missing canoe man".

What police …

2 The alarm was raised only when he failed to arrive at work for a night shift.

It was only when …

3 He spent the next few years hiding inside the house and rarely leaving.

What he did then …

4 A colleague of Anne Darwin's eventually put the pieces of the puzzle together.

It was a …

B Check your answers in the stories on pages 80 and 161.

C What is the effect of starting the sentences with the phrases in italics? Read the rule to check.

> **RULES**
>
> To add emphasis or focus attention on one part of a sentence, we can add certain words or phrases to the beginning of the sentence using another verb (e.g. *It was …/What he knew was …/The reason why … is …/The person who … is …*, etc.). This is called a "cleft sentence".

▶ page 140 LANGUAGEBANK

4 Rewrite the sentences using the prompts.

1 I don't understand why Anne Darwin didn't tell her sons about their father.

What I don't understand …

2 They planned to start a new life in Panama.

The place where …

3 The photograph of the couple buying a house in Panama revealed the deception.

It was …

4 She couldn't understand why Anne had decided to emigrate to Panama.

The thing that …

5 John Darwin flew back to the U.K. from Panama because he was missing his sons.

The reason …

6 He found it difficult coming to terms with what his parents had done.

What he found …

5 A Complete the sentences to make them true for you.

1 Something I have always wanted to do is …

2 The reason why I enjoy … is …

3 The place I would most like to visit is …

4 What I enjoy/dislike most about living where I do is …

5 One thing I would like to change is …

B Use your sentences to start conversations with other students.

A: One thing I would like to change is my job.
B: Really? Why's that?

VOCABULARY
COLLOCATIONS

6 A Complete the common collocations with the words/ phrases in the box.

> an investigation   suffer from   search   shift
> presumed   the alarm

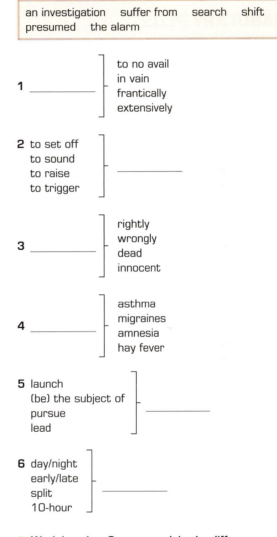

1 _____
  to no avail
  in vain
  frantically
  extensively

2 to set off
  to sound
  to raise
  to trigger
  _____

3 _____
  rightly
  wrongly
  dead
  innocent

4 _____
  asthma
  migraines
  amnesia
  hay fever

5 launch
  (be) the subject of
  pursue
  lead
  _____

6 day/night
  early/late
  split
  10-hour
  _____

B Work in pairs. Can you explain the difference in meaning (if there is one) between the different collocations in each group?

"Search in vain" and "search to no avail" both mean "search without success", but "search frantically" means …

C Work in pairs and answer the questions using appropriate collocations.

1 When was the last time you searched for something?

2 Have you, or anyone you know, ever worked shifts? What kind of shifts?

3 Have you ever suffered from headaches or migraines? What brings them on?

SPEAKING

7 A What would you do if you were stranded on an island? Would you try to raise the alarm or make a break for it yourself? Turn to page 164 and read the rules of a game.

B Work in groups. Decide on a list of five things which you think would be useful to you in this situation. Work out an escape plan.

C Tell other students about your plan. Which group has the best plan?

VOCABULARY *PLUS*
SUFFIXES

8 A Check what you know. Add the headings in the box to the correct columns in the table.

adjectives	nouns	adverbs	verbs

elaborate	elaboration	elaborate/ elaborative	elaborately
deceive	deception	deceptive	deceptively
pretend	pretense	pretend	✗
suspect	suspicion	suspicious	suspiciously

B Underline the suffixes in the words in the table.

9 A One word in each sentence is incorrect. Change or add the suffix to correct it. You may need to change some letters in the original word.

1 Would you care to elaborately on the idea?

2 They traveled to Panama, looking for opportunities to start a new life together, while Mrs. Darwin kept up the pretend that her husband was dead.

3 He apparently had no recollect of his whereabouts or events over the previous five years.

4 In the meantime, in the U.K., several people had become suspicion.

5 A massively search and rescue mission was launched along the northeast coast of the U.K.

6 What police didn't initially realization was that the man in front of them was in fact John Darwin.

7 The rescue teams searched extensive, but to no avail.

8 When visitors came, Mr. Darwin supposed hid in the neighboring house.

B What parts of speech are the corrected words? Find two verbs, two nouns, two adjectives and two adverbs.

10 A Add the corrected words from Exercise 9A to the groups below.

to form verbs

-ate:	motivate, hesitate, renovate, 1_____
-en:	darken, strengthen, brighten
-ize:	prioritize, legalize, modernize, 2_____
-ify:	glorify, electrify, exemplify

to form nouns

-tion/-ation:	exhaustion, production, 3_____
-cy:	immediacy, accuracy, tendency
-ity:	clarity, stupidity, opportunity
-ment:	embarrassment, enjoyment, harassment
-ness:	loneliness, unhappiness, tiredness
-er/-an/-or:	engineer, musician, professor
-ant:	applicant, attendant, disinfectant
-ance/-ense:	clearance, independence, 4_____

to form adjectives

-ant/-ent:	dominant, redundant, independent
-ous/-ious:	scandalous, rebellious, 5_____
-able/-ible:	capable, edible, visible
-ive:	persuasive, elusive, evasive, 6_____
-ful:	respectful, helpful, resourceful

to form adverbs

-ly:	deeply, financially, dramatically, 7_____, 8_____

American Speak out TIP Some suffixes, especially adjectives, have a clear meaning, e.g. *-less* indicates "without" — *hopeless, useless, meaningless*; *-proof* indicates "resistant to the effect of" — *childproof, waterproof, soundproof*. These can help you to guess the meanings of words you do not know. Think about the meaning of these suffixes: *-like* (*childlike, look-alike*), *-worthy* (*trustworthy*), *-ible/-able* (*incomprehensible, habitable*).

B WORD STRESS: suffixes Look at the words in Exercise 10A. Mark the main stressed syllable in each word. Listen to check your answers.

C Listen again and repeat the words, focusing on the correct stress patterns.

D Work in pairs. Take turns choosing words from Exercise 10A. Use them to make questions for your partner.

A: Have you ever hesitated before doing something?
B: Yes, I hesitated before I did my first parachute jump.

▶ page 154 VOCABULARY BANK

pretense / Mrs. / look-alike   pretence / Mrs / lookalike

7.2)) SWITCHING OFF

G participle clauses
P word stress: idioms
V idioms: relaxing

VOCABULARY

IDIOMS: RELAXING

1 Look at the photos. Which of these activities would you find most relaxing? Why?

2 Replace the words in italics in 1–6 with the idioms in the box.

> take time out from (something)   take a breather
> take my mind off (something)   switch off
> let your hair down   unwind

1 OK, run around the field one more time, then you can *take a rest*.

2 Just go to the party and *go wild for a bit*.

3 She's going to *have a month off* work to finish her PhD dissertation.

4 I went traveling in order to *forget about* the tragedy *for a while*.

5 It's hard to *stop focusing on my work* on weekends.

6 If I've been working a sixteen-hour shift, I usually go to the bar to *relax*.

3 A WORD STRESS: idioms Listen to the answers to Exercise 2. Where is the stress on the idioms? Is it on the verb or on another word e.g. noun/adjective?

B Listen again and repeat the expressions.

C Choose three of the expressions in Exercise 2 and write true sentences about yourself. Compare your sentences in pairs.

▶ page 154 **VOCABULARY**BANK

LISTENING

4 A Listen to three people talking about how they spend their free time and answer the questions.

1 What do they do to get away from their day-to-day routine?

2 How does it help them to switch off?

B Listen again. Then write questions for these answers.

Speaker 1:

1 Near where he lives. *Where …*

2 A mountain lion.

Speaker 2:

3 The piano.

4 Elevator music.

Speaker 3:

5 Team sports.

6 His friends.

C Discuss with other students.

1 The first speaker says his hikes are "hard work". What do you think this means? What day-to-day parts of your life can be hard work?

2 The second speaker says "you just go with the flow". What does this mean? What normally flows? In what circumstances might you go with the flow?

3 The third speaker says "it's a remnant of childhood". Remnant has a similar meaning to remains. What do you think "a remnant of childhood" means?

D Which person's method of relaxation is closest to yours? Which would you most like to try? Why?

GRAMMAR
PARTICIPLE CLAUSES

5 A Read about someone who found true freedom by learning a new skill. What did she learn and how did she do it?

<u>Feeling</u> jaded from life at a desk and <u>armed</u> with nothing but a love of Argentinian culture, I decided to learn the tango. Having listened to the music as a child, I already knew the rhythms, so I felt excited walking into my first tango class. However, the tango was harder than it looked, and after the first class, my feet were sore and my knees ached. Not wanting to give up, I decided to take matters into my own hands (and feet!). Using a CD lent to me by a friend, I practiced at home, and after a while, I improved. Encouraged by my teacher, I went to a café where you could hear the music and eventually, having struggled with it for months, I got the hang of it. People looking for something a bit different always love the tango. When you're doing it, you feel completely free: the world disappears – it's just you, your partner and the music.

B Check what you know. Underline the present and past participles in the text. The first two have been done for you.

6 A Match example sentences 1–4 with rules a)–d).

1 **Encouraged by my teacher,** I went to a café where you could hear the music.

2 **Not wanting** to give up, I decided to take matters into my own hands.

3 ... a **CD** (that was) **lent** to me by a friend ...

4 I felt excited **walking into my first tango class.**

> **RULES**
> Participle clauses can:
> a) replace relative clauses.
> b) have an active meaning (when they begin with a present participle).
> c) have a passive meaning (when they begin with a past participle).
> d) describe actions happening around the same time or one immediately after another.

B Read rules e) and f). Find an example of each in the text.

> **RULES**
> e) *Having* + past participle can be used to give background information or show the cause of a second action.
> f) The past participle can be used as an adjective to add extra information.

▶ page 140 LANGUAGEBANK

7 Make one sentence from two. Use participles and the words in parenthesis. Omit some words.

1 As experts have proven, jogging is a stress buster. It's a great exercise. (Proven by / to be)

Proven by experts to be a stress buster, jogging is a great exercise.

2 I honed my technique. Then I spent all my free time painting. (Having)

3 I didn't know how to relax. I always felt tense until I discovered Pilates. (Not)

4 Paul was given the chance to go to a dance school in Colombia. He learned salsa. (Given)

5 She was staying in Toulouse. This is where she learned French cooking. (While)

6 My rollerblades are a great way for me to get around. They were bought for me by my brother. (Bought)

7 He wasn't naturally good at sports. He had to work incredibly hard. (Not)

8 Alternative lifestyles are practiced by many people. These people are looking for freedom from modern life. (looking)

SPEAKING

8 A Discuss. Where do you go to get away from your day-to-day routine and what do you do?

B Work with other students. Look at the list of activities below and answer the questions.

1 What types of people might be interested in these activities? Who are they for?

Going on a survival course is probably for people who ...

2 What might the benefits of these activities be (physical and mental)?

Taking a cooking vacation will help you to ...

3 Which would be the best for a class trip? Why? Share your answer with the class.

We decided that people wanting a way to relax would particularly like ...

- a survival course
- a spa retreat
- a film-making course
- an extreme experience weekend, e.g. skydiving
- a cooking vacation
- a dance course
- a pottery course

SPARNGALL SPA
retreat
relax, rejuvenate, recharge

WELCOME Sparngall Spa Retreat welcomes you to a place of natural beauty, where you can recharge your body and mind. Our mission is to provide the highest quality environment, accomodations, food and activities, so that you can relax completely during your time with us. Our highly qualified staff will provide you with a warm welcome and ensure that you get the most out of your stay.

ACCOMODATIONS Sparngall Spa Retreat boasts eighteen luxury double bedrooms with large en-suite bathrooms and views of Sparngall Mountain. All bedrooms come with stocked refrigerators, fresh flowers that are changed daily, fruit, and spring water from our very own Sparngall Reservoir.

FACILITIES & ACTIVITIES The spa retreat includes a sauna, jacuzzi and swimming pool, all of which are open from 5:00 a.m. until midnight. We are located minutes from Sparngall Mountain and Lake, and we offer seasonal Nordic walking, hiking and fishing. Our other services and activities include:

massage therapy | facials | aromatherapy | yoga | beauty treatments

DINING The Sparngall restaurant includes high-quality, healthy dining with the freshest ingredients. These are grown and harvested on the 4,000 acres of land that surrounds the spa retreat. Our chefs will be delighted to prepare meals to order, including full vegetarian and vegan fare.

RATES Rates vary according to the month. Please go to our website for current rates: www.sparngallspa.net
Sparngall Spa Retreat, Sparngall, SA2 7ND Phone: 01567 887254 Email: sparngall97@com

WRITING
A LEAFLET; LEARN TO USE SUBHEADINGS

9 A What is the purpose of leaflets, brochures and information sheets? What are their typical features?

B Read the guidelines to check.

1 Leaflets, brochures and information sheets inform us about something. They can also advise, warn or persuade. Businesses and organizations use them to promote events, places, services and products.

2 The title must be bold, eye-catching and give a clear idea of the topic.

3 Use short, clear subheadings. They must stand out in a different font.

4 Break the text up into short sections in a logical order.

5 Don't use language that is too complex. The message must be clear and easy to understand.

6 Lay the text out using spaces between sections. Use bullet points for lists of features and include illustrations, charts and photos if appropriate.

10 Read a leaflet about a place to relax and answer the questions.

1 Who is the intended audience?

2 Does the leaflet follow the guidelines above?

3 Would you like to go there?

11 A Find a heading, a subheading and a slogan in the leaflet. How are they different? Think about the types of words that are used and their purpose.

B Why do you think subheadings are useful? Check the ideas you agree with.

1 They help the writer, when he or she is planning the piece, to see what to include and what to leave out.

2 They show the reader how the piece is organized.

3 They allow the reader to jump to the specific information he or she is looking for.

4 They reveal the writer's opinion of the topic.

5 They visually break up blocks of text so that the piece is easier to read.

C Read the additional information about Sparngall Spa Retreat. Think of a suitable subheading.

Sparngall Spa Retreat is accessible by car or train. The nearest railway station is Sparngall Station. From there it is a ten-minute taxi ride to the retreat. We are happy to arrange transportation to and from the station for you.

12 A Read the scenario and think of an idea you can write about. Make notes and think of subheadings.

You own a place where people go to switch off from their daily routine. What type of place is it? Do people go there to learn something or just to relax? What services and facilities do you offer? Is food and accommodation included? How expensive is it?

B Write a promotional leaflet for your idea (250 words).

F exchanging opinions
P polite tone
V risk

When a New York journalist, Lenore Skenazy, wrote about how she had **deliberately** left her nine-year-old son in central New York and let him take the subway home alone, she unleashed a media frenzy. Her son, Izzy, whose idea the expedition had been, was happy. He had arrived home safely, ecstatic with independence. He'd been nagging his mother for weeks to be allowed to travel **unsupervised**. She'd given Izzy a subway map, twenty dollars and a few quarters in case he needed to make a phone call. She hadn't given him a cell phone (in case he lost it). But, Ms. Skenazy's actions landed her in a huge mess. She was labeled "crazy" and "America's worst mom". "My son had not climbed Mount Fuji in flip-flops," she wrote subsequently.

"He'd simply done what most people my age had done routinely when they were his age: gone somewhere on his own." She now runs a blog called Free Range Kids, which **encourages independence** in children and says, "The problem with this everything-is-dangerous outlook is that **over-protectiveness** is a danger in itself. A child who thinks he can't do anything on his own eventually can't." So, are we living in a **risk-averse culture** where we stifle our children's ability to **deal with danger** by never allowing them to **take reasonable risks**? Does Western society **coddle** its children? Or did Ms. Skenazy's actions **expose her son to real and unnecessary danger**? What do you think?

VOCABULARY
RISK

1 Work in pairs and answer the questions.

1 What risks do you think you take in your daily life?
2 Do you think that, as a society, we have become afraid to take risks? Why/Why not?
3 When is it OK to break the rules (at work, driving, at school, etc.)?

2 A Read the article and answer the questions.

1 What did the journalist let her son do?
2 What was her reason for doing this?
3 What kinds of reactions did she receive when she wrote about the experience?
4 What does Ms. Skenazy think is the problem with protecting children too much?

B What do you think the words/phrases in bold in the article mean? Use some of them to complete the sentences below. You may need to use just part of the phrase, or adapt it to fit the context.

1 It's a good idea to get children to cook for themselves from an early age, because it encourages _____.
2 If parents _____ their children by indulging them all the time, the children will never learn to look after themselves.
3 No rational parent would _____ try to _____ their child to unnecessary danger.
4 Children should be encouraged to take _____ _____ like learning how to use sharp knives. This way, they will learn to do things _____.
5 The problem with _____ parents is that the child doesn't learn to deal with problems they will face in the real world.
6 The fact that your coffee cup is labeled "Caution: contents hot" shows that we are living in a _____ society.

C Do you agree with the statements in Exercise 2B? Why/Why not?

FUNCTION
EXCHANGING OPINIONS

3 Listen to people talking about the story in Exercise 2A. Who agrees with the following statements, the man (M) or the woman (W)?

1 It was an amazing idea for the mother to leave her son to go home alone.
2 The boy could have gotten lost, or been attacked.
3 As parents, we have to take a stand against coddling.
4 Doing things by yourself at a young age teaches you how to protect yourself and be streetwise.
5 Children should be thrown in at the deep end.
6 New York is one of the most dangerous cities in the world.
7 It's too dangerous to leave a nine-year-old alone in a city without a cell phone.
8 We're in a hurry to push our kids to grow up too soon.

4 A Listen again and complete the phrases you hear.

a) Oh, come on! You must be _____.
b) That's absolutely _____.
c) Well, I agree with you up to a _____.
d) Surely, you don't _____ that …
e) That goes against my better _____ because …
f) How can you _____ that?
g) It just doesn't make _____ to me.
h) Oh, that's _____!

Ms. / labeled / coddle / an amazing   Ms / labelled / mollycoddle / a brilliant

B Put phrases a)–h) under the correct headings.

Agreeing

1 _____

I couldn't agree more.

Absolutely! I'm with you 100 percent on that.

Agreeing in part

2 _____

I suppose you've got a point, but …

Questioning someone's opinion

3 _____

4 _____

5 _____

6 _____

Where's the logic in that?

You can't honestly think that …

Strongly disagreeing

7 _____

8 _____

▶ page 140 **LANGUAGE**BANK

 American Speak TIP In order to disagree politely, ask questions, for example: *Do you really think so? Don't you think it's a bit long? Isn't that rather extreme?* To make your disagreement seem less forceful, use *Well, Right,* or *Yes, but* at the start of the sentence.

Look at audio script 7.4 on page 172 for examples of these devices.

LEARN TO
CONVINCE SOMEONE

5 A POLITE TONE Listen to the speakers trying to convince the listener of their opinion. How does the speaker try to sound polite?

1 **The point is** that he was only nine years old.

2 **Truly you don't think** he should never be allowed out?

3 **That's the whole point.** We need to encourage independence.

4 **All I'm trying to say is** New York is a dangerous city.

5 **I just think** we're too risk-averse.

6 **Oh, come on!** You can't really think that.

B Listen again and repeat the phrases, copying the tone.

6 A Use the prompts in parentheses to write responses which try to change A's opinion.

1 **A:** Everyone should be a vegetarian.

B: _____?

(surely/think/people/never/eat/meat)

2 **A:** Children shouldn't be allowed to hold knives.

B: _____.

(all/say/children/need/learn/some stage)

3 **A:** Nobody should have to take tests.

B: _____.

(point/exams/useful way/measure progress)

4 **A:** Young drivers shouldn't be allowed to drive with other youngsters in the car.

B: _____!

(come/not make sense)

B Practice the conversations in pairs. Focus on polite tone.

SPEAKING

7 A Look at the situations below. Who do you think should decide in each case? Why? Think of arguments to support your case.

B Work in groups and discuss the situations. Try to convince others of your opinion.

The state versus the individual
Who should decide:

- whether you are allowed to smoke in a public place?
- whether you should be allowed to eat junk food?
- how much exercise an individual should do?
- whether you should be allowed to keep a gun in your house?
- the age at which a child should go to school?
- how often you use your car or how fast you can drive in certain areas?
- the minimum age that someone can start working?

7.4 ◉)) GANDHI: THE ROAD TO FREEDOM

DVD PREVIEW

1 Discuss with other students: what do you know about the topics in the box?

> The history of India   India today
> the British Empire   Mohandas Gandhi
> Jawaharlal Nehru

2 Read sentences 1–8 about Mohandas Gandhi's life story. What do you think the words and expressions in bold mean?

1 Gandhi rose to prominence at a time when India was still subject to **colonial domination**.

2 He is **revered** all over the world for his leadership.

3 He was India's **figurehead** during the struggle for independence.

4 The British were responsible for a violent **clampdown**.

5 The world looked upon these actions with **outrage**.

6 He **galvanized** the nation to action.

7 His **crowning moment** was to come later.

8 The nation's hopes **rested on his shoulders**.

3 Read the program information. True or false: the program will describe how Gandhi helped India gain independence.

▶ Gandhi: The Road to Freedom

India is the world's largest democracy, and a country with a tumultuous history. While it is famed for its cultural achievements and astounding diversity, India also has a legacy of violence, struggle and inequality. This documentary looks at the life of the "father of the nation", Mohandas Gandhi (also known to his followers as Mahatma, "the great-souled one"), and asks how he managed to win India its freedom from the British Empire.

DVD VIEW

4 Look at Exercise 1 again. Watch the DVD. What new information do you know now? Compare your ideas with other students.

5 Watch the DVD again and answer the questions.

1 Why did Gandhi go to Britain in 1931?

2 What was his "crowning moment"?

3 What led to "outrage" and acclaim for Gandhi?

4 How does the narrator describe Gandhi's manner?

5 What impressed Tony Benn about Gandhi?

6 What happened on August 15th, 1947?

6 Work in pairs and retell Gandhi's story. Use as many of the words and phrases from Exercise 2 as you can.

7 Read the extracts from the program and discuss the questions with other students.

1 "Today, Gandhi is revered as the most important Indian of all time … He became the figurehead of the battle to free India." Is anyone from your country revered like Gandhi? Are they regarded as figureheads?

2 "The hopes of a nation rested on Gandhi's shoulders." In your country, in your lifetime, is there a figure who was/is regarded as the nation's great hope?

3 "The modesty of his lifestyle … made … a big impression." Are there any public figures who have made a big impression on you? Who? Why?

galvanize galvanise

American Speakout freedom

8 A Read some answers to the question: "What does freedom mean to you?" Which of these answers do you like?

> It's about living without fear that someone will arrest you or persecute you for following your beliefs.
> **Kwezi**
>
> Freedom is about choices. If I want to speak my own language in public, go to work with my hair dyed bright blue, or wear ripped jeans, no one stops me. That's freedom.
> **Agnieska**
>
> Freedom, to me, means doing what I want, when I want, with whomever I want.
> **Colin**
>
> I'm legally blind. To me, freedom is being able to walk in an open space without traffic or too many people.
> **Lee**
>
> Freedom means not having to worry about time. I only get that feeling when I'm alone in the wilderness or on a beach.
> **Hana**

B Listen to two people discussing what freedom means to them. Who mentions the topics below: the man or the woman?

> voting   religion   speech   travel
> access to information

C Listen again and check the key phrases you hear.

KEYPHRASES

Freedom, to me, means …
We should also bear in mind …
When I think of … [I think of …/what comes to mind is …]
Not only … but …
You could add to that …
While we're on the subject [of …], …
I'd say that one of the biggest issues is …
As I see it, …

9 Follow stages 1—3.

1 What does freedom mean to you? Make some notes and/or an illustration that answers the question.

2 Prepare to talk for 2—3 minutes about your answer.

3 Work with other students and listen to their answers. What do you have in common? What was different about your answers?

writeback what freedom means to you

10 A Read one person's description of what freedom means to them. Is it about personal or political freedom, or both?

WHAT FREEDOM MEANS TO ME

I have three jobs and a young family, and I also study part-time at night for a degree in Social Science. So, you could say I'm pretty busy! On my own, I'm bringing up three kids, all under the age of thirteen, and I really have very little time for myself. I haven't read a book for pleasure or watched TV alone or gone on a date for the best part of a decade. So, when I think about freedom, what springs to mind is me with my feet up, no kids to take care of, no assignments to hand in, and just some quiet music playing in the background.

B Write your own description of what freedom means to you.

G CLEFT SENTENCES

1 A Complete the sentences with the phrases in the box.

> What most impresses me   What you should do is
> The reason I've come   All I want to say
> One thing I've learned is that   The person who
> It was when I was reading that book   What they do

1 _____ is to talk about what we need to do.

2 _____ that I realized what I wanted to do with my life.

3 _____ is his ability to fix any problem.

4 _____ it's generally better to keep your thoughts to yourself.

5 _____ works harder than any of the other students is Kristina.

6 _____ call your manager to discuss the options.

7 _____ is that I think it's too expensive for students.

8 _____ is ask you lots of questions about your preferences and choose a product for you.

B Work in pairs. Make your own sentences using the prompts.

1 All I want to say about ... is ...

2 One thing I'd like to try is ...

3 It was ... who taught me ...

4 What I think we should do is ...

V COLLOCATIONS

2 A Complete the sentences using a suitable collocation.

1 For decades, scientists have searched in v_____ for a cure.

2 If you touch one of the books on the shelf, it will trigger the a_____.

3 We p_____ wrongly that the court case would be the end of the matter.

4 The men were exhausted after their ten-hour s_____ at the factory.

5 My grandmother suffered terribly from a_____, and always carried an inhaler with her.

6 The whistle-blower is the s_____ of an investigation.

B Work in pairs, Student A and Student B. Write down as many collocations as possible for the words in the box.

Student A:

> search   investigation   shift

Student B:

> alarm   presumed   suffer

C Now, test your partner. Say the words from your box. How many collocations can your partner remember?

V IDIOMS: RELAXING

3 A Complete the sentences with one suitable word.

1 To ___unwind___, I usually *play tennis*.

2 The last time I _____ my hair down was *at a New Year's party*.

3 What helps me to take my _____ off work is *dancing salsa*.

4 I think people should take time ____ from work if *they are feeling sick*.

5 *Exercise* helps me when I want to switch _____ from work.

B Work in pairs. Make the sentences in Exercise 3A true for your partner by changing the pronouns and the sections in italics. If you don't know, guess.

To unwind, Davide goes swimming.

C Check your sentences with your partner.

G PARTICIPLE CLAUSES

4 A Imagine your perfect day. Write a paragraph about it using the participle clauses below in any order.

- Refreshed by a good sleep, I ...
- Having eaten, I ...
- Not wanting to ...
- Offered a choice of ...
- Walking to ...
- Having been taken to ...
- Having met up with ...

B Work in pairs and compare your paragraphs. Are they very different? How do they reflect your personalities and lifestyles?

F EXCHANGING OPINIONS

5 A Correct the mistakes in speaker B's responses.

1 A: Everyone has the right to freedom of expression.
   B: I agree with you up a point.

2 A: Freedom of speech means the media are allowed to publish absolutely anything.
   B: That ridiculous! There need to be controls.

3 A: The most important freedom we have is the right to vote.
   B: I could agree more.

4 A: People should be free to choose the country they live in.
   B: I suppose got a point, but there are obvious problems with what you're suggesting.

B Write your own responses to speaker A's statements. Discuss your ideas with other students.

8))) time

HISTORY IN A BOX   p92

I REMEMBER ...   p95

TIME SAVERS   p98

WHAT IS TIME?   p100

SPEAKING	8.1 Choose objects that represent you
	8.2 Talk about memories
	8.3 Discuss ways to save time
	8.4 Talk about a turning point in your life
LISTENING	8.2 Listen to a program about memory and smell
	8.3 Listen to an interview about time management
	8.4 Watch a program about time
READING	8.1 Read about time capsules
	8.2 Read a personal story
	8.3 Read time-saving tips
WRITING	8.2 Write a personal story
	8.4 Write about a major decision in your life

What is the best time of life?

INTERVIEWS

G future in the past
P rhythm: proverbs
V time expressions; proverbs

READING

1 A Read the introduction to the text. What objects would you put in a time capsule to represent your culture?

B Read the article about time capsules. Are any of your ideas mentioned?

2 A Read the article again quickly to find out who, what or when the underlined words refer to.

1 <u>He</u> must be a famous Brazilian singer.

2 Maybe there's a lot of hunting in <u>that place</u>.

3 <u>It</u> is probably a really well-known restaurant in the area.

4 Maybe there's a lot of surveillance <u>there</u>.

5 The recordings were put <u>there</u> because it was probably safer than the Paris Opera House.

6 <u>He</u> believed his capsule would survive over 6,000 years.

7 <u>They</u> collaborated to create time capsules.

8 Only <u>at that time</u> will his grandchildren know exactly what Davisson put in the capsule.

B Discuss. What do the contents of the time capsules tell us about the different societies in the text?

VOCABULARY
TIME EXPRESSIONS

3 A Read extracts a)—f) from the article and answer the questions. Which phrases in bold mean:

1 originates from or starts in (verb)?

2 the beginning of something (noun)?

3 happen repeatedly with the same amount of time between each happening?

4 something that was very close to happening?

5 a situation that will continue far into the future? (2 expressions)

a) ... "history in a box" probably **dates back to** ancient Egypt.

b) ... a new air-conditioning system **was about to** be installed ...

c) His capsule was to remain hidden **for the foreseeable future** ...

d) One of them would be opened **at regular intervals**

e) ... **in years to come** people would find objects like ...

f) From **the outset**, it was to have been the world's biggest time capsule ...

B There are two words missing in each sentence. Add the two missing words to each sentence. Use the expressions in Exercise 3A.

1 In years, we will remember this as a golden age.

2 Scientific breakthroughs don't happen intervals; they occur irregularly.

3 AIDS probably dates the early 20th century but began to spread rapidly in the 1980s.

4 We are enter an age of natural disasters.

5 From, the internet was able to unite people around the world.

6 Poverty will be with us for foreseeable.

C Do you agree with statements 1–6? Compare your ideas in pairs.

Imagine you're burying a time capsule for hundreds of years. When it's finally opened, what will the people of the future find inside it? What will they think of those artefacts? Will they even recognize them? The last few decades have seen more and more time capsules being prepared for the future. Here are some of the things that different cultures have chosen to represent them.

1 People in Curitiba, Brazil, chose a recording of the songs of Antonio Carlos Jobim; processed, packaged meat; an indoor toilet; a pair of jeans and a local tree with yellow flowers.

2 People in Bulawayo, Zimbabwe, chose a bottle of soil, a plastic cup used by beggars, an akierie (a walking stick used for hunting) and a pair of Bata "Toughees" school shoes.

3 People in Fountain, Colorado, USA, chose a piece of barbed wire, a packet of cigarettes, a brick, a high school code of conduct, an issue of *Girl's Life*, a hearing aid, a recording of a high-speed car chase, Prozac, Valium, a TV remote control and a menu from Ralph's Fine Dining.

4 People in Bharatpur, India, chose a bag of soil, a closed-circuit TV camera, a chillum, a gold nose ring and a pair of flip-flops.

5 The idea of "history in a box" probably dates back to ancient Egypt, when the pharaohs were buried with their possessions. Since then, there have been numerous examples of time capsules, all with their own stories attached.

6 On Christmas Eve 1907, members of the Paris Opera placed twenty-four musical recordings into two containers made of iron and lead. They were going to leave these untouched in the opera house's basement for 100 years, but in 1912, they added more recordings, plus a gramophone with instructions on how to use it. The time capsule was supposed to be opened in 2007. However, in 1989, when a new air-conditioning system was about to be installed, it was discovered that someone had broken into one of the capsules and the gramophone was missing. The remaining recordings were taken to France's National Library and opened eighteen years later.

7 Another time capsule was devised by Professor Thornwell Jacobs of Oglethorpe University, Georgia, USA, in 1940. While researching ancient history, he realized historians' lives would be easier if there were more artefacts available, so he created the Crypt of Civilization. He gathered hundreds of objects and sealed them in a waterproof room with a stainless steel door welded shut. His capsule was to remain hidden for the foreseeable future: Jacobs optimistically stipulated that the crypt wasn't meant to be opened until 8113.

8 In 1968, two Japanese companies, Panasonic and Mainichi Newspapers, worked together to create two identical time capsules. One of them would be opened at regular intervals to check the condition of the contents, but the other wasn't going to be touched for 5,000 years. Inside the capsules were 2,090 items, ensuring that in years to come people would find objects like a glass eye, false teeth, dead insects encased in resin, an origami instruction book, fake money and handcuffs.

9 It isn't just big organizations that do it. Harold Keith Davisson, from Nebraska, USA, made a time capsule in 1975 because he wanted his grandchildren to know what life was like in the 1970s. He put it on his front lawn. Of approximately 5,000 items inside it, there was a suit and even a car. From the outset, it was to have been the world's biggest time capsule, but then Davisson learned that other people were building bigger ones. Deciding that actions speak louder than words, in 1983 he built a second capsule on top of the first, including a second car! The capsule will be opened in 2025.

2100

GRAMMAR
FUTURE IN THE PAST

4 A Find sentences a)—d) in the article. Answer questions 1—3.

> **a)** The time capsule was supposed to be opened in 2007. (paragraph 6)
>
> **b)** His capsule was to remain hidden for the foreseeable future. (paragraph 7)
>
> **c)** The other wasn't going to be touched for 5,000 years. (paragraph 8)
>
> **d)** It was to have been the world's biggest time capsule. (paragraph 9)

1 Which grammatical structures in sentences a)—d) talk about plans or intentions in the past? Underline them.

2 Which three structures suggest that the plan did not become a reality?

3 How many other examples of the "future in the past" can you find in paragraphs 6—8 of the article? Which describes a plan that did not become reality?

B How do we make the "future in the past"? Complete the table.

future	future in the past
am/is/are going to	[1]_____ going to
am/is/are to + infinitive	[2]_____ to + infinitive OR [3]_____ to + have + past participle
am/is/are meant to	[4]_____ meant to
am/is/are supposed to	was/were supposed to

▶ page 142 **LANGUAGEBANK**

5 Rewrite the sentences using the words in parentheses.

1 We planned for the opening of our time capsule in 2020. (to be) Our time capsule …

2 The document was secret. No one could see it until 2050. (not / be) The document …

3 The plan was for the safe to be locked for ten years, but someone opened it. (supposed) The safe …

4 The idea was to visit Montevideo, but we didn't have time. (going) We …

5 They expected it to be the world's biggest outdoor festival, but then the rain came. (have) It was to …

6 Jim went to Peru on vacation. He ended up living there for twenty years. (would) Jim went to Peru, where …

6 A Complete the sentences for you, with two true and two false statements.

1 Recently, I was planning to … but …

2 When I was younger I was going to … but …

3 A few years ago I was supposed to … but …

4 A friend and I were thinking about … but …

B Work in pairs. Take turns reading your sentences. Guess which of your partner's sentences are true.

SPEAKING

7 A Look at the objects in the photos. What sort of person is she? What stages of her life are represented by these objects?

B What objects represent you? Choose some items for a "Museum of Me". Include clothing, food or drink, books, magazines or DVDs. What stages of your life do they represent?

C Explain your ideas to other students. How many objects do you have in common?

The first idea on my list is a pair of tennis shoes. I chose this because …

VOCABULARY *PLUS*

PROVERBS

8 A Look at the extract from the article on page 93 and underline the proverb. Do you have a similar saying in your language?

Deciding that actions speak louder than words, in 1983 [Davisson] built a second capsule on top of the first …

B What are proverbs? Think of a definition and compare your ideas.

 American Speak TIP Proverbs are short statements that express a general truth or give advice. They often come from literary sources or refer to ways of life in the past, so may use old vocabulary. It's essential to use proverbs at the right moment and with the exact words. Do you know any proverbs in English? Tell other students.

9 A Work in two groups. Group A: when would you use the proverbs below? Match proverbs 1–6 with situations a)–f). Do you have equivalents in your language? Group B: turn to page 162.

1 A picture is worth a thousand words.
2 Better safe than sorry.
3 Out of sight, out of mind.
4 Home is where the heart is.
5 Practice what you preach.
6 Rome wasn't built in a day.

a) I've enjoyed this trip, but I've had enough now.
b) You should leave early. There may be heavy traffic.
c) You told us to arrive on time, but you were late!
d) The photo of the flood sent a powerful message.
e) I'd been away only a month, but I'd already forgotten my ex.
f) To fulfill your ambitions, you'll need to study hard.

B Work with a student from the other group. Take turns. Show your list of proverbs to your partner. Explain them in any order. Your partner guesses the proverb you are describing.

10 RHYTHM: proverbs Listen to the proverbs. Notice the rhythm and repeat. Many proverbs have two or three main stresses. Listen again and underline the stressed syllables.

11 Work in pairs and discuss. Which of the proverbs do you generally agree with? Think of examples from your own life and tell your partner.

I agree with "practice makes perfect". I played the piano for twenty years. I'm not perfect, but I got much better by practicing.

▶ page 155 **VOCABULARY**BANK

8.2)) I REMEMBER ...

LISTENING

1 Work in pairs. What do the smells in the box make you think of?

> candles   cigarettes   vinegar   fresh bread
> coffee   perfume   disinfectant   sun cream
> lemons   gasoline   paint

2 A Read the radio program listing. What kinds of memories are evoked by particular smells? What is this phenomenon called?

> What does the smell of sunscreen remind you of? Does it evoke strong memories of blue skies and happiness? Then perhaps you have experienced what psychologists have termed the Proust phenomenon. Why is it that particular smells bring back powerful childhood memories? In this radio program, Claudia Hammond explores the link between smell and memory.

B Listen to the program. Which smells from Exercise 1 are mentioned? What do the speakers say about each smell?

3 Listen to the program again, in three parts. Decide if the statements are true. Correct any mistakes.

Part 1

1 The smell of mint sauce reminds the man of Sunday lunches in his childhood home.

2 One man remembers his nursery school when he smells privet (a type of hedge).

Part 2

3 Psychologists think memories associated with photos are stronger than those evoked by smells.

4 Professor Chu uses unfamiliar smells to trigger autobiographical memories.

5 The woman used mints and perfume to cover up the smell of cigarettes.

Part 3

6 When the man smells candles, he is reminded of when he played the church organ.

4 A Complete the extracts with the phrases in the box.

> evocative smell   evoking memories   takes me back
> in time   carried back in time

1 Now, ever had that feeling of being suddenly _____ by a particular odor?

2 There is, it seems, something special about smells when it comes to _____.

3 The smell that always really _____ is the smell of disinfectant.

4 For me, the most _____ is that smell you get when candles have just been snuffed out.

B Check your answers in audio script S8.2 on page 172.

C Work in groups and discuss. Which smells bring back strong memories for you?

GRAMMAR
ELLIPSIS AND SUBSTITUTION

5 A Check what you know. Read the conversations and answer questions a) and b).

a) What words have been left out where you see ▲? Why is this?

b) Look at the words in bold. What do they refer to? What words do they replace?

1 A: ▲ Remember any special smells from your childhood?
B: Yes, I **do** actually. ▲ The smell of my grandmother's perfume.

2 A: The smell of pine trees reminds me of vacations in Greece.
B: Does it ▲? I've never been **there**.

3 A: ▲ Got any photos of your family?
B: Yes, ▲ **lots**.

B Read the rules and answer the questions.

> **RULES**
>
> Use ellipsis to leave out a word, or words, when the context is obvious. In informal speech, we often leave out the beginnings or endings of common phrases.

1 Which words have been left out of the phrases/ questions below?

Ever been to Spain?

See you.

> **RULES**
>
> Use substitution to replace a word or phrase with a single word (e.g. *so, do, many, one, these, some, it, them, there, this, that*) in order to avoid repetition.

2 What does *so* replace?

A: Got everything you need?
B: I think so.

▶ page 142 **LANGUAGEBANK**

sunscreen sun cream

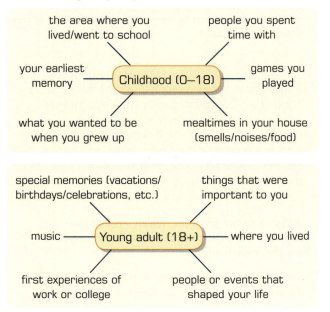

6 A Underline the correct alternatives.

1 **A:** Are you coming to the party?

B: Yes, I think *do/so/not*.

2 **A:** Did you just delete the file?

B: I hope *not/such/do*.

3 **A:** Do you want to try this perfume?

B: No, but I'll try that *some/much/one*.

4 **A:** Do you think we'll have enough time to discuss this later?

B: We'll have *so/a little/one* time.

5 **A:** Are you going away on vacation this year?

B: No. Ann Marie doesn't have enough money, and *more/neither/so* do I.

6 **A:** Are you sure you've got enough copies for everyone?

B: Yes, I've got *none/one/lots*.

B Cross out any words which could be left out of the conversations in Exercise 6A. Listen and check your answers.

C CONNECTED SPEECH Listen to the conversations again. Notice the smooth pronunciation in connected speech. Notice how sounds change and words link together.

You coming‿to‿the party?

Yes‿I think‿so.

D Repeat the conversations with a smooth pronunciation.

7 Work in pairs. Student A: turn to page 163. Student B: turn to page 162. Take turns reading out your sentences and choose the correct responses.

VOCABULARY
MEMORIES

8 A Complete the sentences. Choose the correct word in parentheses and put it in the appropriate place.

1 This place lots of memories for us. (gets/holds)

2 When I hear those old songs, it back a lot of memories. (brings/takes)

3 It's one of my memories. (oldest/earliest)

4 I have very memories of my time at elementary school. (vague/slim)

5 I only have a very recollection of what my grandparents' house looked like. (light/hazy)

6 It was a long time ago, but I remember it. (strongly/vividly)

7 I remember her dress. It was blue with a red belt. (distinctly/heavily)

8 Every time I go there, the memories come back. (flooding/running)

B Which words from Exercise 8A can you use to talk about memories that are not very strong? Which words can you use to talk about memories that are very strong or clear?

▶ page 155 **VOCABULARY**BANK

SPEAKING

9 A Read about the website talkingmemories.com. Would you use or visit a website like this? Why/Why not?

> Do you have vivid memories of your childhood or is it just a hazy blur? At talkingmemories.com you can record your memories of particular stages or events in your life, adding photos and videos. It allows you to preserve meaningful memories of your life, record important milestones and share memories of special events with friends, family and future generations.

B Choose a stage of your life to talk about. Prepare to talk about memories from that stage of your life. Make notes using the prompts below.

Childhood (0–18)
- the area where you lived/went to school
- people you spent time with
- your earliest memory
- games you played
- what you wanted to be when you grew up
- mealtimes in your house (smells/noises/food)

Young adult (18+)
- special memories (vacations/birthdays/celebrations, etc.)
- things that were important to you
- music
- where you lived
- first experiences of work or college
- people or events that shaped your life

C Work in groups and take turns. Talk about the special memories you have. Do others in the group have similar memories from that time?

WRITING
A PERSONAL STORY; LEARN TO IMPROVE DESCRIPTIVE WRITING

10 A Read the story on page 97. Answer the questions.

1 Why was the fig tree so important?

2 What happened to the house?

B Read the advice for writing a story for a magazine. Does the writer of *The Fig Tree* follow the advice?

1 Remember your audience (who is going to read this?) and use a range of structures and vocabulary.

2 Use an informal, chatty style. It makes your article more personal so the reader can identify with you.

3 Capture the reader's attention with an anecdote, something surprising or a strong image.

4 "Close the circle": the ending could echo the beginning or refer to the wording in the task.

elementary   primary

The Fig Tree

11 Read guidelines a)–d) for descriptive writing and follow instructions 1–4 below.

a) Include precise language. Use specific adjectives and nouns and strong action verbs (verbs that carry a specific meaning) to give life to the picture you are painting in the reader's mind.

The lion ate (weak) the antelope.

The ravenous (specific) lion devoured (strong) the antelope.

b) Include all the senses. Remember to describe sounds (using onomatopoeia — where the sound of the word imitates the meaning being described), smells, tastes and textures.

The car screeched to a halt.

The murmuring of innumerable bees.

c) Make use of contrasts. Describe how someone's mood changed from good to bad, or describe a location at different times of year.

d) Use figurative language (metaphor, simile, personification). Imagery can help to engage a reader.

The stars danced playfully in the sky.

(personification — giving human qualities to something that is not human)

Her home was a prison.

(metaphor — when you say one thing is another thing)

She felt as free as a bird.

(simile — when you say one thing is like another thing)

1 Find examples of specific adjectives and strong action verbs in the story *The Fig Tree*.

2 Find an example of onomatopoeia. Where does the writer describe a texture?

3 How does the writer use contrast in this story?

4 Find an example of personification of an object and an example of metaphor.

> **American Speak out TIP** It's important that you communicate to your reader exactly what you mean in the clearest possible way. Using strong verbs and adjectives helps you paint accurate pictures of what you mean in the reader's mind. How do the verbs change the meaning of the following sentences? *"I love you," he said./ "I love you," he screamed./ "I love you," he whispered./ "I love you," he mumbled.* Keep a list of strong verbs.

12 Read the instructions and write a personal story.

1 Work alone. Think about any particular people, objects or places which hold special memories for you. Can you remember particular sights, sounds, smells or textures associated with them?

2 Make notes about the memory, including personal details (how you felt, why it was special, etc.).

3 Write your story (220–250 words). Add a title.

4 Check your writing. Try to improve the description by using more precise language.

I remember we used to visit my grandmother's house on weekends. It was a huge house with gardens leading down to a field, and it seemed almost like a palace to me. At the bottom of the field was an orchard, planted with apples, and twenty-one walnut trees. In the middle of the field stood an ancient fig tree. It was here, in the tree, that my cousins and I would sit and play for hours on end. I can remember the smell of the green leaves, the sticky sap that would leak from the leaves and the figs as they ripened. We each had our own special branch, and we would climb up and then sit looking out over the countryside. I can almost feel the warmth of the sun on our faces and the feeling of safety and security as we hid among the branches. In that tree, we would sit and chatter about life, feast on sweet, crunchy apples, hold meetings, tell jokes, read books, make plans, have fig fights and discuss what we wanted to be when we grew up. The fig tree knew all our secrets.

When I was twelve, my grandmother moved into a small apartment, and we stopped going to the house. But a few years ago, I was in the area, so I drove back there to see if it was how I had remembered it. The house was almost unrecognizable. It had been turned into a doctor's office, with signs all around and cars parked all over the driveway. The gardens had been redesigned, and there were pathways to walk along and benches to sit on and enjoy the views. Gone was my grandmother's wild flower garden. But behind the house, in the middle of the field, just as if time had never passed, stood the fig tree, full of lush green leaves and juicy figs. Its branches hung heavily towards the ground, almost beckoning me to climb up. Just standing in the field brought all the memories of my grandmother and our life there flooding back to me. And touching the smooth bark on the trunk, it was all I could do to resist sprinting to the end of the field to pick an apple or two and then back to the fig tree to enjoy the rest of the warm afternoon.

unrecognizable / doctor's office / driveway   unrecognisable / doctor's surgery / drive

8.3)) TIME SAVERS

- **F** discussing ideas
- **P** word stress: phrases
- **V** collocations with *time*

VOCABULARY
COLLOCATIONS WITH *TIME*

1 Work in groups. Think about your life. Which activities are the biggest time-wasters?

2 A Complete the expressions in bold below with the words in the box. What do the expressions mean?

> in   pushed   the   to   ~~world~~   spare   hands

1 What would you do if you had **all the time in the _world_**?

2 Are you ever _____ **for time**? When?

3 When did you last have lots of **time on your _____**?

4 Do you wish you had more **time _____ yourself**?

5 When you're bored, how do you **pass _____ time**?

6 In your work/studies, do you usually finish tasks **just _____ time** or **with time to _____**?

B Discuss questions 1–6 with other students.

FUNCTION
DISCUSSING IDEAS

3 Work in pairs. Read about three ways to save time at work. Which do you think are good ideas?

> ### Time-savers that will put years on your life
>
> **Prioritize:** Some tasks are important and urgent. Others are important but not urgent. Most are neither. Forget about them until they become important and urgent.
>
> **Don't multi-task:** You think you're doing lots of things well at the same time. You aren't. You're doing lots of things badly at the same time, which will need re-doing later once you realize you've made a bad job of them. Focus on one thing at a time and do it properly.
>
> **Kill distractions:** Ignore email, leave the cell phone in your car, unplug the phone and remove all TVs within sight. If you want to work, work.

4 A You are going to listen to the beginning of an interview with a time management consultant. What do you think the job involves? Listen and check.

B Work in pairs. Listen again and discuss. What does John say about the things in the box?

> what he does   who he works with
> observing   resources
> how people typically start their working day
> lists   distractions

5 A Read audio script S8.5 on page 173. Find expressions for acknowledging an idea or introducing an alternative. Write them in the correct column of the table below.

acknowledging an idea	introducing an alternative
Right. OK.	Having said that, …

B Work in pairs. Add the expressions in the box to the correct column of the table.

> That's true.   You see, …   That's interesting.
> But, you could argue that …   That makes sense.
> Exactly.   I'm with you there.

6 Cross out the incorrect alternative in each sentence.

1 Shopping online is quicker. *On the other hand,/You see,/That's true*, you're taking a risk because you don't see the product or the vendor in the flesh.

2 So you think we should bring a map? *I know what you mean;/But looking at it another way,/I'm with you there*; it's easy to get lost in these parts.

3 Eating fast food saves time, but *I never thought of that,/looking at it another way,/on the other hand,* it's unhealthy.

4 So you think we should leave early in the morning? *That's a good idea./Yes and no./That makes sense.* The traffic gets really bad later in the day.

5 Do you really think I should delegate more? *Having said that./I never thought of that./That's interesting.* I thought I had to do everything myself.

6 I'm always **pressed** for time. *Having said that,/You see,/Alternatively,* my time management is terrible! I do everything at the last minute.

▶ page 142 **LANGUAGE**BANK

prioritize / pressed   prioritise / pushed

LEARN TO
SOLICIT MORE INFORMATION

7 Read some more extracts from the interview in Exercise 4A. Underline three expressions for soliciting more information.

Can you go into more detail? So, let's say I want to restructure my day to get more work done. How would you approach it?

That's a good idea. Can you think of anything else you might look at?

So, you obviously go into a lot of detail looking at what people do every day. Any other suggestions for how I might save time?

8 A Here are five more expressions for soliciting information. Which words do you think are missing?

1 What ___*else*___?

2 Can you tell us _____?

3 Anything to _____?

4 Is there anything we've _____?

5 Anyone managed to _____ up with other ideas?

B The answers are below but in the wrong order. Complete the expressions.

add	missed	more	come	~~else~~

> **American Speak TIP** We use expressions with *any*: any *ideas*, any*thing*, any*one*, etc. when we don't want to be specific. It means that it doesn't matter which or who. Which word beginning with *any* could be replaced by *anybody*?

S8.6

9 A WORD STRESS: phrases Listen to the expressions in Exercise 8A and choose the correct answer.

1 Which words are stressed in these expressions?

   a) the first word in each expression

   b) the last word in each expression

2 What type of words are stressed?

   a) "content" words (usually nouns, verbs, adjectives, adverbs)

   b) grammar words such as prepositions and auxiliary verbs

B Listen again and repeat.

10 Put the words in the correct order to make questions. Add capital letters.

1 **A:** tell / more / us / you / can / ?

   B: Well, for example, we could put a "to do" list on the wall.

2 **A:** you / go / detail / can / more / into / ?

   B: Yes. Every Wednesday, we could discuss the issue.

3 **A:** missed / there / is / we've / anything / ?

   B: No, I think that's everything.

4 **A:** else / of / think / can / anything / you / ?

   B: Yes, we haven't mentioned homework.

5 **A:** ideas / come / anyone / with / to / managed / other / up / ?

   B: Sorry, nothing else from me.

SPEAKING

11 A Work alone. Think of as many ways as possible to save time while working, studying, traveling or doing housework.

B Work in groups and follow the instructions.

1 Choose one facilitator to lead the discussion, solicit ideas and make sure everyone has a chance to speak.

2 Choose one scribe to write down all the ideas.

3 Share your ideas.

4 Divide the ideas into: a) really good, b) interesting but not always practical, c) too difficult to implement.

5 Present your group's best ideas to the class. Which ideas would you like to try?

DVD PREVIEW

1 A Complete the sentence below with two words in the box.

> science   universe   nature   art

While _____ seeks to understand reality through the observation of emotions and the sharing of human experience, _____ relies more on logical reasoning and detailed analysis.

B Compare your answers in pairs. In general, which approach do you tend to accept?

2 Read the program information. What concept is discussed in this episode?

▶ Wonders of the Universe

Who are we? Where do we come from? For thousands of years, humanity has turned to religion and myth to answer these questions. But in this series, Professor Brian Cox presents a different set of answers – answers provided by science. In this episode, Brian seeks to understand the nature of time and its role in creating both the universe and ourselves. Using the Perito Moreno glacier in Patagonia, Argentina, Brian explores the concept of the arrow of time, describing how time is characterized by irreversible change and why sequences happen in the order they do.

DVD VIEW

3 Watch the DVD. Number the ideas in the order they are mentioned.

a) There's a scientific reason for why the world doesn't run in reverse.

b) It's human nature to want to find the answer to these fundamental questions.

c) Permanent change is a fundamental part of what it means to be human.

d) The glacier has been moving down the valley for tens of thousands of years.

4 A Complete the extracts.

1 Events always happen in the same order. They're never _____, and they never go backwards.

2 We never see waves traveling across lakes, coming together and bouncing chunks of ice back _____.

3 We are compelled to travel into the _____.

4 And, that's because the arrow of time dictates that as each moment passes, things _____.

5 I suppose it's kind of the joy and _____ of our lives.

6 In the life of the universe, just as in our lives, everything is _____.

B Watch the DVD again to check.

5 Work in pairs and discuss the questions.

1 What do you think about the point Professor Cox is trying to explain? Do you think the glacier is a useful metaphor for the arrow of time?

2 Are you someone who relishes or resists change?

characterized   characterised

American Speakout a turning point

6 A Listen to someone talking about major turning points in her life. Answer the questions.

1 What were the three important decisions?
2 Does she regret the decisions she made?
3 How is her life different from her sister's?

B Listen again and choose the correct alternatives to complete the key phrases.

> ### KEYPHRASES
>
> My parents gave me the option to *go to a* specialized *performing arts school/stay at home*.
>
> There was *a lot of pressure on me to …/no pressure either way*.
>
> I made the decision to *go to a performing arts school/go to a comprehensive school*.
>
> Luckily for me, *it's panned out/it's turned out OK*.
>
> I found myself faced with *a dilemma/another decision*.
>
> The next major decision … was whether to *move house/have children or not*.
>
> I … wonder *what would have happened if … /if I made the right decision*.

7 A Prepare to talk about a turning point in your life. Think about the questions and make notes.

1 What was the decision? Who was involved? Did anyone or anything influence your decision?
2 How did the decision affect what happened afterwards?
3 How might things have been different now if you had made a different decision?

B Work in groups. Discuss your decisions and how they have affected your lives.

writeback a major decision

8 A Work in pairs and read the forum entry. Do you think Jason made the right decisions?

Tell us about a pivotal moment in your life

Jason, Australia: I'd say that the major pivotal moment of my life early on was when I was eleven years old and my parents decided to divorce. It was up to me to decide who I wanted to live with. At that time, my dad was living in a completely different part of Australia than me and my mom. After some deliberation, I chose to go and live with my dad.

Looking back, it was a hard decision to make for an eleven-year-old, and I do sometimes wonder if I made the right choice. If I could turn back time, I wonder if my relationship with my mother would be any better now had I made a different choice. I suppose I have a sense of regret about that.

However, if I hadn't gone to live with my dad, I wouldn't have met my girlfriend at the time. We were together for over three years, and when she wanted to move to England, I gave up a really good career in Australia to move with her. That was fine for a while, but we eventually split up, and then there was nothing to keep me in the U.K.

I came back to Australia, but it hasn't been easy to rebuild my career. At the end of the day, I think your guiding principle should be that blood is thicker than water, and it's usually best to put your family first.

B Write about a major decision in your life (250–300 words).

specialized · specialised

V TIME EXPRESSIONS

1 A Write sentences about your classmates.

1 For the foreseeable future, _____ will probably …

2 _____ is about to …

3 From the outset of the class, we all realized _____ was …

4 We will all remember _____ in years to come because …

B Work in groups. Read some of your sentences aloud, but don't say the name of the person. Can the others guess who you wrote about?

G FUTURE IN THE PAST

2 A Underline the correct alternatives.

> **Here are some excuses made by absent or late employees.**
>
> • I [1]*meant to/supposed to* be in the office at 8:00, but my dog was stressed out after a family reunion.
> • I [2]*was on the verge of/was to have* written the report on the weekend, but my finger got stuck in a bowling ball.
> • My husband and I [3]*were supposed/ were for* to go away for the weekend, but we had car trouble. It's now fixed, so we're going today (Monday).
>
> **And some excuses for bad behavior in relationships.**
>
> • I was [4]*to go to/going to* call you, but my three-year-old niece dropped my phone in a swimming pool.
> • I [5]*had been/was planning* to break up with you in person, but I thought you'd prefer this email.
>
> **And finally, two excuses for neglected homework.**
>
> • I read the questions, but I didn't realize we [6]*were supposed/were suppose* to answer them.
> • I [7]*meant for/was going* to do it, but I started worrying about the oil crisis, and I couldn't focus.

B Write excuses for the situations below. Use the future in the past. Compare your ideas. Who has the best excuses?

• You were absent from work.

• You forgot to meet a friend.

• You didn't do your homework.

G ELLIPSIS AND SUBSTITUTION

3 A Complete the sentences with a suitable word.

1 A: Do you think we're going to be late?
 B: No, I hope _____.

2 A: Are you enjoying the fish?
 B: My husband hasn't tried it yet, but I _____, and it's delicious.

3 A: Do you expect your decision to have repercussions?
 B: Yes, I expect _____.

4 A: It's a spectacular part of the country.
 B: Is it? I've never been _____.

5 A: Will we see you on Saturday?
 B: No, we'd hoped to be able to come, but I'm afraid we _____.

6 A: Do you mind if I borrow one of these umbrellas?
 B: Of course _____!
 Take _____.

B Cross out words in sentences 1–6 above that could be omitted in casual conversation.

C Practice the conversations in pairs.

V MEMORIES

4 Complete the sentences with the words in the box.

| vague | flooding | earliest |
| holds | distinctly | brings |

1 My grandmother's house _____ lots of memories for me.

2 Looking at photos _____ back wonderful memories of happy times.

3 I have a very _____ recollection of my great-grandfather, an artist, but I can't really remember him well.

4 I _____ remember telling you to leave the key for me.

5 As soon as I walked into the room, the memories came _____ back.

6 One of my _____ memories is of my parents and me on a beach in Mexico.

F DISCUSSING IDEAS

5 A Use a word from each box to complete the conversation.

makes	I'm	another	mind
thought	other	that's	
having	a	know	

| said | you | what | true | with |
| of | sense | hand | good | way |

A: College students should spend their first day getting to know the buildings and staff. This will save them time in the long run.

B: That's [1]_____ _____ idea. I never [2]_____ _____ that.

A: They should also attend a seminar on ways to save money.

B: That [3]_____ _____. Although [4]_____ _____ that, aren't there advisors to help them with that?

A: Yes, there are, but often students don't know where to find them.

B: Yes, [5]_____ _____. But looking at it [6]_____ _____, shouldn't students take responsibility?

A: I [7]_____ _____ you mean. But, on the [8]_____ _____, college is the first time they have had to fend for themselves. Many of them just aren't prepared.

B: [9]_____ _____ you there. I remember how naïve I was when I first left home. [10]_____ _____, I soon learned!

B Work in pairs. Think of things that students/workers at your school/office should do on their first day. Write a conversation using the phrases in Exercise 5A. Practice your conversation and perform it for other students.

9))) inspiration

ICONS p104

FEELING INSPIRED p107

LOVE IT OR HATE IT? p110

THE PHILANTHROPIST p112

SPEAKING	9.1 Choose sculptures to suit clients' needs
	9.2 Talk about boosting creativity
	9.3 Rant or rave
	9.4 Nominate someone for an award
LISTENING	9.2 Listen to people talking about where they get their ideas
	9.3 Listen to rants and raves
	9.4 Watch a program about a philanthropist
READING	9.1 Read about living statues
WRITING	9.2 Write a review
	9.4 Write about an inspirational person

What is the best or worst
advice you've been given?

INTERVIEWS

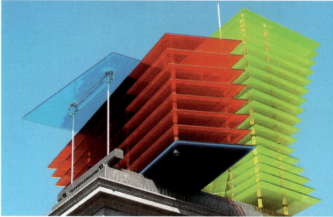

G tenses for unreal situations
P irregular spellings
V adjectives: the arts

VOCABULARY

ADJECTIVES: THE ARTS

1 A Look at three works of art that have been displayed in Trafalgar Square, London. What do you think of each "statue"?

B Look at the words in the box and answer questions 1—4.

> unconventional   thought-provoking   bleak
> compelling   charming   well-received   poignant
> overrated   offbeat   stylish   striking   subtle

1 Which words do you know? Use a dictionary to check the meaning of unknown words.

2 Which art forms do you think these words usually describe?

3 Which words can be used about people?

4 Can you use any of the words to describe the art in the photos?

C Think of movies, books, music or works of art that you can describe with the adjectives in Exercise 1B. Think of as many as you can in two minutes.

I think the X-Men movies are overrated!

D IRREGULAR SPELLINGS Say the words in Exercise 1B aloud. Which three words are spelled differently from their pronunciation? Listen to check your answers. Then listen and repeat.

> **American Speak TIP** English is well known for its irregular spelling. Sometimes combinations of letters in the middle of words are pronounced in unpredictable ways. What are the silent letters in the following words: *whistling, cupboard, leopard, plumber, fascinating, mortgage, foreigner*? Now say the whole word.

READING

2 A Read the title of the article. What do you think it is about?

B Read the article to check your ideas.

3 Match paragraphs 1—6 with headings a)—f).

a) The first and the last

b) Charming or thought-provoking? What the "artists" did

c) Up on the plinth — the artists' viewpoint

d) Antony Gormley's *One and Other*

e) What to do with the fourth plinth

f) The computer's choice: art for everyone by everyone

4 Find words/expressions in the article with the following meanings.

1 show (paragraph 1)

2 leading to (paragraph 1)

3 organize (paragraph 1)

4 worries or concerns (paragraph 2)

5 people who are watching (paragraph 2)

6 unsystematically (paragraph 3)

7 range (n) (paragraph 3)

8 went on longer than (paragraph 4)

9 calm (two words) (paragraph 6)

10 as if someone enjoys watching other people's private lives (paragraph 6)

5 Discuss. What do you think of the project? What would you have done for your hour on the plinth?

spelled   spelt

Sixty minutes of fame: LIVING STATUES

1 _____

In London's Trafalgar Square stand three statues on plinths. These depict historical figures who helped build Britain's empire. The fourth plinth (the base on which a statue stands) stood empty for years, engendering a national debate about what should go on it. Should it be a statue of another British hero – Winston Churchill, for example, or John Lennon? Should it be a striking piece of modern art or something representative of modern multicultural Britain? While the debate went on, Antony Gormley, one of Britain's best-known sculptors, was asked to orchestrate a project to fill the plinth for 100 days.

2 _____

Gormley decided to offer the plinth to members of the public, who would stand, sit or lie on it in their own piece of performance art. While there, they could speak of their preoccupations, stand up (literally) for their beliefs, reveal their fantasies, or simply enact their everyday lives in front of onlookers. It was an unconventional project, bringing the world of reality TV onto the street. It was called *One and Other* and would have a different person occupying the plinth every hour for twenty-four hours.

3 _____

To get a spot on the plinth, the public had to submit their names, which were then chosen at random by a computer. Fourteen thousand five hundred people applied, ranging in age from sixteen to eighty-three. Their professions covered the full spectrum of British life, from professors to blacksmiths to garbage collectors.

4 _____

The first "living statue" was housewife Rachel Wardell. She did it "to show my kids that you can do and be part of anything". The last was a medical photographer, Emma Burns, who read out a moving short story about the ninety-six victims of a disaster at a British soccer stadium in the 1980s. She overran her hour, but as there was no one to take her place, she was allowed to finish.

5 _____

In between Wardell and Burns, there were 2,398 others. They came up with wildly different ways to spend their sixty minutes of fame, some thought-provoking, some poignant, some charming. Darren Cooper performed a silent disco for an hour, while fifty of his friends stood below, listening to the same music at the same time on their headphones. Jane Clyne dressed up as a bee to highlight the decline in the numbers of bees due to environmental damage. David Rosenberg, a designer from London, used a folding pink bicycle to generate electricity to light up his suit.

6 _____

And what was it like up on the fourth plinth? Did the performers have to put up with nerves and noisy onlookers? "I was quite nervous at first," Darren Cooper said, "but once I started dancing, the nerves went away, and I had the best time." Rachel Lockwood said, "It felt very peaceful and serene on the plinth looking down at everyone living their lives. All I could hear was the noise of the fountains and the traffic below. I felt like I was isolated and in a bubble." Martin Douglas said, "It was strangely voyeuristic watching people go about their daily lives. Not many people look up, you know!"

garbage · rubbish

GRAMMAR
TENSES FOR UNREAL SITUATIONS

6 A Read some comments on the *One and Other* project. Which ones do you agree with?

1 This is great. <u>It's about time people realized</u> that art is for everyone.

2 These are normal people acting <u>as if they were</u> artists, but what they're doing isn't art.

3 <u>I wish I was</u> brave enough to do something like that in front of everyone. I admire them for their courage.

4 <u>Imagine you had</u> sixty minutes to perform in public. I think it would be hard.

5 <u>I'd prefer nobody noticed</u> me in public. I'd hate to be up there.

6 <u>What if I had been</u> on the plinth? I'd have done something about world peace.

B Look at the underlined clauses in the comments above and answer the questions.

1 What is the tense of the final verbs in each underlined clause? One of the verbs is a different tense. Which one?

2 Do the underlined clauses refer to a) the past, or b) an imaginary/hypothetical situation?

▶ page 144 **LANGUAGEBANK**

7 Complete the sentences with the words in the box.

> time   prefer   would   imagine   if   had
> was   hadn't

1 He walked in here as though he _____ a hero.

2 If only I _____ lost my lottery ticket, I'd be rich!

3 It's _____ you stopped complaining and did something!

4 Supposing you _____ seen her! What would you have said?

5 I'd _____ nobody knew about my plans.

6 Hey, _____ you could speak twenty languages! Wouldn't that be amazing?

7 What _____ you could retire right now? Would you?

8 I _____ rather do a research paper than take the test.

8 Answer the questions. Then compare your answers with other students.

1 Would you rather somebody took you to a movie or to the theater? A rock concert or a ballet?

2 Imagine you could own any painting or sculpture in the world. Which would you choose?

3 Supposing you were asked to act in a soap opera. Under what conditions would you accept?

4 If someone from your hometown said, "It's time we did something cultural," what would you suggest?

SPEAKING

9 A Work in groups. You are art dealers. Look at page 163 and read about your clients 1–3 and look at the sculptures. Decide which sculpture to recommend to each company.

B Compare your ideas with other groups.

VOCABULARY *PLUS*
THREE-PART MULTI-WORD VERBS

10 A Read three extracts from the article on page 105 and answer the questions below.

a) While there [on the plinth], they could ... stand up for their beliefs.

b) They came up with wildly different ways to spend their sixty minutes of fame.

c) Did the performers have to put up with nerves and noisy onlookers?

1 Underline the multi-word verbs. What do they mean?

2 Is it possible to split three-part multi-word verbs? (Can we say: *he came up with an idea* and *he came up an idea with*?)

3 Where is the main stress on three-part multi-word verbs?

B Read the advice for learning multi-word verbs. Which pieces of advice do you agree with?

1 Write full examples of multi-word verbs in your notebook because they are best understood in context.

2 Learn all the meanings of the most common phrasal verbs by heart. The top ten are *go on, carry out, set up, pick up, go back, come back, go out, point out, find out, come up.*

3 Never use phrasal verbs in formal English.

4 Don't learn long lists of multi-word verbs because there are too many and they have different meanings. Instead, "discover" them in texts.

5 Learn the general meanings of some particles (see page 61) because you can sometimes guess the meaning of the multi-word verb from the particle.

6 Group the multi-word verbs either by topic (e.g. friendship: *get on, fall out*), main verb (e.g. *get up, get over*), or particle (e.g. *come up, eat up*) in your notebook.

 11 Choose the correct multi-word verb to complete each sentence.

1 You stole the money, but you'll never *get away with/get around to it!*

2 I've been meaning to write to Sally, but I never *get away with/get around to* it.

3 I don't really *go along with/go in for* dangerous sports; I prefer golf.

4 I'm happy to *go along with/go in for* your plans.

5 Because of the price, I don't know if we'll buy the apartment; it'll all *come up with/come down to* money.

6 We have twenty-four hours to *come up with/come down to* a plan to save this company!

7 I'm not going to *put down to/put up with* this noise for one minute longer!

8 He had problems reading, which he *put down to/put up with* his poor education.

9 You have to *stand up for/stand up to* that bully, or he'll walk all over you.

10 My father taught me to *stand up for/stand up to* my beliefs.

11 I hope to *catch up with/catch on to* you at the party next month.

12 The police will never *catch up with/catch on to* this little scam!

12 Choose three questions to answer. Compare your answers in pairs.

1 Is there anything you've wanted to do for a long time but haven't **gotten around to**?

2 When you need ideas desperately, how do you **come up with** them?

3 What irritations of modern life do you find difficult to **put up with**?

4 Is there anyone from your past you'd love to **catch up with**?

5 Do you **take part in** any dangerous sports, or do you prefer a quiet life?

6 Can you think of a time when you **stood up for** your beliefs?

▶ page 156 **VOCABULARYBANK**

get around to it / take part in   get round to it / go in for

9.2)) FEELING INSPIRED

LISTENING

1 A Work in pairs and discuss the questions.

1 Where do you think people in different jobs might find inspiration, e.g. musicians, artists, business people, chefs, architects?

2 Write a list of six ways to find inspiration.

B Listen to four people talking about where they get their ideas. Make notes about what their job is and where they get their inspiration.

C Did the speakers mention any of the ideas from your list in Exercise 1A?

2 A Answer the questions.

1 Why does Speaker 1 like to do the dishes?

2 What happens when Speaker 2 goes skiing?

3 Why does Speaker 3 enjoy using old recipe books that he has had for a while?

4 What did Speaker 4's teacher tell her? How has this helped her?

B Listen again to check your answers.

C Discuss. What do you think of the ideas suggested? What do you do when you're looking for ideas or trying to solve a problem?

VOCABULARY

IDEAS

3 A Write a list of all the phrases you can think of that use the words *idea* or *ideas*. You have two minutes.

have an idea, think of an idea …

B Look at the list of common collocations below. Does it include the phrases on your list? Can you think of other ways to express the phrases in bold?

1 He's always **coming up with novel ideas**.

2 I'm **toying with the idea of** going back to college.

3 What **gave you the idea** for the book?

4 **The idea came to me** while I was taking a bath.

5 Can we **brainstorm ideas for** the new advertisement?

6 We **hit on the idea of** renting a cottage.

7 **Whose bright idea was it** to leave the clothes out in the rain?

8 The company is looking for people who can **come up with original ideas**.

9 It seemed like **a good idea at the time**.

10 Camping in winter was **a ridiculous idea**.

C Answer the questions.

1 Which phrase is often used ironically (to mean the opposite of what you say)?

2 Which phrases talk about having new ideas?

3 Which phrase is used when you're considering something?

4 Which phrases refer to bad ideas?

4 A Which phrases in Exercise 3B could you use to talk about the following situations?

1 Your younger brother is thinking about going to college, but isn't sure if he wants to.

2 Your business has a new product and is looking for some new ideas for ways to sell it.

3 You've been wondering what to do for your birthday, and when you were out today you suddenly had an idea.

4 You organized a family walk, but the weather got bad, and now everyone's in a bad mood.

B Think of examples from your own life where you or someone you know has had a bright idea/a ridiculous idea/an original idea. Tell your partner.

> **American Speak TIP** Most monolingual dictionaries will show lists of common collocations. Find some common collocations for the word *creativity*. Write them in your notebook.

5 A PRONUNCIATION: 'O' Look at the words in the box. Put them in the correct group below according to how the 'o' is pronounced.

> ~~coming~~ ~~book~~ novel toying going to
> brainstorm cottage whose out company
> looking who original good ridiculous

1 /ʌ/ (some): *coming,*

2 /ʊ/ (took): *book,*

3 /ɒ/ (on):

4 /ɔɪ/ (coin):

5 /ə/ (actor):

6 /uː/ (shoot):

7 /aʊ/ (mouth):

8 /ɔː/ (door):

9 /əʊ/ (show):

B Listen to check your answers.

C Think of some more words with the same sound to add to each line. Practice saying the words.

▶ page 156 **VOCABULARYBANK**

do the dishes / take a bath   do the washing up / have a bath

How do you get your INSPIRATION?

1 Cultivate your imagination. Write everything down. Charles Darwin kept a rigorous system of notebooks _____, and he reread them frequently. These days, we have Google Docs. Use a "spark file" to keep track of interesting ideas and websites you come across.

2 Create a "coffee house" culture in your brain by extending your sphere of interests with hobbies. Many great inventors worked on several projects _____. Darwin had no fewer than sixteen hobbies.

3 Take a reading sabbatical. Bill Gates takes two weeks off _____ just to read. This isn't practical for most people, but you can adopt the principle. Save up everything you want to read around a topic, and then take a long weekend to do nothing but read.

4 Learn to share. George Bernard Shaw said, "If you have an apple and I have an apple and we exchange these apples, then you and I will still each have one apple. But if you have an idea and I have an idea and we exchange these ideas, then each of us will have two ideas." Share your ideas _____, both online and offline.

5 Spend time _____. Every once in a while, find space and time to just relax and be by yourself. Solitude bears surprising fruit.

6 Try new things. Doing the same thing every day does little to spark your creative genius. Put yourself in new situations and try new experiences. This will _____ allow your brain to make new and interesting connections.

GRAMMAR
ADVERBIALS

6 A Read the text. What information do you think could go in the spaces? What do you think of the ideas?

B Look at the adverbial phrases below. Match phrases in box A with phrases in Box B with possible similar meanings.

> **A** on your own   almost certainly   a year   readily   record his ideas   simultaneously

> **B** most probably   alone   at the same time   to keep track of his observations   willingly   annually

C Complete the text using the words/phrases from box B in Exercise 6B.

---

7 A Read the rule and answer the questions.

> **RULES**
>
> An adverbial gives us additional information about a verb, an adjective or another adverb. It can be a single word (_frequently, eventually_) or a group of words (_on your own, for his ideas_) which act together to give detail.

Which adverbials in the text describe:

1 how something happens/should happen? (adverbial of manner)

2 when something happens? (adverbial of time)

3 how often something happens? (adverbial of frequency)

4 the probability of something happening? (adverbial of probability)

5 why something happened? (adverbial of purpose)

B Find at least three other examples of adverbials in the text.

▶ page 144 **LANGUAGE**BANK

8 A Expand sentences 1–6 using the adverbials in a)–f). Make sure you put each adverbial in the correct position.

1 I ¹_totally_ forgot to call you ²_yesterday_ ³_to tell you about this great idea I have_.

2 We ¹_____ go walking ²_____ ³_____.

3 I can ¹_____ change the appointment ²_ ³_____.

4 I ¹_____ like to chat with friends on Facebook ²_____ ³_____.

5 I ¹_____ like to take things easy ²_____.

6 I'll ¹_____ try to visit my family ²_____.

a) to make it more convenient / easily / for you

b) to find out what they've been doing / generally / at night when I'm at home

c) next time I'm in the area / probably

d) totally / to tell you about this great idea I have / yesterday

e) on the weekend / usually

f) in the mountains near our house / regularly / during vacation

B Choose two sentences from Exercise 8A. Expand them in a different way to make them true for you. Compare your sentences in pairs.

vacation the holidays

SPEAKING

9 Discuss the questions in groups.

1 Would you try any of the ideas in the text on page 108? Why/Why not? Add two more suggestions to the text.

2 Do you think that people today are more or less creative than they used to be? Why?

3 Do you think the way people cultivate their imagination or look for inspiration has changed in recent decades?

WRITING

A REVIEW; LEARN TO USE A RANGE OF VOCABULARY

10 **A** Read the review of an exhibit and answer the questions.

1 What kind of exhibit is this?

2 Who is it suitable for?

3 Is the review positive or negative?

4 Would you visit this exhibit based on the review?

B Read the guidelines for writing a review. Which ones does the British Invention Show review follow? How could it be improved?

1 Try to be both informative and entertaining.

2 Give an account of the subject in question (the book, movie, play or event) and offer a reasoned opinion about its qualities. Report on the content, the approach and the scope of the work.

3 Your audience may or may not have heard about the work in detail. Make sure your review caters to all.

4 Even with a short review, try to follow a clear structure. Include:

• a brief introduction.

• a description of contents.

• an assessment of value.

• a comparison with others.

• a conclusion.

The British Invention Show

From the sublime to the ridiculous, The British Invention Show has everything. Designed as an exhibit to showcase ideas for new inventions from around the world, this is the place to come if you're looking for financial backing for your latest eccentric gadget idea. Combining technology with innovation and invention, the show is held annually and lasts for four days.

As a gadget fan myself, I was really delighted to be able to check out some of the new ideas. The first to catch my eye was a plant pot that moves around in search of the sun. Initially, I thought this was a joke, but actually the pot has wheels and a solar panel, and it wheels itself around your garden or balcony looking for a sunny spot. Clever.

Next, I spotted a pillow you can write messages on, and later erase them. This idea had come from Barcelona, and although entertaining, it's perhaps not that useful. In fact, it seems that many of the ideas being presented are here simply because of their entertainment value.

Among the 200 inventions, there are some really fascinating and highly intelligent ideas too though, like the hydrogen-powered car and the new stereo systems. My personal favorite? An absolutely stunning James Bond-style submarine. The only problem with this is that you'd need to be a millionaire to buy one.

If you like technology and you've got a good sense of humor, the British Invention Show is an entertaining day out. Definitely worth a visit.

11 **A** Work in pairs. Think of synonyms for the words/phrases below.

1 unusual/peculiar

2 very pleased

3 at first

4 funny and enjoyable

5 extremely interesting

6 very clever

7 extremely attractive or beautiful

B Find synonyms for words/phrases 1–7 in the review. Compare them with your own ideas.

> **American Speak TIP**
>
> Make your review interesting by using a variety of adjectives, e.g. *good = excellent, superb, top-quality, terrific, exceptional*, etc. Qualify the adjectives you use in a review with adverbs, e.g. *absolutely gripping, completely credible, quite heavy-going*. Find examples of adverb + adjective combinations for 1–7 in Exercise 11A in the review.

12 You have been asked to write a review of an exhibit for a magazine. Read the exhibit description below. Then turn to page 164 and read some notes about it. Write a review based on the notes (200–250 words).

Exhibit: Iconic Inventions

Folio Society Gallery, The British Library **Price: FREE**

In a celebration of great ingenuity, this exhibit explores the stories behind some iconic inventions. Whether they are changing the world of sports, fighting climate change or just making life a bit easier, each inventor has challenged the established way of doing things. From Dyson's revolutionary bladeless fan to President Obama's favorite dog bowl, trace the journey of an idea from that first spark of inspiration to the development of a business. See original drawings, patent specifications and the finished products.

exhibit / humor   exhibition / humour

9.3)) LOVE IT OR HATE IT

F ranting/raving
V express yourself
P positive/negative intonation

VOCABULARY
EXPRESS YOURSELF

1 A Read the website extract and discuss the questions.

1 What kind of website does it talk about?

2 What can you read about on this site?

3 Do you know of any other websites like this?

4 Do you think they are a good idea? Why/Why not?

B What do you think the following words/phrases from the extract mean?

1 rave (v, n)

2 rant (v, n)

3 crave a fresh perspective

4 speak their mind

5 let your feelings fly

6 a piece of your mind

C Complete the sentences with the correct form of words/phrases in Exercise 1B.

1 Everything I read in the newspapers is the same. I really _____.

2 He went on a _____ about the evils of modern society.

3 That's not acceptable. You should give the manager _____.

4 Don't tell him he is wrong all the time. Let him _____.

5 I've never seen you so animated before. You really _____.

6 Rick loves to _____ about how wonderful life is in Australia.

FUNCTION
RANTING/RAVING

2 A Choose three of the topics below. What do you think people would rant or rave about for each one?

• arts and entertainment

• culture and lifestyle

• economy

• food

• news and politics

• people

• products

• science and technology

• sports

• travel *speaker 1*

B Listen to people ranting and raving about different things. Match each rant/rave with a topic in Exercise 2A.

C What did each person say about their topic?

Do you ever find yourself hating something that everyone else raves about?

For me, it's football and junk food. For my husband, it's opera and modern art. Now you have the chance to celebrate your individuality on rantrave.com. This website claims to have a community of independent thinkers who crave a fresh perspective and are always willing to speak their mind. You can find more than just reviews here – this is a place for people to rant and rave about anything that's on their mind, whether it's paying for an overpriced ticket, raving about a new album you've bought, or simply complaining about football scores.

Sign up to rantrave.com and start to let your feelings fly. Why not give the world a piece of your mind, whether they like it or not?

3 A Listen again and complete the phrases below.

Raving

It was the most wonderful/amazing/awesome …

It was absolutely [1]_____/incredible.

It's really the best (show) [2]_____.

There's (absolutely) nothing [3]_____ than …

(It was) one of the most [4]_____ (sunsets) I've ever seen.

I couldn't believe my [5]_____ when …

It was idyllic.

It's an all-time [6]_____.

Ranting

If there's one thing I can't [7]_____, it's …

It drives me up the [8]_____.

It was absolutely [9]_____.

It was a total [10]_____ of money.

It's not my style/kind of thing/cup of tea at all.

B POSITIVE/NEGATIVE INTONATION Listen to the phrases. Notice how the intonation changes for the positive and the negative comments. Repeat the phrases.

LEARN TO
USE COMMENT ADVERBIALS

5 A Listen to extracts from the rants/raves in Exercise 2B and complete the sentences.

1 _____, it drives me up a wall.

2 I have, in the past, _____ raised my voice at tourists.

3 I'd _____ go back there again.

4 She was _____ good, honestly.

5 The restaurant was _____ overpriced.

6 _____, it's hard to cook for a lot of people.

> **American Speak TIP**
> Listen out for comment adverbials (*absolutely, definitely, obviously, totally, simply, undoubtedly, completely, surprisingly, incredibly,* etc.) to help you understand someone's viewpoint. Also, when you are talking, comment adverbials which come at the beginning of the sentence can give you thinking time (*Honestly, Basically, Seriously,* etc.).

B Choose the correct alternatives.

1 *Honestly/Undoubtedly*, I have no idea where you could possibly find more delicious chocolates!

2 *Incredibly/Basically*, he's just lazy.

3 *Clearly/Completely*, this was one of the more luxurious hotels.

4 Not *clearly/surprisingly*, with high unemployment young people are struggling to find jobs.

5 It's quite *basically/simply* the most ridiculous idea I've ever heard.

6 *Undoubtedly/Completely*, this is one of the top bands of the moment.

C Work in pairs. Are the sentences in Exercise 5B rants or raves? Choose one of the sentences and develop it into a short conversation. Include two more comment adverbials.

SPEAKING

6 A Choose two or three topics from the list below. Prepare to rant or rave about each topic. Make notes and try to use comment adverbials.

• a restaurant you've enjoyed/been disappointed by

• a spectacular/ugly place you have visited

• an item of clothing you love/hate

• an actor or movie you love/hate

• a piece of music/album you love/hate

• something you bought recently which was a success/disaster

B Work in groups. Take turns talking about your topics. Do you agree with the other students? If not, offer your own opinion.

4 Match the sentence halves.

1 If there is one thing I can't

2 We went to an exhibit at the Tate Modern, but I'm afraid

3 The hotel had great reviews, but the service was

4 It was most definitely one of the funniest movies

5 There's nothing better than

6 It's one of the most

a) absolutely horrendous.

b) a really well-made coffee, in a friendly and welcoming café.

c) stand, it's having to read a boring book.

d) spectacular shows ever. That's why it's been such a raving success.

e) I've ever seen. I was on the floor with laughter.

f) it wasn't my cup of tea.

▶ page 144 **LANGUAGEBANK**

9.4 ▶)) THE PHILANTHROPIST

DVD PREVIEW

1 A Look at the pictures and the lesson title. What type of person do you think of when you hear the word philanthropist? What job might a philanthropist have?

B Read the program information. Were you correct about this philanthropist?

▶ BBC News: The vegetable seller

This BBC News clip tells the story of an extraordinary woman named Chen Shu-chu. Shu-chu is a vegetable seller in Taitung City, Taiwan. Although she has experienced a lot of hardship in her life and is not a rich woman, she gives away a large proportion of the money she earns and has become a famous philanthropist, contributing to schools and various other charitable causes. The recipient of several awards and now in her sixties, Shu-chu remains humble and continues to give away her money.

DVD VIEW

2 Watch the DVD clip and complete the Fact File about Chen Shu-chu.

FACT FILE: Chen Shu-chu, philanthropist	
Job:	Vegetable seller
Works:	¹_____ hours a day, 6 days a week
Childhood:	mother and ²_____ died young
Donates to:	school, ³_____, children's homes
Awards:	many, including one from the President of ⁴_____
Gave:	⁵$_____ to hospital
Philosophy:	better to give money away because you can't take it with you when you die

3 A Answer the questions below.

1 What does Miss Chen say about the usefulness of money?
2 What originally inspired Miss Chen to help others?
3 How do people frequently react to her generosity?
4 What were the results of her giving money to a local hospital?
5 When will she retire?

B Watch the DVD again to check.

4 Work in pairs and discuss the questions.

1 What do you think of Miss Chen's story?
2 Do you know of other people who do similar things?

American Speakout an award nomination

5 A Read about an award. What is it for and who can nominate candidates?

> The Inspiration Award recognizes an individual for their ability to make a difference in the lives of others. The award-winner will be someone who has demonstrated commitment to a cause through organizing, developing projects and/or showing leadership skills. Anyone may nominate a candidate for the award. Go to our website for more information.

B Listen to a speaker talking about a nominee for the award. How has the nominee helped others? What personal qualities are mentioned?

C Listen again. Check the key phrases the speaker uses. Which phrase is an idiom? What does it mean?

KEYPHRASES

He ...

goes under the radar.

has made a huge difference in people's lives.

is my hero.

has worked tirelessly.

provides moral support.

is an example to us all.

must have helped thousands of people.

would be a worthy winner.

is a shining light.

6 A Choose someone you'd like to nominate for the award. Make some notes on who they are and why they'd be a worthy winner.

B Work in groups. Take turns describing your nominee. Decide on who should win the award and tell the class.

writeback an inspiring person

7 A Read the description of an inspirational person below. Who has she inspired? How?

My Inspiration: Simin Behbahani

Simin Behbahani was one of Iran's greatest modern poets and a tireless advocate for human rights. She was twice nominated for the Nobel Prize in Literature, and Barack Obama quoted one of her verses when addressing the Iranian people in 2011.

As a writer, she was best known for reviving an ancient type of sonnet used by the classical Persian poets. However, her subject matter was the daily lives of Iranians: the challenges they faced and their hopes and dreams. She was often called Iran's national poet, because she spoke for the people. Her most famous poem is probably *My Country, I Will Build you Again*, which has been widely anthologized.

Behbahani was nicknamed "the lioness of Iran". She frequently spoke out about human rights and refused to be intimidated by the authorities, who persecuted her for years. In fact, she once called them "my children". From a prominent family with international connections, she had opportunities to leave Iran, but she chose to stay because of her love for her country and her people.

Behbahani was an inspiration to a whole nation and to women everywhere. Many of her nineteen books of poetry have now been translated into English, so perhaps her work might become better known throughout the world. She died in 2014 at the age of 87.

B Write a description of an inspirational person (200–250 words). You can choose the person you described in Exercise 6A or someone else.

C Read other students' descriptions. Who should get the award?

anthologized   anthologised

V ADJECTIVES: THE ARTS

1 Underline the correct alternatives.

1 I thought the painting was *striking/overrated*. I'm amazed it won an award.

2 What a *compelling/well-received* program. I couldn't stop watching.

3 The song is very *poignant/subtle*. It reminds me of some hard times.

4 Her photos are really *charming/ unconventional*. She breaks all the rules!

5 The novel was quite *bleak/ offbeat*. It was full of bizarre surprises.

6 That actress is extremely *stylish/thought-provoking*. She always dresses well.

G TENSES FOR UNREAL SITUATIONS

2 A Read about a wish list for the arts. Find and correct six mistakes.

It's high time art forms like opera are made accessible to the public. Tickets should be cheap, and free for children. Opera and theater are treated as though they're for the elite, but they're about the same things that are in the papers every day: jealousy, passion, murder and blood feuds, and it's about time the public is having a chance to enjoy them.

I'd prefer that TV isn't overtaken by sites like YouTube. The do-it-yourself culture has its benefits, but people talk as if anyone can make a masterpiece on camera. They can't, and that's why TV will survive.

Finally, it's time school teachers will think outside the box. What if circus skills were taught in schools? Supposing kids having a chance to learn how to juggle, swing on a trapeze and be real clowns? I'm sure millions of kinesthetic learners would rather spend their days doing this than sitting at desks doing worksheets.

B Write three sentences to describe your own wish list for the arts. Remember to use language for unreal situations.

V IDEAS

3 A Choose the correct option to complete the sentences.

1 Oh, no! The whole bookcase has fallen over now. Whose _____ idea was it to move it?

    a) toy **b)** novel c) bright

2 We were completely at a loss until we _____ on the idea of renting out the office.

    a) hit **b)** had c) held

3 **A:** What _____ him the idea of becoming a circus performer?

    B: I have no idea.

    a) hit **b)** gave c) had

4 If we don't know what to do, I suggest we _____ a few ideas.

    a) toy **b)** original
    c) brainstorm

5 I've never heard of that before. What an _____ idea!

    a) original **b)** origin
    c) originate

6 I've never heard of such a _____ idea in all my life.

    a) ridiculous **b)** ridicule
    c) ridiculously

B Work in pairs. Test each other on the phrases above.

A: We thought it was a good idea at the time …
B: It seemed like a good idea.
A: Correct.

G ADVERBIALS

4 A Work in pairs. Try to expand the sentences as much as possible by adding different adverbials.

1 I eat chocolate.

A: I always eat chocolate.
B: I always eat chocolate at the end of the day.
A: I always greedily eat chocolate at the end of the day.

2 I like music.

3 He left the office.

4 We agreed to pay.

5 We went there.

6 I love the way she speaks.

7 He cooks.

B Compare your sentences with other students.

F RANTING/RAVING

5 A Complete the conversations with the words in the box.

> horrendous   amazing
> ever   idyllic   luck   all-time
> waste   thing

1 **A:** What did you enjoy about the movie?

    B: The most _____ thing about it was the cinematography. It was spectacular!

2 **A:** Did you like his latest book?

    B: Yes, it's an _____ classic. It's his best one yet.

3 **A:** Did you enjoy your vacation?

    B: Yes, it was the best vacation _____.

4 **A:** Did you enjoy the exhibit?

    B: I'm afraid I didn't. It's not my kind of _____.

5 **A:** Did you manage to get tickets?

    B: Yes, I couldn't believe my _____ when I saw there were still some available.

6 **A:** It's a four-star restaurant.

    B: I can hardly believe that. The service was absolutely _____.

7 **A:** What was the island like?

    B: Oh, it was _____. The beaches were sandy and deserted, and the sea was a beautiful turquoise blue.

8 **A:** Is that new computer game you bought good?

    B: No, it was a total _____ of money because it was the wrong version for my computer.

B Work in pairs and practice the conversations.

kinesthetic   kinaesthetic

10)) horizons

ON THE ROAD p116

DREAMS COME TRUE? p119

MAKING A PLAN p122

SPEAKING
10.1 Plan your dream adventure
10.2 Talk about real-life success stories
10.3 Negotiate a plan for a film festival
10.4 Talk about your ideal job

LISTENING
10.2 Listen to an author reading from his memoir
10.3 Listen to a talk about stages in a negotiation
10.4 Watch a competition to become a wildlife filmmaker

READING
10.1 Read about an epic car journey
10.2 Read an essay about celebrity

WRITING
10.2 Write a "for and against" essay
10.4 Apply for your dream job

What are your goals in life?

INTERVIEWS

WILDEST DREAMS p124

115

10.1))) ON THE ROAD

G inversion
V collocations
P stress/unstress

VOCABULARY
COLLOCATIONS

1 Work in groups and discuss the questions.

1 Do you think travel can broaden your horizons? How?

2 Have you (or anyone you know of) traveled around the world?

3 If you could travel around the world, how would you travel?

4 What do you think would be the good/bad things about such an experience?

2 A Use your knowledge of collocations to match 1–8 with a)–h).

1 set	a)	experience
2 Twenty-six years on	b)	touring the continent
3 a trial	c)	off on an epic journey
4 a valuable learning	d)	his job
5 spend a couple of years	e)	the road
6 After quitting	f)	straight for the Sahara Desert
7 The couple headed	g)	the beaten path
8 Traveling off	h)	run of the trip in Africa

B STRESS/UNSTRESS Listen to the phrases to check your answers. Where do the main stresses fall? Which syllables are unstressed? Listen and repeat the phrases.

C Discuss. How do you think the phrases above could relate to a story about two people traveling around the world in their car?

READING

3 A Read the article to check your ideas from Exercise 2C. Discuss the questions. How far has Gunther Holtorf traveled? What do you think about his journey?

B Put sentences a)–g) in the correct places 1–6 in the article. There is one extra sentence.

a) Holtorf has glowing memories of these desert areas "beyond civilization".

b) "I take pills, my fever goes down, and the next day the sun is shining again, and everything is all right."

c) Holtorf and his wife Christine enjoy reminiscing about their many trips into the wild.

d) His next step was to put an ad in the *Die Zeit* personal column, to which Christine, a single mother from Dresden, replied.

e) Remarkably, this is the first accident Holtorf and his car, Otto, have experienced in twenty-six gripping years on the road.

f) Another is positive thinking.

g) Before meeting Christine, Holtorf had originally embarked on a trial run of the trip in Africa, with his third wife, Beate.

4 Work in pairs and answer the questions.

1 What caused the car to crash?

2 Has Gunther experienced many crashes?

3 What did he learn from his trial trip to Africa?

4 What gave Gunther the idea to go traveling in Africa?

5 How do you think Gunther's attitude has helped him?

6 Would you consider going on a journey like this? Why/Why not?

GUNTHER, CHRISTINE AND OTTO:
A Love Story

How a man met a woman and they set off on an epic journey across six continents in one amazing, unbreakable car

It's an hour before sunset in northern Madagascar.

The bush stretches to the horizon and surges up to the edge of the road. Light floods the scene from left to right and pours through the open window.

Another vehicle is coming towards Gunther Holtorf without slowing. It's going to be a tight fit.

He brakes and steers the Mercedes G-Wagen towards the edge of the road.

The ground is soft, and the thick vegetation conceals a steep slope. Slowly the car slips, then starts a slow-motion roll. Mid-roll, it stops for a second, then it turns again – but hits a tree, just strong enough to hold it in position on its side.

[1]_____ There have been minor incidents – a kangaroo flying into a side door, an Indian truck reversing without looking – but in 177 countries and 884,000km (549,000 miles), nothing worse than a dent.

Holtorf, seventy-six, undoes his seat belt and lifts himself out of the open passenger window. He's unharmed – not a scratch.

For most of this epic journey, Holtorf was accompanied by his fourth wife, Christine. They formed an extraordinary twenty-year partnership, in which Otto the car was a third and equal member.

off the beaten path / truck off the beaten track / lorry

²_____ It had been a valuable learning experience, with two immediate consequences.

First, the couple split up. Then, Holtorf got Otto refitted, creating a spacious storage area under a comfortable bed.

³_____ They hit it off, and before long he had a question for her: "I said, 'Why don't we do a little bit of travel?'"

Christine agreed, and in November, once her son had been settled in a boarding school, Otto set off for Africa again. Holtorf was fifty-three, Christine thirty-four.

The plan was to spend a couple of years touring the continent, spending as little time as possible in towns or cities, and as much as possible out in the wild.

In thirty years working for Lufthansa, more than twenty of them in offices overseas, Holtorf had spent hour after hour in the air looking down at roads. After quitting his job, he decided this was where he wanted to be. The couple headed straight for the Sahara desert.

⁴_____ He met other Western travelers who were, he says, "addicted" to the Sahara, returning again and again, and he can understand why.

"The Sahara doesn't mean sand, only 13 percent is sand, the rest is gravel, rocks, dry nature. There is no grass, no animals, no insects, no wind," he says. "You can listen to the silence."

One of the secrets of traveling off the beaten path, Holtorf says, is patience. ⁵_____

All problems can be solved in time, he believes, and malaria – which he has now had eight times – is one that he reckons to overcome in two days.

"Fifty percent of sickness is sickness you have mentally," he says. "You get malaria, and mentally you add another malaria – but I cut it by 50 percent. ⁶_____ There are some people who, faced with ninety-nine positive things and one negative, focus on the negative thing," he suggests. "I am the other way around. If there are ninety-nine negative and one positive, I focus on the positive."

SPEAKING

5 A Work in groups and read the brochure below. Would you like to go on one of these trips? Why/Why not?

Dream Journeys

Have you ever considered going on an adventure you will never forget? Try one of our Dream Journeys.

NORTH WEST PASSAGE
Follow in the footsteps of legendary explorers across the Arctic Circle from Alaska (USA) to Resolute (Canada). Discover the beauty of polar bears, whales and icebergs on this epic sea voyage.

TRANSPORT: ship
TIMING: 20 days

BERBER TRAIL Marrakesh, Morocco
After the excitement of a night in the exotic city of Marrakesh, your mission is to climb Toubkal (4,167m), in the Atlas Mountains. With beautiful flowers and picturesque villages on the lower slopes, this is not a difficult climb.

TRANSPORT: by foot
TIMING: 7 days

HO CHI MINH TRAIL Vietnam
Bicycles are still a favorite way to get around in Vietnam. Pedal your way along rice fields and mountain paths from Ho Chi Minh in the south to Hanoi in the north.

TRANSPORT: bicycle
TIMING: 19 days

B Plan your own dream adventure. Where would you go and what would you do? Read the information below and plan a trip for your group.

There is one constraint: you can only make one journey by commercial airplane. For the rest, you can use any other means of travel. Think about the following questions.

- How are you going to travel?
- What countries will you visit?
- What will be the main aim of your trip?
- How long will the trip take?
- Could you use the trip to highlight any particular issues? Which ones? How?
- What problems do you think you might have? How will you deal with them?

C Tell the class about your plans. Which group has the most interesting idea for a dream adventure?

GRAMMAR
INVERSION

6 A Read the text. What is so special about Otto the car?

OTTO THE CAR

When Gunther Holtorf first embarked on what was supposed to be an eighteen-month tour of Africa in his Mercedes called Otto, he had no idea that the same car would take him 550,000 miles, on a twenty-six-year-long journey. Never before has a car traveled so many miles. The Mercedes has been to more single countries than any other car. It's a world record, and one that Holtorf says would have been impossible to achieve had he tried with a modern car. Holtorf says he drove the car like a granny and mastered the mechanics himself. Not once did the car break down so badly that he couldn't fix it. He carried huge numbers of spare parts, and a healthy dose of patience. Having finished its epic journey, the car is now in a museum in Stuttgart.

B Read the sentences. What do you notice about the word order? Rewrite the sentences beginning with *if*.

1 Had the car been a modern car, it would never have completed the journey.

2 Had he not mastered the mechanics himself, they might have experienced more breakdowns.

C Choose the correct alternative to complete the rule. Then find another example of inversion in a conditional clause in the text.

RULES

In *formal/informal* written texts, the word order in conditional clauses may be inverted.

D Look at sentences 1–4. Notice how inversion is also used after negative adverbials to add dramatic effect. Find two examples in the text in Exercise 6A.

1 **No sooner had they finished** one trip than they were planning another.

2 **Rarely/Never before/Seldom had they seen** such scenery.

3 **Not once/At no point did they stop** to question their decision.

4 **Only later/Not until the journey was finished did they appreciate** some of the places that they had visited.

▶ page 146 LANGUAGEBANK

7 A Complete the second sentence so that it has the same meaning as the first.

1 He didn't think about leaving until they argued.
Not until …

2 I then saw the danger that we were in. Only …

3 As soon as we left the tent, it collapsed. No sooner …

4 If we had remembered, we would have taken extra fuel. Had …

5 They had never ridden motorcycles for such extended distances. Never before …

6 They did not consider giving up the expedition at any point. At no point …

B Think about a difficult journey you have experienced. Complete the sentences for you and tell a partner.

1 Had I known … then …

2 Never before had I …

3 No sooner had I … than …

4 Not only … but also …

C Write a short description of your/your partner's journey using inversions where appropriate.

VOCABULARY *PLUS*
SYNONYMS

8 A Look at six extracts from the texts on pages 116, 117 and in Exercise 6A. Can you think of words/phrases with similar meanings to the words in bold?

1 they set off on an epic **journey** across six continents

2 the thick vegetation **conceals** a steep slope

3 in twenty-six **gripping** years on the road

4 Holtorf had originally **embarked on** a trial run of the trip in Africa

5 creating a **spacious** storage area under a comfortable bed

6 [He] **mastered** the mechanics himself.

B Which word in each set has a different meaning?

1 **journey**: trip, tracker, expedition

2 **conceal**: hide, cover up, extract

3 **gripping**: thrilling, exhilarating, dull

4 **embark on**: undertake, complete, set off on

5 **spacious**: minuscule, extensive, immense

6 **master (v)**: train, grasp, get the hang of

American Speak out TIP Use a thesaurus to help you expand your vocabulary range. Look up the word *interesting* in a thesaurus. How many alternatives does it offer? Think of example sentences for each word and write them in your notebook.

9 Replace one word in each sentence with the correct form of a synonym from Exercise 8. Do not change the meaning of the sentence.

1 He hid the documents under his coat.

2 The book is a thrilling account of his journey.

3 He began a new career as a photographer.

4 I never quite grasped the art of walking in high heels.

5 He went on a journey to Borneo to film the wildlife there.

6 Exhibits are regularly held in the spacious reception area.

10 Write down five words from the lesson. Work in pairs and think of as many synonyms as possible for each word.

▶ page 157 VOCABULARYBANK

10.2)) DREAMS COME TRUE?

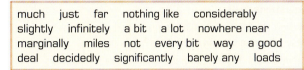

G comparative structures
V ambition
P intonation: emphasis; rhythm

SPEAKING

1 Read the text below and discuss.

1 Which story is the most interesting?

2 Are stories like these becoming more common?

3 How would your life change if something similar happened to you?

Real-life success stories

How would your life change if you suddenly became famous? Read about some real-life success stories.

Cheng Guorong, thirty-four, went from being homeless to becoming a fashion icon. Spotted by a photographer on the streets of Ningbo, China, Guorong's image went viral. A movie is planned about his life.

At age ninety-three, **Lorna Page** published her first novel: *A Dangerous Weakness*. With her royalties, she bought a big country house and invited three friends who were living in a nursing home to move in with her.

Dancer **Sarah "Paddy" Jones**, aged seventy-nine, reached the finals of the TV show *Britain's Got Talent*. Five years earlier, she'd won $100,000 and global fame for coming in first in the Spanish talent show *Tú sí que vales*. She started dancing in 1936.

GRAMMAR
COMPARATIVE STRUCTURES

2 Read three answers to question 3 above. Which phrases in bold mean a small difference, and which mean a big difference?

1 My life would be **barely any different** to now.

2 Life would be **significantly more** stressful in the public eye.

3 I'd receive **far more** opportunities to make money.

3 A Which words in the box can complete sentences 1 and 2 below?

much	just	far	nothing	like	considerably
slightly	infinitely	a bit	a lot		nowhere near
marginally	miles	not	every bit	way	a good
deal	decidedly	significantly	barely any		loads

1 My life now is ___ better than it was before I became famous.

2 My life now is ___ as good as it was before I became famous.

B Discuss the questions.

1 What type of difference do the words in Exercise 3A describe: a small difference, a big difference or no difference?

2 Which words are formal, and which are informal?

C Read about two other comparative structures. Match structures 1 and 2 with rules a) and b).

1 Double comparatives

The harder you search for fame, the more difficult it is to find it.

2 Progressive comparatives

She gets more and more beautiful every time I see her.

RULES

a) A _____ comparative describes how something increases or decreases by repeating the same comparative. We put *and* between the forms.

b) A _____ comparative describes how a change in one thing causes a change in another. We use two comparative forms with *the* and a comma after the first clause.

▶ page 146 LANGUAGE**BANK**

4 Imagine you are the world's most famous celebrity, photographed by the paparazzi every day. What might you say about your life?

1 My life would be considerably better if …

2 Being a celebrity is nothing like as …

3 One good thing about fame is that it's far …

4 Even for a celebrity, it's every bit as …

5 I find it more and more difficult to …

6 The more famous I become, …

7 The more money I make, …

8 Life gets better and …

5 A INTONATION: emphasis Listen to completed sentences 1–4 from Exercise 4. Notice how we emphasize differences by stressing the modifier (*considerably, nothing like,* etc.). Read your sentences aloud, emphasizing the modifier where appropriate.

B RHYTHM: in double comparatives What do you think expressions 1–3 mean? Do you have equivalents in your language? Listen to the rhythm of double comparatives. Then listen and repeat.

1 The more, the merrier.

2 The sooner, the better.

3 The bigger they come, the harder they fall.

LISTENING

6 A Read about a writer named Frank McCourt and discuss questions 1–3.

1 Why do you think Frank McCourt published his first book only when he was in his sixties?

2 How do you think his life changed after *Angela's Ashes* became a bestseller?

3 Who do you think he met after becoming famous?

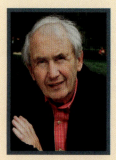

Frank McCourt came from an extremely poor Irish–American family. His ambition was to be a writer, but the longer he waited, the more unlikely it seemed that his dream would come true. So, having spent most of his adulthood as a teacher, he was delighted when his memoir, *Angela's Ashes*, was published. By now in his sixties, he was every bit as surprised when the book became a bestseller. Life became a good deal better for him with his sudden fame. He went on to write two more books: *'Tis* (1999) and *Teacher Man* (2005), which cemented his reputation as a first-class memoirist.

B Listen to an extract from *Teacher Man*. Were your answers to questions 1–3 correct?

7 A Listen again. What is the significance of the numbers and names below?

1 thirty years	6 hundreds of times
2 a few hundred copies	7 President Clinton
3 thirty languages	8 Sarah, Duchess of York
4 1996	9 Elton John
5 five a day	10 William Butler Yeats

B Find words 1–6 in audio script S10.4 on page 174. What do you think they mean?

1 a scrap (of attention) (n)	4 clamor (n)
2 dazzled (adj)	5 geriatric (adj)
3 ascension (n)	6 a beacon (of hope) (n)

C Turn to page 163 to check your answers.

8 Read the extracts from the recording and discuss the questions.

1 "The book was my second act." What do you think this means?

2 "A woman in a coffee shop squinted and said, 'I seen you on TV. You must be important.'" What does the narrator think of the woman's comment? What is his tone of voice?

3 "I was asked for my opinion on Ireland, conjunctivitis, drinking, teeth, education, religion, adolescent angst, William Butler Yeats, literature in general." What is the narrator's tone of voice here? (Serious? Ironic? Humorous?)

4 "I traveled the world being Irish, being a teacher, an authority on misery of all kinds." From this comment, what can you guess about the book *Angela's Ashes*?

VOCABULARY
AMBITION

9 A Read the pairs of sentences. Do they have similar or opposite meanings? What do the phrases in bold mean?

1 a) I know people who **crave** fame and fortune.

   b) Nobody I know has ever **hankered after** fame.

2 a) It's hard to **be in the spotlight** all the time.

   b) I like to be the **center of attention**.

3 a) You need to **serve an apprenticeship** to get good at something.

   b) In a profession, you have to **pay your dues** even if it takes years.

4 a) It's important to **be held in high esteem** by your peers.

   b) It's not important to **be renowned** for work.

5 a) I'd love to **become an overnight success** like Frank McCourt.

   b) I'd love to **shoot to fame** like Frank McCourt.

6 a) I'm **set on** becoming an expert in my field.

   b) I **have aspirations** to become known in my area.

B Choose three or four sentences that are true for you. Explain your choices to a partner.

▶ page 157 **VOCABULARY**BANK

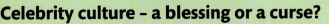

SPEAKING

10 **Work in groups and discuss the questions.**

1 What were your ambitions when you were younger? Are they the same today?

2 Have you had any experiences that made your dreams come true? How was your life different before and after the experience?

3 Are any of these your dream come true? If not, what is?

- getting a job that you really love
- living in a magnificent house
- finding the "perfect" partner
- winning the lottery
- speaking English perfectly
- passing an upcoming test

WRITING

A "FOR AND AGAINST" ESSAY; LEARN TO DESCRIBE PROS AND CONS

11 **A** **Work in groups. Read the quotes and discuss questions 1–4 below.**

> "If you become a star, *you* don't change; everyone else does."
>
> (Kirk Douglas, actor)

> "A celebrity is a person who works hard all their life to become well known, then wears dark glasses to avoid being recognized."
>
> (Fred Allen, comedian)

1 Do you think the quotations are true?

2 What is "celebrity culture"?

3 Do you read gossip columns or magazines about celebrities? Do you watch talk shows or look at websites that focus on celebrities?

4 Do you think celebrity culture is a good or a bad thing?

B Read the essay. What arguments does the writer give for and against celebrity culture?

Celebrity culture – a blessing or a curse?

The world's first celebrity was Alexander the Great. Not only did he want to be the greatest man in history, but he also wanted everyone to know it. Alexander employed historians, sculptors and painters to tell his story for posterity, and they succeeded. But, of course, his achievements were astonishing. Today, many people become celebrities by doing little more than craving to be the center of attention. With so many magazines, talk shows and websites needing content, such "celebrities" fill a void, but many would argue that they fill a void with another void. The question is, does celebrity culture matter? Is it just harmless fun or does it erode our values?

On the one hand, there is the fame industry: *Hello* and *OK* magazines, gossip columns, Oprah Winfrey-style talk shows. These give us insights into the rich and famous. They show us the ups and downs of people whose lives seem far larger than our own. Most of us enjoy a bit of gossip, and what could be better than hearing about some superstar finally getting what he deserves (whether good or bad)? This view sees celebrity culture as a branch of the entertainment industry. In addition, fame has become democratized. On reality shows like *Big Brother*, the participants don't need to have any talent, and many see this as a good thing. Not everyone can be an Einstein or a Messi.

On the other hand, there are those who believe celebrity culture has got out of control. They argue that people now idolize mediocrity. It is no longer the greatest who win our hearts, but the loudest. A recent poll discovered that almost fifty percent of teenagers simply want to "be famous", without specifying the profession and presumably without making any effort to learn a skill. The danger is that fame can be confused with achievement. Appearing on TV is not the same as spending years mastering an instrument or working for peace or inventing a cure.

So, is celebrity culture a blessing or a curse? Those in favor say it entertains us, sells newspapers and allows us to dream. Those against say it promotes "fame for fame's sake" and doesn't value effort or skill. One thing we know is that the actions of most of today's celebrities will soon be forgotten, while real achievements won't. William Shakespeare, Joan of Arc, Helen Keller, Mahatma Gandhi, Nelson Mandela: their work will live on. And we're still making movies about Alexander the Great two thousand years after he died.

12 **"For and against" essays often follow the structure below. To what extent does the essay in Exercise 11B follow this structure?**

1 Introduction to the issue

2 Points for (plus examples)

3 Points against (plus examples)

4 Conclusion

13 **A** **Which phrases in the table were not used in the essay above?**

contrasting arguments	
On the one hand … on the other hand … While … is true, it is also true to say …	
pros	**cons**
What could be better than … ? One of the benefits is … Those in favor (say) …	The danger is … One of the drawbacks is … Those against (say) …

B Add the expressions in the box to the correct column of the table.

> In contrast to this, …   On the positive side, …
> One disadvantage is …   The arguments against … include …
> The arguments for … include …   On the negative side, …
> We also need to take … into consideration   One advantage is …

14 **Choose one of the topic statements below. Write down as many pros and cons as you can think of. Write a "for and against" essay (350–450 words).**

- Modern celebrities are poor role models.
- All books should be available for free on the internet.
- Fast food should be prohibited.
- College education should be free for everyone.

talk show / democratized / idolize   chat show / democratised / idolise

F negotiating
V negotiation
P polite intonation

VOCABULARY
NEGOTIATION

1 Think about the questions. Then discuss them in groups.

1 Why might the people in the photos need to negotiate?

2 What negotiations do you think the following people sometimes have? What experience do you have of these types of negotiations?

- parents and children
- bosses and employees
- companies and customers

3 What do you think makes a good negotiator?

2 A Read seven tips for negotiating. Which three are the most important for you?

1 Approach the negotiation in the right way. Don't think of the other negotiator as your enemy. There are bound to be similar things that you both want, so try to **establish common goals**.

2 Be realistic when **haggling** or bargaining. Don't start with an insultingly low offer. This will only annoy the other party and make a successful conclusion less likely.

3 Be aware that you won't get everything you want. You will need to surrender some points. This means you need to **make compromises**.

4 Always be **tactful** and diplomatic. Never talk badly about anyone or anything. If you do, it may come back to haunt you.

5 Don't be afraid to postpone or **defer** a decision. As the negotiation progresses, you may find that the conditions aren't right. You can always come back the next day and start again.

6 Don't **bluff**. If you don't know something, say you don't know. If you say "this is my final offer", it must be your final offer. If you are caught bluffing, you will lose your credibility as a negotiator.

7 Keep your eye on the main goal. Once the main deal is done, **make concessions** on small details. The idea is not to "win", but to make sure both parties are happy.

B Can you think of any other tips for negotiating?

C Which words/expressions in bold in the text can be replaced by definitions a)–g)?

a) let the other person have something in order to reach an agreement

b) careful about what you say so that you don't upset or embarrass anyone

c) pretend something in order to achieve what you want

d) delay (until a later date)

e) accept less than what you originally wanted in order to reach an agreement

f) find out what you both want

g) arguing to agree on the price of something

FUNCTION
NEGOTIATING

3 A Put the stages of a negotiation in the correct order.

> make an offer   follow up the deal
> establish common goals
> refuse or accept the deal
> name your objectives

B Listen to a conversation about negotiating and check your answers.

4 A Work in pairs and answer the questions.

1 In a negotiation, what does "exploring positions" mean?

2 What is the most important word in a negotiation?

3 What should you do if you switch off and miss something during a negotiation?

4 What is "always delicate" during a negotiation?

5 What word should you never say in a negotiation, according to the man?

6 What might you need to do in a business negotiation?

7 What is the purpose of following up the deal?

B Listen again to check.

C Discuss the questions.

1 Do you think the advice is relevant to all types of negotiation or only some types, e.g. business?

2 Did the man say anything that you particularly agree or disagree with?

5 A Read the phrases for negotiating. Which ones did the man use? Check your answers in audio script S10.5 on page 175.

naming your objectives	refusing an offer
We want to sort this out as soon as possible. By the end of the day, we want to resolve this.	That would be difficult for me because of … I'm not sure I can do that because …
exploring positions	**accepting an offer**
What do you have in mind? Can you go into more detail?	Good. That sounds acceptable to me. Great. We've got a deal.
making conditional offers	**following up the deal**
If you do … for me, I'll do … for you. What if we supported your idea?	Let me know if you have any questions. Get in touch if anything needs clarifying.

B Can you think of any other expressions that could go under the headings in Exercise 5A?

▶ page 146 LANGUAGEBANK

6 Circle the correct alternative to complete the sentences.

1 We want to sort this *over/through/out* as soon as possible.
2 Can you go *into/through/onto* more detail?
3 Great! We've *got/played/had* a deal.
4 What do you have *in/to/on* mind?
5 If you sponsor this idea for me, I'll *have/try/make* concessions for you.
6 *How/Why/What* if we supported your project from the beginning?
7 Let me know if you have any *discussions/questions/agreement* about the arrangements.
8 Get *to/on/in* touch if anything needs clarifying.

LEARN TO
STALL FOR TIME

7 A The speaker mentions "stalling for time". What do you think this means? Read the expressions below. Which one is not used to stall for time?

1 I'd like to think about it.
2 I'll have to ask about that.
3 I need more time to consider it.
4 I can give you an answer to that right now.
5 Can I get back to you on that?

B POLITE INTONATION Listen and repeat the expressions in Exercise 7A. Copy the intonation.

SPEAKING

8 A Read some notes about a plan to hold an International Film Festival at your school. Which unresolved issues are the most important?

- Name of event: International Film Festival
- Who for: all students at the school
- Place: the school
- Movies: ?
- Dates: ?
- Times: 5:30 first movie, 8:00 second movie
- Cost: ?
- Food and drink: ?
- Advertising the event: ?

B Work in two groups. Group A: turn to page 159. Group B: turn to page 161. Read your roles and answer the questions.

C Work with a student from the other group. Negotiate a deal.

D Tell the class what you decided.

questions   queries

DVD PREVIEW

1 Read the program information and answer the questions.

1 Where do the contestants travel to and why?

2 What do they hope to win, and what happens if they are not good enough?

3 Would you be interested in entering this competition? Why/Why not?

▶ Wildest Dreams

Wildlife filmmaking is one of the most difficult jobs on earth. Thousands want to do it, but few get the chance. The BBC has chosen nine people with ordinary jobs to see if one of them has what it takes to become a wildlife filmmaker. Presented by Nick Knowles, *Wildest Dreams* puts them through their paces in one of the natural world's greatest arenas – Africa – with the ultimate prize for just one of them: a job at the BBC's prestigious Natural History Unit. In this episode, the hopefuls face their first challenges in the vast swamps of Botswana's Okavango Delta. If any of them aren't good enough, this will be the end of their journey, and they'll be sent home.

DVD VIEW

2 Watch the DVD and number the statements in the order you hear them.

a) The bees are obviously getting a bit more angry now. Please don't sting me.

b) I've never even been on a plane before, so to be going over African wilderness is just absolutely amazing.

c) We've got to throw ourselves into it. We've got to put ourselves on the line.

d) I've never been anywhere like this in my life, so this is all a really, really amazing experience for me.

e) I'm feeling really under pressure, and I'm gonna lose my temper in a minute.

f) It's exhilarating, but it's made my day. I can't stop smiling.

3 A Complete the extracts.

1 It takes people with a very special mix of _____ and _____.

2 How will this factory worker from Rotherham cope filming thousands of _____?

3 And when _____ to the limits, how does it feel to track the most powerful _____ on earth?

4 Today, nine ordinary people are on a journey to one of the world's remotest spots, the Okavango Delta in Botswana, to start a _____ in wildlife filmmaking.

5 East London mum Sadia Ramzan dreams of _____ and loves animals, so this could be just the _____.

6 For one of you, this will be a _____ experience.

B Watch the DVD again to check.

4 Work in groups and discuss the questions.

1 What skills and qualities do you think are important for this job?

2 Do you think you have the skills/qualities necessary for this job? Why/Why not?

American Speakout a dream job

5 A Listen to someone talking about his dream job. How does he answer the questions?

1 What is your dream job?

2 What skills/qualifications/experience do you have that would help you qualify for the job?

3 What qualities are important for the job?

4 What could you do to help you on your path to your dream job?

B Listen again and choose the correct alternatives to complete the key phrases.

KEYPHRASES

I guess my dream job *would have to be/has to be* a (filmmaker).

I'd *relish having the opportunity/love to have the opportunity* to work in an environment like that.

I'm fairly qualified in that *I'm doing a degree in … /I have a degree in …/I studied at …/I have previous experience in …*

I'd like to think that I'm a fairly *organized/motivated/creative* individual.

I'm not afraid to *try out new ideas/tell people what I think/get stuck in/put myself on the line.*

I've got quite a good eye for *detail/a product/things that are going to work.*

I think it's essential to be *hardworking/open-minded/flexible.*

I'm also doing *some work experience/a part-time course in … .*

---

6 A Think of your own dream job. Prepare to answer the questions in Exercise 5A. Take notes.

B Work in groups and take turns presenting your ideas. You each have three minutes for your presentation. At the end, decide who you would give the dream job to.

writeback a job application

7 A Read about Francesca's dream job. What do you think the job is?

Get-your-dream-job.com

Do you want to apply for your dream job?

If you want to be sure of getting the job, send us a short paragraph explaining why it's your dream job and how your skills and experience qualify you.

Francesca: My absolute dream job by far would be an _____. I've always been fascinated by people who taste food and drink for their jobs, like chocolate tasters, restaurant critics, etc. I'd like to think that I have a very fine palate. I'm what you'd call a real foodie, always cooking and enjoying fine food. Perhaps that's because of my Italian background. In the summer, one of the things I most enjoy is going out in the evening with a few friends to have an ice cream. In Italy, there's an ice cream shop on nearly every street corner, selling a frightening number of different flavors of ice cream. I think I've tried them all, including some of the strangest combinations, like English trifle and pistachio. To my mind, my passion for flavor combined with my creative instinct would make me ideal for the job.

B Write a short paragraph about the dream job of your choice (150–200 words). Don't include the name of the job.

C Read other students' descriptions of their dream jobs. Can you guess the jobs?

V COLLOCATIONS

1 Complete the sentences with the words/phrases in the box.

> an epic   quitting   run   valuable   headed   beaten

1 _____ life in the city to live near the sea was a decision she wouldn't regret.
2 Working in the slums was hard, but proved to be a _____ learning experience.
3 He set off on _____ journey through South America.
4 Most of the time, they traveled off the _____ path.
5 The manager _____ straight for his office.
6 Before embarking on the expedition, they decided to go for a trial _____.

G INVERSION

2 A Put the phrases in the correct order to make sentences. Add capital letters and punctuation.

1 a knock at the door / than / no sooner / had she / there was / sat down
2 the last chocolate, / did you eat / any more / but you / not only / also didn't buy
3 called you earlier / realized / had I / would have / to happen, / I / what / was going
4 they / like it / see / would / never again / anything
5 can I / been / it / how difficult / only now / must have / appreciate
6 have overslept / might not / they gone / had / earlier, / they / to bed

B Work in pairs. Use the prompts to write a five-line story using only inversions.

1 Never before …
2 No sooner …
3 Had she known …
4 On no account would she have agreed …
5 Only now would she …

> *1 Never before had she seen the beautiful mountain flower.*
> *2 No sooner had she picked it than …*

C Read your stories to other students. Who has the best story?

G COMPARATIVE STRUCTURES

3 A Work in pairs. Student A: look at box A. Student B: look at box B. Write four comparative sentences using the phrases in your box.

> **A** nothing like as   every bit as
> the more …, the more …   bigger and bigger

> **B** better and better   a good deal
> the more …, the more …   nowhere near

B Compare your sentences.

V AMBITION

4 A Complete the words/phrases in bold by adding the missing letters.

1 What you would do if you suddenly **s _ _ _ to fame**:
2 Someone who became an **o _ _ _ _ _ _ _ t success**:
3 Someone who always has to be the **c _ _ _ _ _ of attention**:
4 One reason someone in your field might be **h _ _ _ in h _ _ _ esteem**:
5 A job for which you need to **s _ _ _ _ an apprenticeship**:
6 Someone who is **renowned _ _ _ outstanding work**:
7 Something you were **set _ _ doing** when you were younger:
8 Something you **cr_ _ _** regularly:
9 An **asp _ _ _ tion** that most people in your country have:
10 Something you used to **hanker a _ _ _ _**, but no longer care about:

B Write an example sentence for the phrases in Exercise 4A. Are your answers similar to other students'?

> *1 If I suddenly shot to fame, I would go and hide on an island!*

F NEGOTIATING

5 A Sentences a)–g) are from a meeting about a company's annual party. Cross out the extra word in each sentence.

a) OK, so you'd like to take everybody to Sweden instead of having a party. Can you go into the more detail?
b) Get in to touch if anything needs clarifying.
c) Welcome, everybody. By the time end of the meeting, we want to have some concrete plans for our Christmas party.   *1*
d) If that you can pay for some of the trip, I can ask the board to subsidize the rest.
e) Good. That sounds acceptable for to me.
f) First, can you tell me a little about what you have taken in mind?
g) I'm not of sure we can do that because of the cost.

B At what stage of the meeting did the sentences occur? Put them in a logical order. The first one has been done for you.

C What do you think were the responses from the other people in the meeting?

Response to sentence c): "Fine. That sounds good."

subsidize   subsidise

)) IRREGULAR VERBS

Verb	Simple past	Past participle
be	was/were	been
beat	beat	beaten
become	became	become
begin	began	begun
bend	bent	bent
bet	bet	bet
bite	bit	bitten
bleed	bled	bled
blow	blew	blown
break	broke	broken
bring	brought	brought
broadcast	broadcast	broadcast
build	built	built
burn	burned/burnt	burned/burnt
burst	burst	burst
buy	bought	bought
catch	caught	caught
choose	chose	chosen
come	came	come
cost	cost	cost
cut	cut	cut
deal	dealt	dealt
dig	dug	dug
do	did	done
draw	drew	drawn
dream	dreamed/dreamt	dreamed/dreamt
drink	drank	drunk
drive	drove	driven
eat	ate	eaten
fall	fell	fallen
feel	felt	felt
feed	fed	fed
fight	fought	fought
find	found	found
fly	flew	flown
forbid	forbade	forbidden
forget	forgot	forgotten
forgive	forgave	forgiven
freeze	froze	frozen
get	got	gotten
give	gave	given
go	went	gone
grow	grew	grown
hang	hung	hung
have	had	had
hear	heard	heard
hide	hid	hidden
hit	hit	hit
hold	held	held
hurt	hurt	hurt
keep	kept	kept
know	knew	known
lay	laid	laid
lead	led	led
leap	leapt	leapt

Verb	Simple past	Past participle
lean	leaned/leant	leaned/leant
leave	left	left
lend	lent	lent
let	let	let
lie	lay	lain
light	lit	lit
lose	lost	lost
make	made	made
mean	meant	meant
meet	met	met
mistake	mistook	mistaken
pay	paid	paid
put	put	put
read	read	read
ride	rode	ridden
ring	rang	rung
rise	rose	risen
run	ran	run
say	said	said
see	saw	seen
sell	sold	sold
send	sent	sent
set	set	set
shake	shook	shaken
shine	shone	shone
shoot	shot	shot
show	showed	shown
shrink	shrank	shrunk
shut	shut	shut
sing	sang	sung
sink	sank	sunk
sit	sat	sat
sleep	slept	slept
slide	slid	slid
speak	spoke	spoken
spend	spent	spent
spill	spilled/spilt	spilled/spilt
split	split	split
spread	spread	spread
stand	stood	stood
steal	stole	stolen
stick	stuck	stuck
sting	stung	stung
swim	swam	swum
take	took	taken
teach	taught	taught
tear	tore	torn
tell	told	told
think	thought	thought
throw	threw	thrown
understand	understood	understood
wake	woke	woken
wear	wore	worn
win	won	won
write	wrote	written

GRAMMAR

1.1 The Continuous Aspect

An aspect is a way we look at something. With verb forms, there are three aspects: simple, continuous and perfect. The simple aspect emphasizes that an action is complete. The perfect aspect emphasizes that an action is completed before another time.

The continuous aspect focuses on the action and its duration (how long it lasts), rather than the result. It is used to show that an activity is temporary and its duration is limited.

In contrast to the continuous aspect, we usually use simple tenses to talk about facts, permanent situations, finished actions and habits. Some verbs — called state verbs — are not usually used in the continuous, e.g. verbs that describe personal feelings (*love, prefer*), the senses (*hear, smell*) and thoughts (*believe, understand*).

Use the continuous aspect to talk about:

- actions that we see happening over a period of time.
  They've been waiting here for an hour.
- actions in progress when another thing happens.
  John was crying when I arrived.
- temporary or incomplete situations.
  He's living with his parents until he can find a house.
- repeated actions (that may be annoying).
  She's always playing her music loudly.
- situations in the process of changing.
  The economy is getting worse.
- plans (often using the past continuous).
  I was thinking of going home this weekend.
- tentative ideas (to avoid being too direct with a request).
  I was wondering if I could borrow some money.
- actions in progress at a particular time.
  Everyone seems to be working at the moment.

1.2 Describing Habits

Use *will* to describe present habits and behavior (both good and bad).
She'll tell you everything she has done during the day, even if you're not interested.
He'll always bring me flowers.

Use the present continuous + *always*, *keeps* + *-ing* and *will keep* + *-ing* in the same way. This often implies annoyance.
He's always telling me what to do.   She keeps texting me.
They will keep nagging me to go and visit them.

Use *used to/would* to describe past habits and behavior (both good and bad).
My parents wouldn't drive me to parties on Saturday nights.
They used to make me stay at home.

Note: We can only use *will/would* to describe habits, not states.

He would get angry very easily.
NOT *He would be angry very easily.*

Use past continuous + *always*, *kept* + *-ing* and *would keep* + *-ing* in the same way.
They were always complaining.
We kept asking for a refund, but we were ignored.
He would keep going on about his brother. It drove me mad.

Use *keep on* to emphasize that the action is repeated frequently.
Sorry, I keep on forgetting your name!

Use *tend to* to describe typical states.
She tends to shout a lot.
My parents tended to be very laid-back.

Spoken Grammar

Will and *would* may be stressed to emphasize the annoyance at a habit.
He will turn up late.
They wouldn't listen to me.

Other Expressions

I'm inclined to …/I have an inclination to …/I'm happy to …

I tend to …/I have a tendency to …

I'm prone to …

I'll spend hours …/I'd spend hours …

As a rule, I …

Nine times out of ten, I …

Andy is inclined to act first and think later.
I'm prone to falling asleep in front of the TV in the evenings.
He has a tendency to be very critical, and this makes him unpopular with colleagues.

1.3 Speculating

Use the following phrases to speculate about people or situations.

I suppose/guess/imagine he's/she's around …	There's something … about him/her.
I'd say he's/she's …	He/She gives the impression of being …
I wonder what he/she …	He/She could be/could have been …
I'd make a guess (that) …	It seems like he/she …/It seems to me …/It looks to me as if he/she
If I had to make a guess, I'd say (that) …	It makes me think (that) maybe he/she …
I'm pretty sure he/she …	It might suggest (that) …

PRACTICE

1.1

A Choose the best option, a) or b), to complete the sentence.

1 The photocopier a) **isn't working** b) **doesn't work** at the moment, but the technician will fix it later.

2 You can't go because you a) **haven't been finishing** b) **haven't finished** your work.

3 I a) **was having** b) **had** a great time when my dad came and dragged me home!

4 The mail carrier a) **is weighing** b) **weighs** the package right now.

5 That's a tricky question, and I a) **am not knowing** b) **don't know** the answer.

6 I a) **was looking** b) **looked** through my old papers, and I found a letter from you.

7 Can you turn down the volume? I a) **am talking** b) **talk** on the phone.

8 I a) **wasn't hearing** b) **didn't hear** the doorbell, so I carried on watching TV.

9 She has a) **been studying** b) **studied** all morning.

10 I live in Krakow, but I a) **am doing** b) **do** a course in Warsaw this summer.

B Complete the questions. Use the correct continuous form of the verb in parentheses where possible. Which sentences need a simple form?

1 A: _____ (cry)?
   B: Because I just fell off my bike, and it hurts!

2 A: _____ (work) there before they fired him?
   B: About twenty years. He was devastated.

3 A: _____ (do) since you graduated?
   B: I've mainly been looking for a job, but no luck so far.

4 A: _____ (live) in Miami?
   B: Twenty-seven years. I moved here when I was twenty.

5 A: _____ (talk) to when I saw you earlier?
   B: Oh, she's an old schoolmate.

6 A: _____ (want) to be when you were a child?
   B: A firefighter. I loved the uniform!

7 A: _____ (wait) long?
   B: About an hour. The hospital is always busy on Saturdays.

8 A: _____ (not finish) your degree?
   B: Because I ran out of money and couldn't pay the tuition fees.

1.2

A Add *will/won't/would/wouldn't* to the sentences in the correct place.

1 On Sunday mornings, I get up early and go for a run along the river before anyone else is awake.

2 I sometimes wait for hours before a bus arrives.

3 My mother-in-law always bake a cake for us when we visit.

4 He keep bothering me for my telephone number, but I don't want to give it to him.

5 The children stop fighting. It's driving me crazy.

6 She spend the first half an hour chatting before she even starts work.

7 My parents take us on camping vacations in the rain. We hated it.

8 My grandfather shout or tell you off. He was a very gentle man.

B Complete the sentences using the prompts in parentheses.

1 The drug _____ headaches if used for prolonged periods. (tendency/cause)

2 He _____ paintings which cost far too much money. (inclined/buy)

3 We're _____ about politics at the dinner table. (prone/argue)

4 I _____ whether or not I've been given the job. (keep/wonder)

5 She's _____ a fuss about the way I dress. (always/make)

6 They _____ at cards, so I decided not to play with them. (kept/cheat)

7 As _____, I _____ a lot of herbs and spices in my cooking. (rule/not use)

8 My father _____ me back a present from his travels. (would always/bring)

1.3

A Complete the conversations with the words in the box.

| sure | seems | wonder | guess | give | ~~imagine~~ | say | make | looks |

1 A: I _____*imagine*_____ it might rain later.
   B: Yes, it _____ as though it could.

2 A: How much do you think that painting is worth?
   B: I'd _____ a guess at about $500.
   A: Not quite. It's worth $1.2 million.

3 A: What time do you think they'll arrive?
   B: I'm pretty _____ they'll be here by six.

4 A: What do you think it's supposed to be?
   B: I _____ it could be an animal of some sort.

5 A: I _____ if she'll remember we're coming.
   B: If not, we'll surprise her.

6 A: If I had to make a guess, I'd _____ it was that way.
   B: It _____ to me that we're lost.

7 A: Have you seen that Rafael and Lina have a fancy new car?
   B: Yes, they _____ the impression of having plenty of money.

GRAMMAR

2.1 Hypothetical Conditional: Past

The most common conditional sentences refer to permanent facts (zero conditional), future possibility (first conditional) or imaginary situations (second conditional).

Hypothetical Conditional: Past (Third Conditional)

Use to talk about something that could have happened, but didn't, or should not have happened, but did.

If I hadn't eaten that shellfish, I would have been fine.

other forms with a third conditional meaning

Supposing you'd met the president, what would you have said?
Imagine you'd missed the flight, what would you have done?

In more formal contexts, it is possible to replace *if* by inverting the subject and *had*.   *Had I known her, I would have said hello.*

Or replace *if* with *If not for* + noun (+ gerund)

If not for Wilkinson's heroics, they would have lost the match.

Mixed Conditional

Use to say how, if something had been different in the past, the present or future would be different.

If she'd listened to me, she wouldn't be in debt now.

Regrets

Use *regret* + gerund, *if only* + past perfect or *wish* + past perfect to say we want something in the past to have been different.

I regret going out last night.
If only I hadn't left the oven on.
He wishes he'd gone to college.

Use *if only* + simple past or *wish* + simple past to say we want something to be different now.

If only we had some matches!
I wish you were here.

Note: After *if only* and *wish*, we often use *were* instead of *was*.

Were is considered more correct in formal English, although *was* is often used in spoken English.

Use *if only* + *would* or *wish* + *would* to show we are annoyed by something now.

If only you'd be more sensible!
I wish you would be quiet!

2.2 Verb Patterns

verb + -ing

Many verbs can be followed by a verb in the *-ing* form.

Some of these verbs are related in meaning: *like, dislike, adore, love, detest, can't bear/stand*. Some can also be followed by the infinitive, but the meaning may change.

We regret to inform you … (We are sorry **before** we speak.)
He regrets telling her … (He is sorry **after** he speaks.)

Prepositions are followed by an *-ing* form.

Are you still interested in buying the property?

-Ing forms when they function as nouns (gerunds) are often the subject of a sentence.   *Smoking is bad for you.*

Infinitive with *to*

Use an infinitive with *to*:

• after certain verbs including *appear, decide, fail, need, offer, refuse, want, wish*. Verbs with a future meaning (*hope, expect, promise*, etc.) are often followed by the infinitive.
They hoped to negotiate a better deal.

• after certain verb + object combinations, e.g. *advise, allow, ask, cause, encourage, forbid*.
The police asked everyone to remain calm.

• with some nouns, often as part of semi-fixed phrases (*It's time to …*, etc.).

• after most adjectives.   *I was happy to help.*

Passive Infinitive or -ing form

Use the passive *-ing* form (*being done*) to describe actions which are done to the subject.

I hate being told what to do.

Use the passive infinitive (*to be done*) after some verbs (especially reporting verbs).

He was considered to be the right person for the job.

Perfect Infinitive or -ing form

Use the perfect *-ing* form (*having done*) or the perfect infinitive (*to have done*) to emphasize when one action happened before another.

She mentioned having seen him leave.
They seem to have solved the problem.

After verbs of preference (*would like/love/hate/ prefer/rather*), we can use the perfect infinitive to talk about an action in the past.

We would hate to have lost the match.

Negative Infinitive or -ing form

Not + infinitive and *not* + *-ing* are also important.

It's quite common not to understand at first.
Not understanding is quite common.

Infinitives can be the subject of a sentence.

To learn is important.
Not to thank her would be impolite.

2.3 Introducing Opinions

Use the following phrases to introduce opinions or knowledge.

If you want my honest opinion, …	Quite frankly, …	The reality is, …/In reality, …
According to (the statistics), …	From what I can gather, …	As far as I'm concerned, …
To my knowledge, …	Look at it this way.	If you ask me, …

PRACTICE

2.1

A Complete the sentences with the correct form of the verbs in the box. Use the negative form where necessary.

> take over   know   be   spend   find   cause   stay   pull
> die   become   tell   arrive   win   listen   call   cook

1 If you _____ to my advice, you _____ in such a terrible situation now.

2 I regret _____ a manager so young; I wish I _____ more time in the industry first.

3 We _____ your house if we _____ you on the cell phone.

4 Imagine if Donner Textiles _____ the company, it _____ all kinds of problems.

5 Had they _____ us about that hotel, we _____ there now, instead of in this dump!

6 But for the emergency services _____ so quickly, many more people _____ in the fire.

7 If I _____ she didn't eat wheat, I _____ pasta.

8 It's such a shame: had she _____ a muscle, she _____ the race.

B Rewrite the sentences using the word(s) in parentheses.

1 We gambled on red. We lost.
(If/won) _____.

2 They only asked him to the party because he's famous.
(wouldn't) _____.

3 The boys feel bad about borrowing your car.
(regret) _____.

4 She didn't know you were a vegetarian! She bought fish!
(Had) _____.

5 I forgot my keys. Now we're locked out!
(If only/wouldn't) _____.

6 I'm working in a boring, low-paid job. I shouldn't have dropped out of college.
(If) _____.

7 Ahmed is sorry he didn't speak to you before you left.
(wishes) _____.

8 He had been injured. Otherwise we would have won.
(If not for) _____.

2.2

A Underline the correct alternatives.

We all know how important ¹*make/making/to make* a good first impression is. We've heard the statistics: when you meet someone for the first time, only seven percent of their impression is based on what you say, thirty-eight percent on how you say it, and a massive fifty-five percent on your appearance and manner. So, it's vital not ²*underestimate/underestimating/to underestimate* the importance of choosing your clothes carefully when you go to that key meeting or job interview. This is your opportunity ³*impress/impressing/to impress*. On ⁴*walk/walking/to walk* into the room, most people are likely ⁵*to have form/to have forming/to have formed* an opinion of your character based on your appearance in less than three seconds. It's difficult ⁶*say/saying/to say* why people insist on ⁷*judge/judging/to judge* by appearances, even when we know that it's so unreliable ⁸*do/doing/to do* this. Even in courtrooms, juries and judges appear ⁹*give/giving/to give* lighter sentences to people who are well dressed.

B Find and correct the six mistakes in sentences 1–8.

1 I can't stand seeing people smoke in cars.

2 I don't know why you waste all your time sit in front of the computer.

3 Cody was encouraged play the guitar by his father.

4 They hoped meet up with some of the stars after the show.

5 They were rumored to have get married in secret.

6 I gave up the idea of go into politics when I was in my thirties.

7 We were tempted ask if we could stay the night, but we thought it might seem rude.

8 I would prefer to have seen it for myself.

2.3

A Match the sentence halves.

1 If you want my

2 The reality

3 Look at it

4 As far as

5 If you ask

6 According to

7 Quite

8 From what I can

9 To my

a) honest opinion, there isn't much evidence to support this theory.

b) frankly, this is the best movie of the decade.

c) is, we can't keep sending them money.

d) gather, he's very well established in his field.

e) knowledge, Yum Yums is the best brand for baby food.

f) me, you should put aside more time for your family.

g) the boss, we're making a profit of $100,000 every month.

h) I'm concerned, this company is living on borrowed time.

i) this way: we must do something now or things will get worse.

GRAMMAR

3.1 Noun Phrases

A noun phrase is a group of words which function as a unit to describe the noun. Information can be added before or after the noun to add further information about it.

before the noun (pre-modification)

Compound nouns are formed when another noun is added to help describe the main noun. These can be written as two words, with a hyphen, or as one word. *coffee cup   build-up   fingerprint*

Compound adjectives can be used for expressions of measurement. **Note:** Plural expressions become singular.

*a **forty-five-minute** journey* (It takes forty-five minutes.)

*a **six-year-old** boy* (He is six years old.)

Adverb + adjective combinations can be used to give more information about the noun. *an amazingly simple process*

Adjectives before a noun need to be in a specific order.

determiner	value	size	age	shape	color	origin	material	compound	noun
two	lovely		old			French			vases
my	shabby				black		leather	biker	jacket
some		small		oval			silver	ear	rings

after the noun (post-modification)

Prepositional phrases can be used to help modify the noun.

*the light **from the setting sun***
*a suggestion **for how to arrange the meeting***

Participle clauses also give more description.
*people **rushing in and out of their offices***

Relative clauses can also be used to modify the noun phrase. See 3.2 below.
*the man **whom I spotted in the restaurant***

Sometimes, the relative clause can be rewritten as a noun phrase.
research that has been conducted recently → recent research

3.2 Relative Clauses

defining relative clauses

Defining relative clauses give essential information about a noun. Compare:

1 *My uncle, who lives in New York, is coming to Oxford.*
2 *My uncle who lives in New York is coming to Oxford.*

In sentence 1, *who lives in New York* is a non-defining relative clause. It gives extra non-essential information about the uncle. In sentence 2, it is a defining relative clause. The speaker has more than one uncle so he/she identifies which uncle he/she is talking about.

In defining relative clauses, we can omit the relative pronoun if it is the object of the verb.
I've eaten the cake (which) I made yesterday.

Non-Defining Relative Clauses

Non-defining relative clauses give extra information about a noun. Use a comma before and after the relative clause.
*That project, **which I started years ago,** still isn't finished.*

Relative Pronouns

Use: *who* for people, *which* for things/groups of people, *where* for places, *whose* for possessions belonging to people and things. *That can* replace any pronoun except *whose* in defining relative clauses.

Use a relative pronoun after *some of, all of, a few of, none of.*
*She has four sisters, **none of whom** are married.*

Fixed Prepositional Phrases and Relative Clauses

There are a number of fixed phrases which use a preposition in a non-defining relative clause.
*The company ran out of money, **at which point** I quit my job.*
*He may work late, **in which case** I'll get home first.*
*We watched the final, **the** result **of which** was never in doubt.*

In informal sentences, the preposition stays with the verb. In formal sentences we put the preposition before the relative pronoun. Compare:

He completed the book which he'd been working on. (informal)
He completed the book on which he'd been working. (formal)

3.3 Making a Proposal

Introducing your Proposal
Just to give a bit of background information, …
To start with, I'm going to talk briefly about …

Stating the Purpose
The aim of the project is to …
The main goal/objective of our proposal is to …

Describing your Idea
What we plan to do is …
We're going to build/develop/come up with …

Justifying your Idea
This solution will help us to …   This idea is feasible because …

Listing the Benefits
In the first instance, this would mean …
The short-term/long-term benefits include …

Summarizing your Proposal
So, basically, what we're proposing (to do) is to …
To sum up, we're proposing …

Soliciting Questions
Does anyone have any questions?
Is there anything that needs clarification?

PRACTICE

3.1

A Make one sentence by adding the information in parentheses to the noun phrase. Pay attention to word order.

1 I like coffee. (black / strong / small cups of / freshly ground)

_____

2 He bought the house. (by the river / little / pretty)

_____

3 She made cakes. (with strawberries and fresh cream on top / delicious / dark chocolate / two)

_____

4 He smokes cigars. (which Juan gives him / hugely expensive / Cuban / those / enormous)

_____

5 They carried the books. (ridiculously heavy / massive pile of / all the way up seven flights of stairs)

_____

6 It was a dog. (incredibly smelly / hairy / guard / but rather friendly)

_____

B Rewrite the sentences to make one sentence with a complex noun phrase.

1 I went to the store. It sold shoes. It was advertised on television.

I went _____.

2 The man was old. He was walking with a stick.

He was _____.

3 We ate the cakes. They were homemade. They were absolutely delicious. We were sitting in the sunshine.

We ate _____.

4 They rented a house. It was nice. It was near the airport. It had a swimming pool.

They rented _____.

5 We went to a restaurant. It was big. It was a pizza restaurant. It was on the outskirts of town. It was run by two Italian brothers. They were called Gino and Rino.

We went _____.

3.2

A Complete the text with one word in each space.

In my early twenties, [1] *when* I was a student, I used to hang out in a few places, none [2] _____ which were exactly fancy. There was one seedy dive called Schubert's, [3] _____ an acquaintance of mine, [4] _____ name I've forgotten, played the piano. But my favorite haunt, [5] _____ which I remember everything including the decor (a Matisse poster [6] _____ edges were peeling off the wall), was Johnny Bee's Café.

The table [7] _____ I regularly sat faced a window from [8] _____ you could see the street. I must have gone to Johnny Bee's every day until I graduated, by which [9] _____ I was virtually living there. Most of the dissertation [10] _____ which I was working was conceived in Johnny Bee's. I went back last year and saw the same people, none of [11] _____ had changed except for a few gray hairs.

B Complete the second sentence so it has a similar meaning to the first. Use the word in parentheses.

1 There were lots of children there and all of them sang really well. (whom)

There were lots of children there, _____.

2 When the fire alarm went off, the lesson ended. (point)

The fire alarm went off, _____.

3 We stayed in that woman's house. (house)

That's the woman _____.

4 Claire the person I learned the most from. (whom)

The person _____.

5 If you get a scholarship, you won't need to pay. (case)

You may get a scholarship, in _____.

6 There are two photocopiers in the office, which are both out of order. (of)

There are two photocopiers in the office, both

_____.

3.3

A Underline the correct alternatives to complete the proposal.

Just to give a bit of [1]*background information/ information background*, we're computer programmers who have traveled all over the world and have contacts everywhere. To start [2]*up/with*, we're going to talk briefly about our plan for a website to organize student trips abroad.

The main goal [3]*to/of* our proposal is to get funding for this internet start-up, and the [4]*target/aim* of the project is to help students travel abroad for life-changing trips.

OK, [5]*how/what* we plan to do is create personalized trips according to the client's interests. We're going to come [6]*up with/down to* a menu of travel options linked to the client's profile.

This idea is [7]*possible/feasible* because students book everything online and they love traveling, but they also want to avoid the problems of independent travel. This [8]*opportunity/solution* will help them to realize their dreams.

Here are the benefits: in the first [9]*instance/case*, our idea would mean the client didn't have to organize anything. Secondly, there is the [10]*term-long/long-term* benefit of security. We will plan safe itineraries and we'll always know where the traveler is.

So, basically, [11]*that/what* we're proposing is to tailor trips for the client using our contacts abroad. To [12]*sum up/the sum up*, we want to provide amazing experiences for future generations, and you can be a part of this by providing start-up funds for our site.

GRAMMAR

4.1 Introductory *it*

Use *it* as an 'empty' subject to introduce or identify something later in the phrase.
'What's the problem?' 'It's nothing. It's just that I'm worried about work.'

Use *it* + *be* to talk about:

- weather.
  It's a bit chilly for this time of year.
- time/dates.
  It's about half past two.
- situations.
  It's a very peaceful place.
- distance.
  It's about thirty miles away.

Use *it* before some phrases to describe probability.
It looks as though we're going to lose.

Use *it* before some phrases to report events.
It would appear that they have left without us.

Use *it* as an 'empty' object after certain verbs to introduce a clause.

(subject + verb + *it* + complement + infinitive/clause)
I'd appreciate it if …
I find it impossible to …

Other Common Expressions With *it*

it + *be* + adjective
It's hard to know if …
It's easy to believe that …

it + verb phrase
It always amazes me that …
It looks/seems as if …

it in the middle of the phrase
I'll leave it to you to decide …
I find it easy to …

Fixed Expressions

It's no wonder/no coincidence that …
It's considered rude to …
It's pointless/no use + -ing …

4.2 The Perfect Aspect

The perfect aspect looks back from one time to another and emphasizes that an action is completed before another time. In some cases, the exact time may be unimportant or unknown. Sometimes the event is incomplete. It started in the past and is still relevant now.

Present Perfect

Use the present perfect to look back from now to a time before now.
I've been here since June.

Use the present perfect continuous to focus on the length of time the action takes.
She's been waiting for hours.

Past Perfect

Use the past perfect to look back from a time in the past to a time before that.
I had to go back because I'd forgotten my passport.

Use the past perfect continuous to focus on the length of time the action takes.
She'd been doing the same job for fifteen years.

Future Perfect

Use the future perfect to look back from a time in the future to a time before that.
By next week, we will have finished the project.

Note: We also use *will have* + past participle to make predictions about the present or the future.
Don't call the house, she'll have left for work by now.

Use the future perfect continuous to focus on the length of time the action takes.
In 2020, I'll have been living here for fifty years.

Perfect Infinitive

Use the perfect infinitive after verbs like *seem* and *appear* to look back to a previous time period.
He seems to have forgotten us.

It can be used with different time periods.
It's great to have finished my exams.
He said he was sorry to have missed your party.
We hope to have done the work by 5:00.

4.3 Expressing Hypothetical Preferences

Use the following phrases to express hypothetical preferences.

Hypothetical Preferences	
If it was up to me, I'd …/I'd have (+ past participle)	Far better to … than …
I'd rather (+ infinitive)	This would be by far the best option.
I'd just as soon (+ infinitive) … as	My preference would be to …
Given the choice, I'd …	Without a shadow of a doubt, I'd …
If I ever found myself in this/that situation, I'd …	No way would I (+ infinitive).

PRACTICE

4.1

A Add *it/it's* in the correct place(s) in sentences 1–8.

1 I can't stand when all does is rain for days on end.

2 I'd appreciate if you could give me a little more notice next time.

3 No use just standing there. You'd better get on with it.

4 I find hard to believe that the summer is here already.

5 Appears that the police have video footage of the incident.

6 Pointless arguing with her when she's in that kind of state.

7 I'll leave to the others to decide what time we should meet.

8 I've always made clear that my family has to take priority over my work.

B Complete the second sentence so it has a similar meaning to the first. Use three to six words including the word in parentheses.

1 Don't cry about the situation now. It won't help. (pointless)

It _____ about the situation now.

2 Being trustworthy is vital in this profession. (essential)

It's _____ in this profession.

3 He appears to have misplaced his keys. (seems)

It _____ his keys.

4 We need to be hospitable to them as they were welcoming to us. (owe)

We _____ hospitable as they were welcoming to us.

5 I am not surprised by her lack of enthusiasm as she has heard the talk before. (wonder)

It's no _____ when she had heard the talk before.

6 It's easy for me to keep abreast of the latest news online. (find)

I _____ of the latest news online.

4.2

A Underline the correct alternatives.

1 UNICEF *will have provided/has been providing/ is to have provided* humanitarian assistance to developing countries since 1946.

2 My family *will have lived/has lived/had been living* in that house for over 100 years by the time we were forced to move.

3 Next year, it *had been/will have been/ has been* twenty years since we met.

4 They *have closed/have been closing/ will have closed* that store because it wasn't making money.

5 Judging by the state of the garden, she *will have abandoned/had been abandoning/ appeared to have abandoned* her home.

6 By 2018, Tom *will have been running/ has been running/is to have run* the company for twenty years.

B Complete speaker B's responses using the prompts. Use perfect tenses.

1 **A:** Is the protest still going on?

B: Yes. The workers / march / since 8:00 this morning.

2 **A:** Why did you shout at the students at the end of class?

B: They / talk throughout the whole lesson.

3 **A:** Eliana is the most experienced person in the office, isn't she?

B: Yes. This time next year she / work / here / for forty years.

4 **A:** Do you think they'll be at the airport now?

B: Yes. It's 8:00. They / arrive / by now.

5 **A:** Why is he losing so badly?

B: He / seems / forget / how to play!

6 **A:** I hear Mary lost her job because the company went bankrupt.

B: That's right. She / only / work there for two months when the company closed.

4.3

A Match the sentence halves.

1 If I found myself in

2 This would be by

3 I'd just as

4 Far better

5 Given the

6 No way would

7 My preference would

8 I'd rather eat at home

9 Without a shadow of

10 If it was up to

a) than go to Grisky's.

b) soon listen to the radio as watch TV.

c) choice, I wouldn't take any tests.

d) that situation, I'd panic.

e) far the best option.

f) be to speak to the manager.

g) me, I'd have told her earlier.

h) to tell the truth than to make up a story.

i) a doubt I'd buy it if I had the cash.

j) I ever steal anything.

GRAMMAR

5.1 Modal Verbs and Related Phrases

Use modal and semi-modal verbs and phrases to express degrees of obligation or whether or not something is necessary, desirable, permitted or forbidden. Modals are also used to refer to people's abilities.

have to, must, should, ought to, had better for obligation
*We **ought to set** the alarm for an hour earlier.*

Had better is stronger than *ought to* and implies a warning.
*We'**d better leave** now. We don't want to be late.*

need for talking about obligation or lack of it

*We **needed to ask** for directions.* (If we had done this, we wouldn't be lost.)

Notice the difference between *didn't need to* and *needn't have*.

*We **didn't need to ask** for directions.* (We had a map.)

*We **needn't have asked** for directions.* (We asked for directions, but it was unnecessary as we found a map.)

can, (be) allowed to, (be) supposed to, (be) permitted to for talking about what is permissible/possible

*We **couldn't leave** the premises after 6 p.m.* (It wasn't allowed.)

Be supposed to implies that someone expects you to do this (maybe it's a rule). We can use this when we don't obey the rule.

*We'**re supposed to leave** the key on the desk when we finish.* (But we may not, we may take it with us.)

Other phrases which can be used with modal meaning
(be) allowed, (be) permissible; (be) forbidden, (be) banned; (be/feel) compelled, (be) compulsory; (be) forced to, (be) obligatory; have the courage to, dare to
*They **were forced to wear** army uniforms.*

(Army uniforms were compulsory.)
*We **weren't allowed to contact** the teachers.* (It wasn't permissible to contact them.)

5.2 The Passive

Use the passive to sound objective and impersonal. The passive is particularly common in formal writing, e.g. academic writing and news reports.

Use the passive to emphasize the important information at the beginning of the sentence.

*Penicillin **was discovered** by Fleming.* (The most important point is the invention of penicillin.)

Use the passive if who performs the action is unknown or unimportant. The emphasis is on the action itself.
*The museum **was built** in the seventeenth century.* (We aren't interested in who built it.)

Use the passive to show that we are not certain.
*It **is believed** that this ancient society used aspirin.* (There is no proof. It's just a theory.)

Use the passive to distance ourselves from a statement.
*It'**s said** that it's unlucky to walk under a ladder.* (The speaker might not believe this.)

The passive is often used in formal English to describe rules, processes or procedures.
*Membership cards **must be shown** at the door before entry.*
It is common to use the passive with an infinitive or with *to have* + past participle.

*She **was thought to be** the best swimmer in the city.*
*He **is known to have been** present during the crimes.*

We can use a causative form with a passive meaning. The form is *have/get* + object + past participle.
*We **had** the walls **painted** blue.*
*He **had** his laptop **upgraded**.*

Spoken Grammar

Get is more informal than *have*.

A spoken form of the causative *have* is common in the U.S.A.
*I **had** the mechanic **fix** my car.*

5.3 Making a Point

Making a Point	Clarifying a Point	Challenging a Point
There are several reasons why I think that …	What I'm basically saying is …	Do you think that's always the case?
The reason (why) I say that is …	The point I'm trying to make is that …	Can you be sure about that?
The facts suggest …/The evidence shows …	Actually, …/In fact, …	Is there any way/evidence to prove that?
After all, …	Let me put it this way …	But that's not the point.
The point is …	I think you'll find that …	I don't see how you can say that.
If you think about it, …		But that doesn't take account of the fact that …

PRACTICE

5.1

A Complete the second sentence so it has a similar meaning to the first. Use the correct form of the word in parentheses.

1 We couldn't bring our own food to school. (allow)

We weren't. _____.

2 I wish I hadn't told him that I cheated in the exam. (should)

I _____.

3 Turn your cell phones off. They are not allowed in the movie theater. (better)

You'd _____.

4 You must hand this work in first thing in the morning. (have)

You _____.

5 I didn't have the courage to tell them the truth. (dare)

I didn't _____.

6 They aren't allowed to have their lights on after 10 p.m. (supposed)

They're _____.

B Find and correct the mistakes in sentences 1–8. There is one mistake in each sentence.

1 You didn't need rush. There's another five minutes before the film starts.

2 We'd better to leave plenty of time to get to the airport in case of heavy traffic.

3 You didn't have got to buy a present. That's very kind of you.

4 You should don't drive a car if you're tired.

5 We didn't had to stop at all on the way.

6 They were supposed deliver the furniture today.

7 You ought to trying this program — it's very good.

8 You shouldn't to talk to people like that. It's rude.

5.2

A Complete the second sentence so it has a similar meaning to the first. Use the passive or causative and the word in parentheses.

1 Police are investigating the case. (being)

The _____.

2 The college lets you borrow a car for official business. (allowed)

You _____.

3 They are delivering Mike's washing machine today. (having)

Mike _____.

4 Some people say the tradition began in the nineteenth century. (claimed)

It _____.

5 There's a possibility someone recognized Wilhelm. (might)

Wilhelm _____.

6 She instructed the players to stretch before the game. (had)

She _____.

7 Someone is checking in our luggage right now. (being)

Our _____.

8 The researchers have only tested the product on volunteers. (been)

The _____.

B Why might sentences 1–8 be better in the passive? Which might be formal written English?

C Rewrite the underlined phrases in the passive. Omit the "doer" of the action.

[1]They say that the world's greatest keepers of secrets are spies. While this may be true, there is another secret connected to spies that is less well known. They are a huge problem for their employers. Why? Like most workers, spies retire when they get old. However, unlike most workers, spies retain numerous high-level secrets. [2]They need to keep these secrets even after the spies retire. So [3]what can the authorities do with retired ex-spies? In the 1960s, [4]they considered brainwashing. But [5]they discovered that brainwashing didn't work. They also tried hypnotism, in the hope that [6]they could erase certain memories from the mind. But it turned out to be impossible to erase some memories and not others, e.g. the names of your family members and your street address. So what did they do in the end? We don't know, of course. It's a secret.

1 _____

2 _____

3 _____

4 _____

5 _____

6 _____

5.3

A Put the underlined words in the correct order to complete the conversations.

A: [1]saying I'm is what we need to be very careful who we give the information to. [2]suggest facts the that the more people who know about the idea, the riskier the situation.

B: I guess so. But we need to tell people about the product before we launch to get people excited about it.

A: That's true, but [3]the is point if the competition find out about it, they will probably steal the idea.

B: [4]think always you is that case the do?

A: Yes. [5]all after, what have they got to lose?

C: [6]are several think reasons there why I this is the right thing to do and [7]about think it if you, we don't have any other options.

D: [8]say you don't can how see I that. I just don't think the idea will work in practice.

C: Well, [9]way put this me it let, we don't have any more time to consider options. We need to decide.

D: I know there are time pressures, but [10]that trying make is I'm point to the we need to think about the costs as well.

GRAMMAR

6.1 Future Forms

be going to

Use *be going to* + infinitive to:

- express personal intention. The action has been considered in advance and some plans have already been made.
  We're going to stay with John next summer.

- make a prediction based on present evidence.

I think she's going to fall! (She is off balance.)

Will

Use *will* to:

- make predictions.   *We'll win the Cup this year.*

- talk about future facts.   *He'll start school next year.*

We often use *will* with adverbs of probability.
I'll probably see you tomorrow.

We also use *will* for decisions made at the moment of speaking.   *I think I'll have a nap.*

Present Continuous

Use the present continuous to talk about a pre-arranged action in the future. *Be going to* is for intentions, while the present continuous is for planned events or arrangements for a specific time.
I'm visiting Sheila on Sunday.

Present Simple

Use the simple present to talk about fixed future events in timetables or programs.
My train arrives at 5:00..

Future Continuous

Use the future continuous to:

- talk about an action that will be in progress at some time in the future.
  This time next week, I'll be lying on a beach.

- make a deduction about the future based on normal practice.
  I expect the Smiths will be having their annual party soon.

- talk about something that will happen as part of the normal course of events, not because you planned it.
  I'll be seeing Jackie at college, so I'll give her the note.

Future Perfect and Future Perfect Continuous

Use the future perfect to talk about a future event which will be finished at a certain point in the future. Use the future perfect continuous to talk about the length of an action as seen from a moment in the future.
The builders will have finished our house by January.
By 2018, I'll have been studying French for twenty years.

Modal Verbs

Could, *might* and *may* are also used to make predictions. They have similar meanings, but *may* is more formal.

Be To

Use *be* + *to* + infinitive to describe official plans and arrangements.
The company is to provide insurance for all of its workers.

Be Due To

Use *be due to* + infinitive to describe a formal arrangement.
The plane is due to land at 6:00.

6.2 Concession Clauses

Use concession clauses to give information that contrasts with the information in the main clause.

The clauses can be introduced with conjunctions such as *although*, *however*, *even though*, etc.
Although he was a good linguist, he took five years to learn Mandarin.

We can also use *while* and *whilst* (formal) to replace *although*.
While/Whilst I'd like to be with you, I have to attend a meeting.

Use *much as* to replace *although* with verbs of liking and hating to talk about strong feelings.
Much as we appreciate your efforts, sadly we won't be able to use the report.

Use adjective/adverb + *as/though* + subject + verb clause for emphatic sentences.
Hard as we tried, we failed to get hold of anybody.
Difficult though it was, we eventually secured the premises.

Use *however/whatever/wherever*, etc. to express the idea of 'no matter what/who/where', etc.
Whatever he says, I'm going anyway.

Use *in spite of* and *despite* + noun phrase/-ing form to express contrast.
In spite of the fact that we had no ID on us, the porter let us in.
Despite feeling awful, we stayed until the end.

Note: Sentences using *in spite of/despite* are not concession clauses, as the linker is not followed by a verb clause, but is followed by a noun/-ing form.

We can use adverbs and adverbial phrases to introduce contrast.
We were exhausted but we carried on all the same.
We were exhausted. Nevertheless, we carried on.

6.3 Describing Cause and Effect

Cause

Informal and Neutral	Formal
It all started ...	It has its origins/roots in ...
It originated in/from ...	It can be traced back/attributed to ...
It's because of ...	It stems from ...

Effect

Informal and Neutral	Formal
It led to ...	It resulted in ...
It has caused ...	It gave rise to ...
Because of this, ...	It brought about ...

PRACTICE

6.1

A There are ten words missing from the speech. Complete it by adding the missing words.

'Yesterday we announced that we are merge with Jonas Inc. We are due do this in May, so today I'm going speak about the company's history and the decision to merge. This time next year, the company will have building houses for twenty-five years. By January, we will built more than 100,000 homes, and I hope that we'll still be houses in 2050. Although we be discussing the new situation with you individually, we are sure your jobs will secure. Through this merger, we be expanding and so we will be moving into unknown markets. By February, we will sent you a document about the company's plans. For now, I promise there will be opportunities for all.'

B Complete the second sentence so it has the same meaning as the first. Use the words in parentheses and a future form.

1 It's our twentieth wedding anniversary tomorrow. (married)

By tomorrow, we will _____.

2 The arrival time for the London-Brussels flight is 2:00. (at)

The London-Brussels flight _____.

3 The government will pass a law prohibiting guns. (is)

The government _____.

4 I work in the same office as John, so I can speak to him. (seeing)

I'll _.

5 We arrived here in July five years ago. (living)

By July, we'll _____.

6 The committee has scheduled a meeting with the owners. (due)

The committee is _____.

7 Roger always puts up his Christmas decorations in November. (putting)

I imagine Roger will _____.

8 My son celebrates his eighteenth birthday next March. (old)

My son _____.

6.2

A Complete the sentences with the words in the box.

however	despite	although	as	whenever
whereas	matter	spite		

1 American cars are generally too large for the Japanese market, _____ Japanese cars are popular in the USA.

2 Hard _____ she tried, she couldn't get the door to open.

3 No _____ how difficult it is, I'm determined to do my best.

4 They explained that we could leave _____ we wanted to.

5 She went to Spain _____ the fact that her doctor had told her to rest.

6 We went out in _____ of the rain.

7 I really want the car, _____ much it costs.

8 We decided to take the room, _____ we knew we couldn't really afford the rent.

B Rewrite the sentences using the words in parentheses. Write one or two sentences.

1 I spend much too much time on the internet. I know that it's bad for me. (Despite)

_____

2 My grandmother is still fully independent. She is nearly ninety-six years old. (Even though)

_____

3 He's an excellent manager. He can be a bit scary to work for. (… although …)

_____

4 They tried hard. They couldn't persuade him to give up his work. (Hard as)

_____

5 I understand how difficult the situation is. I'm afraid I can't help. (Whilst)

_____

6 He's very charming. I wouldn't trust him at all. (… However, …)

_____

6.3

A Underline the correct alternatives.

The Second World War gave [1]*rights/arise/rise* to the term 'The First World War'. Impossible? No. It's all because of 'retronymy'. A 'retronym' is a word invented for an object/concept whose original name has gone out of date. Retronyms are invented because new developments change the way we perceive the world. The term 'The First World War' can be traced [2]*up/on/back* to 1939. Before that date, nobody knew there would be a World War II, and World War I had, until then, been called 'The Great War'.

Another example is the guitar. All guitars used to be acoustic.

The invention of the electric guitar [3]*caused/led/moved* to the term 'acoustic guitar'. Similarly, nobody said 'black and white TV' before the invention of color TV [4]*developed/resulted/traced* in the need for the term. Many retronyms [5]*affect/stem/rise* from modern technology. The invention of laptops brought [6]*with/for/about* the term 'desktop computer' and the proliferation of cell phones resulted [7]*on/in/to* the word 'landline'. The word 'retronym' is [8]*attributed/given/caused* to Frank Mankiewicz, an American journalist.

retronym

GRAMMAR

7.1

Cleft Sentences

Cleft means 'divided'. In cleft sentences, one sentence is divided into two parts, each with its own verb. This adds emphasis to part of the sentence.

John loves Mary. (one verb)

It's Mary that John loves. (two verbs, emphasizes Mary)

The following structures are commonly used to begin cleft sentences.

It + ...	What + ...
It was a ... who ...	What I like about ... is
It was in ... that ...	What they didn't realize was ...
other structures	

The person who ...	The reason why ... is/was ...
The place that ...	The only thing that ... is/was ...
The thing that ... is/was ...	All that I would ... is/was ...
Something that ... is/was ...	

Note: We use the singular form after *It + ...* and *What + ...* sentences.

*It **was** my parents I had to thank for this.* NOT ~~It were my parents ...~~

*What **is** really annoying are the arguments.*
NOT ~~What are really annoying ...~~

We can use *Wh* - words with cleft sentences. To emphasize the action, we use a form of *do*.

*Jane invested well. → **What** Jane **did was** invest well.*

Emphasizing with *what*, *all* and *it*

To emphasize an action or series of actions, we can use sentences beginning with *What*.

*He dropped the vase. → **What happened was (that)** he dropped the vase.*

We can use *Wh-* clauses as introductory phrases.

What I would like to know is where the money went.

We can use *all* instead of *what*.
All I'd like to say is that the company appreciates your work.

Use *It + be + that/who* to emphasize parts of a sentence.

*Karin left her bag on the train. → It was **Karin** who left her bag on the train.* (Karin — not Fatima)

*It was **her bag** that Karin left on the train.*
(not her umbrella)

*It's **because you have such a good sense of humor** that I enjoy your company.* (emphasising reason)

*It was **only yesterday** that I discovered the documents were missing.* (emphasising time)

*It was in **Paris** that they first met.* (emphasizing place)

7.2

Participle Clauses

Participle clauses are used to make our writing and speaking more economical, efficient and, sometimes, more elegant. They can also be used to add information about reason, condition and result.

Past Participles

Past particle clauses have a passive meaning. Use past participles to add extra information. They sometimes serve the same purpose as adjectives (describing a noun).

***Loved** by everyone, Don was a wonderful soul.*
(describes Don)

***Exhausted** from her efforts, she struggled on.* (describes 'she')

Present Participles

Present particle clauses have an active meaning. Use present participles (*-ing* form):

• as reduced relative clauses. Here the present participle serves the same purpose as an adjective.
*The **woman who is smiling** in the photo is my grandmother. →*
*The **woman smiling** in the photo is my grandmother.*
*I smelled the **bread that was burning**. → I smelled the **burning bread**.*

• as adverbial clauses (like adverbs): expressing manner, conditions, cause, result, etc. This is especially common in formal or literary texts. To make the negative, use *not* before the present participle.

***Moving silently**, the lion follows its prey.*
***Lying face down in the sand**, he looked like some strange sea beast.*
***Not being qualified**, she couldn't work there.*
*There was a fire, **resulting in serious damage**.*

Having + past participle

Having + past participle is used:

• to show the cause of a second action.
***Having won** every competition, he decided to retire.*

• to show a sequence of actions.
***Having made** breakfast, she sat down and read the paper.*

7.3

Exchanging Opinions

Agreeing
That's absolutely right.
I couldn't agree more.
Absolutely! I'm with you 100 percent on that.

Agreeing in Part
I agree with you up to a point.
I suppose you've got a point, but ...

Questioning Someone's Opinion
Oh come on, you must be joking.   Surely you don't think that ...
That goes against my better judgement because ...
How can you say that?   Where's the logic in that?
You can't honestly think that ...

Strongly Disagreeing
It just doesn't make sense to me.   Oh, that's ridiculous!

PRACTICE

7.1

A Complete the second sentence so it has a similar meaning to the first. Use the word in parentheses.

1 He lost his job because he kept breaking the rules. (reason)

The _____

kept breaking the rules.

2 He only realized who she was when he left the theater. (recognized)

It was only _____ her.

3 I want to persuade them to come with us. (do)

What I _____

to come with us.

4 The thing that concerns me is whether she will have enough money. (worry)

All _____

whether she will have enough money.

5 They have such a fantastic range of spices. (amazing)

What is _____

such a fantastic range of spices.

B Rewrite the sentences in three different ways using the prompts. You may need to change some words.

1 Elections have given these people their first real opportunity to decide who will govern them.

a) What elections have done is _____.

b) The thing that _____.

c) It's the elections _____.

2 Heavy snow and severe weather caused widespread disruption to the country's airports, roads and rail systems.

a) It was the airports, _____.

b) It was heavy snow _____.

c) What caused disruption _____.

3 Hundreds of students marched downtown to protest against the new laws.

a) What caused students _____.

b) The reason hundreds of _____.

c) What happened was _____.

7.2

A Complete the pairs of sentences using the same verb, once as a present participle and once as a past participle.

1 a) _____ as much noise as she could, Lola attracted the attention of the rescuers.

b) _____ in China, this new gadget will be cheap and efficient.

2 a) _____ he had six months to live, he shocked everyone by living another twenty years.

b) _____ his staff he was visiting a client, Jones disappeared with all the company's money.

3 a) _____ for her ticket, she suddenly realized she had never been to a theater before.

b) _____ by the hour, the employees rarely worked on the weekend.

4 a) Many of the clothes _____ by famous people are kept in the museum.

b) All participants _____ a badge will receive a free meal.

5 a) In my opinion, it's one of the best books ever _____.

b) _____ on his blog today, Mick Davies says the economic crisis is over.

B Find and correct five mistakes in the text.

Arming with nothing but a donated caravan, a solar laptop and toothpaste made from crushed cuttlefish bones, Mark Boyle lives without cash. Having graduate in economics, he was a food company manager. One afternoon while to discuss the world's problems with a friend, he decided to act on Gandhi's words: 'Be the change you want to see in the world.' Giving a camper by a stranger, he moved out of his home. A friend donated a bike and he got himself a stove and began his new life. He now lives off the land, bikes everywhere and writes a blog. Is it true freedom? Asking what he misses about his old life, he says stress, traffic, bank statements and utility bills. He's joking.

7.3

A Complete the conversations with the words in the box.

| honestly   suppose   where   more   sense   100 percent |

1 A: The sales department has asked us to talk through the material with them.

B: Why do they want to do that? It just doesn't make _____ to me.

2 A: No one would ever want to actually wear something like that. It's too uncomfortable.

B: I _____ you've got a point.

3 A: I think we've done more than enough for today.

B: Absolutely! I'm with you _____ on that.

4 A: When we finish the tour, we need to go back to the beginning and start again.

B: _____'s the logic in that?

5 A: Excellent. I think that's an excellent idea.

B: I'm sorry, but you can't _____ tell me you think that is a good idea.

6 A: We'll have trouble finishing everything in time.

B: I couldn't agree _____.

GRAMMAR

8.1 Future in the Past

Sometimes when we're talking about the past, we want to mention something that was in the future at that time. To do this, use future structures but make the verb forms past, e.g.

is going to → was going to
I was going to help you, but I didn't have time.

present continuous → past continuous
They were hoping to have a picnic, but it rained all weekend.

will → would*
I arrived in Recife, where I would spend ten years of my life.*

*This is a different use from *would* for repeated actions in the past. Compare:

At sixteen, I got a job at Lizmo Company, where I would later become CEO.
(future in the past)

For years, I would go running at 5:00 a.m. every morning.
(repeated actions in the past)

We can also use *was/were to* + infinitive and *was/were to have* + past participle. These are quite literary and more commonly found in writing than speech. The expression *was to have* is usually used when the plan did not become a reality.

They told me I was to give a speech the following day.
I was to have taken a job with my father's company, but it went bankrupt.

Other expressions to talk about the future in the past

To describe a plan that did not become reality, use:

- *was/were supposed to.*
  I was supposed to go to Nick's house, but my car broke down.

- *meant to.*
  I meant to mention the cost of tickets, but I forgot. (active)
  We were meant to check in an hour ago! (passive)

For events that very nearly happened, use:

- *was/were on the verge of* + gerund.
  She was on the verge of giving up her dream when she received a letter from an agent.

- *was/were on the point of* + gerund.
  They were on the point of leaving when the boss arrived.

- *was/were about to* + infinitive.
  Hi! I was about to text you!

8.2 Ellipsis and Substitution

Ellipsis

Sometimes words which we might expect to be present from a grammatical point of view are left out because we can understand the meaning from the context (the preceding or following text). Often the words which are left out are auxiliary verbs, modal verbs or subjects.

She immediately got up and (she) left the room. (subject)

Should we wait for a while or (should we) call him right away? (modal verb)

They have finished lunch and (they have) gone for coffee. (subject + auxiliary verb)

It is possible to leave out repeated verb phrases or adjectives and just repeat the auxiliary or modal verb.

Marisa has never tried Asian cooking, but I have (tried Asian cooking).
Harry always thinks he's right about things, but he isn't (always right about things).
I thought we'd be able to finish this before Monday, but we can't (finish this before Monday).

Spoken Grammar

Ellipsis is very common in spoken English as the situational context is usually very clear between the speakers.

Didn't know you were going. (*I didn't know* …)
Sounds good to me. (*That/What you've just suggested sounds good.*)

This means that some common phrases are often shortened.
Did you have a nice weekend? → Nice weekend?
I suppose so. → Suppose so.   It's nice to meet you. → Nice to meet you.

Substitution

Instead of repeating a word/phrase, they are sometimes replaced with a substitute word/phrase. Determiners (*many, a little, some,* etc.), *so, do* and *not* are all used for this.
A: *Do you know a lot of the people coming tonight?*
B: *Not many.*
A: *What do you think of this dress?*
B: *Actually, I prefer the other one.*
A: *Do you think they'll be here soon?*
B: *I think so.* (*so* = them to be here soon)
A: *Who ate all the chocolate cookies — you?*
B: *No, Max did.* (*did* = ate all the cookies biscuits)
A: *Will you have to pay a fine?*
B: *I hope not.* (*not* = I won't have to pay a fine)

8.3 Discussing Ideas

Acknowledging an Idea
Right. OK.   That's a good idea.   Sure.   I know what you mean.
Definitely.   That's interesting.   I never thought of that.
That makes (perfect) sense.   Yes, it's true/That's true.
Exactly.   I'm with you there.

Introducing an Alternative
Having said that, …
But looking at it another way/But I'm looking at …
But on the other hand   Yes and no.   You see, …
But you could argue that   Alternatively, …

PRACTICE

8.1

A Match the sentence halves.

1 I was supposed to
2 The three musicians were going
3 At the time, I didn't know that
4 Paul was on the verge of
5 Honestly, I was
6 You were about to

a) I would never see her again.
b) planning to help you in the garden, but I got a backache.
c) giving up when he saw the top of the mountain.
d) to be the greatest band in history.
e) make the biggest mistake of your life.
f) call home, but I forgot.

B Find and correct the seven mistakes in sentences 1–10.

1 We are about to ascend the mountain when snow started to fall.
2 Just as Clancy was on the point of escaping, a guard entered the hallway.
3 Melissa meant tell you about the dinner invitation, but she forgot.
4 We were to had taken the 6:02 train to Boston, but it was canceled.
5 She got sick when she was on a verge of becoming a superstar.
6 He was going to stay with his brothers for a while before emigrating.
7 Thompson then traveled to Bali, where he will later meet his sixth wife.
8 I was but hoping to work with Donna again, but she left the company.
9 It was to have been a surprise party, but she found out about it.
10 I was to meeting Daley and his gang in the subway at midnight.

8.2

A Complete the sentences with words in the box.

| mine so one there do some ones not |

1 This jacket is in a terrible state. I need to buy a new _____.
2 Louise loves Italian food, and I _____ too.
3 A: Is it safe to come out?
   B: I think _____.
4 They'll probably lose the match, but I hope _____.
5 These batteries are too small. I need those _____ over there.
6 I've been to Europe. We went on vacation _____.
7 A: Is that your car?
   B: No, _____ is parked across the street.
8 A: Do you know where all the tools are?
   B: There are _____ in the garage.

B Decide which words can be omitted in sentences 1–8.

1 I'm not sure if they've finished, but I think they have finished.
2 We could have met them later, but I didn't want to meet them later.
3 Do you want a coffee? I've just made some coffee.
4 I'd be happy to help if you need me to help.
5 A: What time were we supposed to arrive?
   B: We were supposed to arrive at six.
6 Erica had ice cream for dessert and Bill had chocolate cake.
7 They'll be here soon, but I don't know exactly when they'll be here.
8 A: Have you got the time?
   B: The time is half past two.

8.3

A Put the underlined phrases in the correct order to complete the conversation. Capitalize letters where necessary.

A: Teachers, my idea is that from now on students set their own homework.
B: That's interesting, ¹of I that thought never.
A: If they set the homework, there's more chance they will do it.
B: ²with there you I'm. ³sense makes that.
C: ⁴way another at but it looking, won't they set very small amounts of homework?
A: ⁵mean you what know I, but I don't think it will happen. Students know what is good for them.
C: Yes and no. Many of them want to learn, but ⁶hand the on other, my students hate homework. They prefer going to parties at night!
A: Mine too.
C: ⁷that said having, maybe they can write about their parties for homework.
B: Nice idea!

GRAMMAR

9.1 Tenses for Unreal Situations

After some expressions, we use past tenses to describe unreal or imaginary situations. These ideas may refer to the past, present or future.

it's time

Use *it's time* + simple past to say that something is not happening but it should be.
It's time you went home.

We can also use *it's high time* + simple past or *it's about time* + simple past. These are more emphatic than *it's time*.
It's high time she left her boyfriend!
It's about time you found a job!

what if/suppose/supposing

Use *what if/suppose/supposing* + simple past to ask about imaginary situations and their consequences in the present or future. These are similar to second conditional questions.
What if you missed the plane?
Suppose you got injured, what would the coach say?
Supposing they gave you the prize, how would you feel?

We can also use these expressions with the past perfect. This is similar to the third conditional.
What if you'd failed your exam last week, what would you have done?

would rather/would sooner

Use *would rather/would* sooner + simple past to describe preferences.
I'd prefer you didn't play football inside.
I'd rather they gave me a check than a watch when I retire.

If the person expressing the preference is also the subject of the preference, use the infinitive (not the past tense).
I'd rather go to Madagascar than Hawaii.
I'd rather eat bread than cake.

as if/as though

Use *as if/as though* + simple past to say that appearance is different from reality.
She treats me as if I had a disease.
(The speaker knows he doesn't have a disease.)

They use this place as though it was a playground.
(It isn't a playground.)

Use the simple present/present perfect with these expressions when the situation may be true.
He acts as if he knows what he's doing.
(Maybe he knows what he's doing.)

You look as though you haven't slept for days.
(Maybe she hasn't slept for days.)

9.2 Adverbials

Adverbs or adverbial phrases give us information or detail about how, when, why, how often, where, etc., something happens. They can be single words or groups of words.

Adverbials of Manner

These describe how something happens.
He left the room quietly.   She spoke in a soft voice.

Adverbials of Time

These describe when something happened.
In 2008, the government was overthrown.
We saw him yesterday.

Adverbials of Frequency

These describe how often something happened.
We must have gone there pretty much every day for ten years.
I often blog about this topic.

Adverbials of Probability

These describe how probable or improbable something is.
He is right, without a doubt.   She is undoubtedly right.

Adverbials of Purpose

These describe the reason behind/for an action.
They play chess to work on their strategic thinking skills.
She apologized for being so insensitive.

Comment Adverbials

These describe someone's viewpoint.
The clothes in that store are ridiculously expensive.

For more examples, see page 111.

Adverbs and adverbial phrases usually go at the end of a sentence in the following order: how, where, when. Adverbials of purpose generally come last.
They wandered aimlessly (how) around the park (where) at the end of the concert (when) in search of the keys (purpose).

Some adverbials can go at the start of the sentence for emphasis.
On the radio, they played his music all day long.

Adverbs/Adverbials of frequency usually go before the main verb (or after the verb *to be*/auxiliary verb).
Our paths have frequently crossed.

9.3 Ranting/Raving

Raving
It was the most wonderful/amazing/awesome …
It was absolutely fantastic/incredible.   It's really the best (show) ever.
There's (absolutely) nothing better than …
(It was) one of the most spectacular (sunsets) I've ever seen.
I couldn't believe my luck when …   It was idyllic.   It's an all-time classic.

Ranting
If there's one thing I can't stand, it's …
It drives me up a wall.
It was absolutely horrendous.
It was a total waste of money.
It's not my style/kind of thing/cup of tea at all.

PRACTICE

9.1

A Cross out the incorrect alternative.

1 I'd *prefer/sooner/rather* we went somewhere picturesque than stay here.

2 He scores goals *as if/as were/as though* it was the easiest thing in the world.

3 *What if/Suppose/How about* that half-baked idea became a reality?

4 It's *the/high/about* time she started living up to her name.

5 She'd *rather/want that/prefer* they came up with some ideas than just criticize.

6 *Supposing/Rather/Suppose* your career went downhill, what would you do?

7 Isn't it *one time/time/about time* you took her feelings into consideration, too?

8 In meetings, I'm treated *as if/as though/as* I was an idiot.

B Rewrite the sentences using the words in parentheses and the simple past.

1 You really should speak to your mother. (high time)

_____

2 What would happen if I pressed this button? (Suppose)

_____

3 The way they treat that girl, you'd think she was a princess. (as though)

_____

4 Given the choice, I would learn Chinese instead of German. (sooner)

_____

5 Imagine a volcanic eruption in a densely populated area. (What if)

_____

6 She ought to stop smoking now. (about time)

_____

7 Anyone would think they own the place, the way they behave. (as if)

_____

8 I don't want you to go there. (prefer)

_____

9.2

A Choose the correct option, a), b) or c), to complete the text.

The $40 Art Collection

Tom Alexander, began ¹_____ collecting British modern art after moving to the Isle of Arran, U.K., in 1947. Having ²_____ established a store ³_____ with his brother in the village of Brodick, he joined the Officers Emergency Army Reserve in order to do something 'public spirited'. ⁴_____, the Officers Emergency Army Reserve paid him an ⁵_____ sum of money – around $40. With the encouragement of his wife Catherine, he decided to use this money to buy one work of art per year. Alexander had acquired an interest in avant-garde British art after purchasing his first piece in 1943 and visited the Tate and National Gallery ⁶_____. In a fashion that would be impossible today, Alexander wrote ⁷_____ to artists whose work he liked and asked them to send him a piece of their own choosing, for inclusion in an exhibition. Many famous artists ⁸_____ responded to Tom Alexander's direct and eloquent approach, often enjoying the idea of having works on Arran. The exhibit includes examples of correspondence Alexander had ⁹_____.

1 a) often   b) clearly   c) regularly
2 a) obviously   b) successfully   c) frequently
3 a) here   b) there   c) everywhere
4 a) To his surprise b) Surprised   c) For a surprise
5 a) per year   b) per month   c) annual
6 a) always   b) whenever possible c) impossibly
7 a) straight   b) immediately   c) directly
8 a) generously   b) often   c) used to
9 a) obviously   b) usually   c) with the artists

B Put the phrases in the correct order to make sentences. There may be more than one possible order.

1 I / just grab / if / at lunchtime / I'm in a hurry / quickly / a sandwich / to eat

2 generally / sit / too tired to talk / in front of the television / At night / my husband and I

3 to reduce the number / carefully plan / in English / I / always / of mistakes / anything I write

4 in front of / too much time / I / the computer / consistently / spend / Unfortunately

5 enjoyed each other's company / online / for a while / They met / and

6 about six months ago / painting / I / took up / to help me relax

7 when I left this morning / my things / I left / on the kitchen table

8 have more time / probably / I'll / when my exams are finished / to see my friends

9.3

A Find and correct the six mistakes in the conversations below.

1 **A:** Did you enjoy the concert?

   B: It was awesome — really, the best concert never!

2 **A:** How was the exhibit?

   B: I didn't really like it. I wasn't my mug of tea.

3 **A:** Did you enjoy the movie last night?

   B: No, it was a horror movie and if there's one thing I can't stand for it's violence. I walked out halfway through.

4 **A:** Did you like the book?

   B: Yes, it's a classic.

5 **A:** What did you think of the acting?

   B: Oh, I thought it was absolute incredible.

6 **A:** Was the restaurant good?

   B: No, the food and the service were terrible. It was total waste of money.

GRAMMAR

10.1 Inversion

Inversion is when we put an auxiliary verb before the subject of a clause.
I never saw such a wonderful sight again.

auxiliary + subject + clause
*Never again **did I see** such a wonderful sight.*

Inversion is common in written formal texts, but it is also used in informal spoken English to add dramatic effect or emphasis.

*No way **would I** ever **go** on a trip like that!* (There is no way/chance that I would ever go on a trip like that.)
*Not in a million years **would I agree** to cross Africa on a motorcycle!*

Negative Adverbials

In formal English, it is common to use inversion after negative adverbial expressions and restrictive words such as *only, never, hardly* and *little*.
***At no time** did they stop to think about the consequences.*
***Not until** the ambulance arrived did we realize how serious it was.*
***The meeting had hardly** begun when they started to argue.*
***Never before/Rarely/Seldom** had I seen such landscapes.*
***Little** did they realize how stupid they had been.*
***No sooner** had we heard that prices were increasing than we accepted the deal.*
***No longer** will we accept these poor conditions.*
***Only then** did they see what a fantastic chance they'd been offered.*

Only now that I am pregnant has he finally agreed to stop riding his motorcycle.
***Not only** did they leave their families for more than two months, **but** they **also** traveled to some of the most dangerous places on the planet.*
***Under no circumstances/On no account** should you leave the bike unattended.*
***They had scarcely left** the room when people started talking about them.*

Conditional Clauses

Inversion can be used with conditional sentences to make them sound more formal.
If we had known how much it was going to cost, we would never have chosen it.
***Had we known** how much it was going to cost, we would never have chosen it.*
If you were to have approached from the other direction, you might have seen the signs.
***Were you** to have approached from the other direction, you might have seen the signs.*

10.2 Comparative Structures

Modifiers

	Big Difference	Small Difference
Formal	considerably, infinitely, decidedly, significantly, nothing like, nowhere near	marginally
Neutral	much, far, a lot, a good deal	slightly, a bit, barely any
Informal	miles, way, loads	

*Their technology was **considerably** more advanced than ours.*
*We're **way** better than you at football!* (spoken English)

Modifiers with *as + as*

We also use modifiers to give more detail about *as* + adjective + *as* statements.

To show a big difference, use *nothing like*, or *nowhere near*.
*He's **nothing like** his brother.*
*She's **nowhere near** as good as me at chess.*

To show a small difference use *almost* or *nearly*.
*He's **almost as** neurotic **as** me.*

To emphasize no difference use *just* or *every bit*.
*I'm **just as** smart **as** you.*
*We're **every bit as** good **as** our competitors.*

Double Comparatives

Use double comparatives with *the* to say that one situation leads to another.
***The bigger** the lie, **the more** people believe it.*
***The more** you read, **the more** you'll learn.*

Progressive Comparatives

Use the progressive comparative form to say something is escalating. Use the comparative word twice (separated by *and*) to emphasize the adjective.
*House prices are getting **lower and lower**.*

10.3 Negotiating

Naming your Objectives
We want to sort this out as soon as possible. By the end of the day, we want to resolve this.

Exploring Positions
What do you have in mind? Can you go into more detail?

Making Conditional Offers
If you do … for me, I'll do … for you. What if we supported your idea?

Refusing an Offer
That would be difficult for me because of … I'm not sure I can do that because …

Accepting an Offer
Good. That sounds acceptable to me. Great. We've got a deal.

Following Up the Deal
Let me know if you have any questions. Get in touch if anything needs clarifying.

PRACTICE

10.1

A Match the sentence halves.

1 No sooner had I reached the car than
2 Little did I know what
3 At no time did she
4 Only after the movie had started
5 Scarcely had I walked in through the door
6 Had I suspected that he was untrustworthy,

a) admit that it was her own mistake.
b) I obviously wouldn't have given him the package.
c) I realized I had left my keys inside.
d) did I realize that I'd seen it before.
e) surprises they had in store for me.
f) when the phone rang.

B Find and correct the five mistakes in sentences 1–8.

1 Seldom I have seen him looking so miserable.
2 Not only have they decided to move cities, but they are leaving the U.S.A. altogether.
3 Under no circumstances you should leave the office.
4 We had known there would be a water shortage, we would have been more prepared.
5 Only later she realized her mistake.
6 Had he invited us, we would have been delighted to accept.
7 At no time did she consider giving up her campaign.
8 Were they to apologized more quickly, I might have forgiven them.

10.2

A Complete the sentences with a suitable word.

1 She's nothing _____ as intelligent as her father.
2 We are _____ lot stronger than them.
3 I'm _____ any bigger now than I was twelve years old.
4 This tastes a good _____ better than it did yesterday.
5 He's _____ bit as famous as his mother.
6 Some sprinters just get faster and _____ as they get older.
7 The closer you come, _____ more dangerous it'll be.
8 I'm nowhere _____ as ambitious as my brother.

B Put the words in bold in the correct order to complete the text.

Four of the Baldwin brothers, Alec, Daniel, William and Stephen are actors. While they are [1]**as famous nothing as** some acting families such as the Redgrave dynasty, their story is [2]**interesting bit as every**. When they were young, the boys were always getting into trouble. This continued into adulthood! The oldest of them, Alec, is [3]**the by talented far most**, and he landed acting roles in movies like *Beetlejuice* and *The Hunt for Red October*. Daniel, the second brother, followed suit, starring in *Hawaii Five-O* on TV. His acting career looked set to flourish, but his personal problems [4]**worse got worse and** and he ended up getting arrested after some strange behavior in a hotel. Brother number three, Billy, [5]**talented near as as nowhere** Alec, was initially a New York model, but [6]**than years little in more two** became a Hollywood actor, appearing in *Born on the Fourth of July* and *Flatliners*. The fourth brother, Stephen, is [7]**a closer deal good** to Alec in terms of acting talent, and he is best known for his performance in *The Usual Suspects*. While they all followed the same career path, the brothers are [8]**more famous considerably** for their personal lives than their acting. They still get into fights with one another and regularly appear in the tabloids.

1 _____ 5 _____
2 _____ 6 _____
3 _____ 7 _____
4 _____ 8 _____

10.3

A Two words in each sentence are in the wrong order. Correct them.

1 **A:** We want to sort out this as soon as possible.
  B: Can you go into detail more about your proposal?
2 **A:** By end the of the meeting, we want to have a concrete plan.
  B: What do you have mind in?
3 **A:** If you do for this me, I'll help you with the project.
  B: I'm sure not we can do that because of our contract.
4 **A:** Good, that sounds to acceptable me.
  B: Let know me if you have any questions.
5 **A:** Great! We've a got deal.
  B: Get in touch if anything clarifying needs.
6 **A:** What if supported we your idea for the pension scheme?
  B: OK, but the rest of the proposal would difficult be for us as it still means cutting jobs.

LESSON 1.2 PERSONALITY

1 A Find pairs of opposite adjectives in the box.

> considerate   circumspect   conservative   temperamental   impetuous
> easy-going   gregarious   selfish   liberal   introverted

B Match the adjectives in the box with statements 1–10.

1 She expects everyone to help her, but she never does anything for anyone else!

2 My boss is happy one minute and screaming the next.

3 The manager doesn't like new ideas; he wants to do everything the old way.

4 That child talks to very few people; he prefers to sit quietly and read or just think.

5 That girl is so relaxed that she never seems to worry about anything.

6 She's very cautious; she thinks carefully before she decides to do something.

7 She's tolerant and she wants her employees to be free to do what they want.

8 That man makes too many quick decisions without thinking about the consequences.

9 When he sees me, he always brings a gift and asks about my family.

10 She loves socializing; she goes to parties every night.

C Can you think of people (friends, famous people, fictional characters) who match the adjectives above?

LESSON 1.2 IDIOMS FOR PEOPLE

1 A Read sentences 1–6 and look at the pictures. How could you complete the idioms?

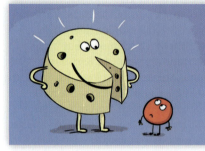

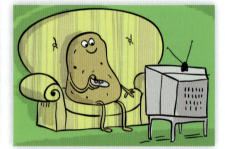

1 She has a lot of power. In that organization she's a ...

2 He must be the laziest person I've ever met. He's a total ...

3 She sometimes gets out of control. She's a bit of a ...

4 He ruined the company's reputation. He was a ...

5 She broke her arm and still refused to give up. She's a ...

6 He complains whenever we try to have fun. He's a bit of a ...

B Check your ideas. Match idioms a)–f) in bold with sentences 1–6 above.

a) **rotten apple**: one bad person who has a bad effect on all others in the group

b) **loose cannon**: an unpredictable person who may cause damage if he/she is not controlled

c) **couch potato**: a person who lives a sedentary lifestyle, never doing any exercise

d) **wet blanket**: a negative person who ruins other people's good times

e) **big cheese**: an important, influential person

f) **tough cookie**: someone who is strong enough to deal with difficult or violent situations

LESSON 2.1 METAPHORS

1 Underline the metaphors in sentences 1–12. Match the metaphors with the meanings in the boxes.

Intelligence as light

> a smart idea that comes suddenly intelligent
> was especially good at something not very intelligent

1 As a small child, Akiko was obviously bright.

2 Nico shone at math from an early age.

3 The solution came to me in a flash of inspiration.

4 Everyone thought I was dim, but I eventually passed all my exams.

Theories as buildings

> help prove developed basis
> fails because of a particular reason

5 We analyzed the findings and then constructed a theory.

6 Do you have any statistics to support this theory?

7 Your evidence is very weak; that's where your idea falls down.

8 The foundations of the argument aren't very strong.

Business as war

> began an intense series of actions aimed at
> merge together a big profit

9 We made a killing from his latest investment.

10 The marketing department launched an aggressive campaign to promote the product.

11 Our new ads are targeting eighteen-year-olds.

12 The two companies decided to join forces in 2009.

LESSON 2.2 OPINIONS

1 A Choose the correct alternatives to complete the phrases in bold.

1 If an opinion is one that is commonly agreed on, it is the *general/usual* **opinion**.

2 Sometimes it can be diplomatic to *keep/hold* **your opinions to yourself**.

3 If you have an idea about something that doesn't represent your company's view, it is your *individual/personal* **opinion**.

4 If someone has strong opinions and lets them be known, they might be considered *opinionated/idealistic*.

5 If you disagree with someone, you might have a *split/difference* **of opinion**.

6 If there are two sides to the argument, and equal numbers of people on both sides, then we can say **opinion is** *divided/half*.

7 If there is no right or wrong answer, then it is just a *matter/case* **of opinion**.

8 People have a right to make their own decisions about things. In other words, they are *entitled/open* **to their own opinion**.

B Complete the sentences with the correct answers from Exercise 1A.

1 Sandy suggested splitting the work between us, but if you want my _____ opinion, I think it's a bad idea.

2 I honestly couldn't stand him. I found him both _____ and arrogant.

3 I'm afraid I don't agree. We seem to have a _____ of opinion on this one.

4 We asked over a thousand people and found that opinion was _____, with nearly forty percent against the decision.

5 I don't see how you can say that. It's a _____ of opinion.

6 You can't tell him what to believe in. He's _____ to his own opinion.

7 I think in this instance it might be better to _____ our opinions to ourselves.

8 The _____ opinion seems to be that it would be a good idea to start now.

))) VOCABULARY BANK

LESSON 3.2 ADJECTIVES

1 A Match sentences 1–4 with photos A–D.

1 It's a vast, overpopulated metropolis.

2 It's a quaint, secluded village far from any big cities.

3 It's a scenic town with awe-inspiring mountain views.

4 It's a sprawling, ramshackle slum.

B Match meanings a)–h) with adjectives in sentences 1–4 above.

a) extremely large

b) extremely impressive in a way that makes you feel great respect

c) surrounded by views of beautiful countryside

d) spreading over a wide area in an untidy or unattractive way

e) unusual and attractive, especially in an old-fashioned way

f) in bad condition and in need of repair

g) very private and quiet

h) there are too many people in a place

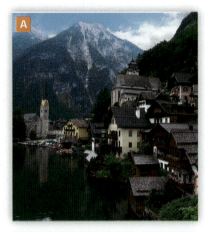
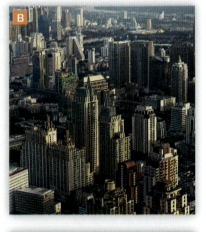

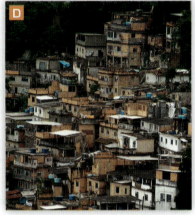

LESSON 3.2 PREFIXES

1 A Underline two prefixes in each sentence.

1 She was a supermodel when miniskirts first became fashionable.

2 Camping in sub-zero temperatures, the team soon learned to cooperate.

3 I became bilingual by interacting with French speakers from an early age.

4 I'm semi-retired now, but I outlasted many younger men in this business.

B Complete the second column of the table with the words in the box.

> below   small   half   more/more powerful/larger
> between/among   bigger/greater than something else

C Which words are described in definitions 1–8 below? Use prefixes from the table in Exercise 1B.

1 twice every month   *bimonthly*

2 a hero who has amazing powers

3 grow too big for some of your clothes

4 a secondary plot that isn't the main story

5 between or among nations

6 a circle cut in half

7 two people who founded a business together

8 a small bar, or drinks in a small fridge, in your hotel room

D Add more examples to the third column of the table.

Prefix	Meaning	Example Words
bi-	two	**bi**monthly, **bi**centenary
co-	joint	**co**-author, **co**-pilot
inter-		**inter**changeable, **inter**continental
mini-		**mini**cab, **mini**mize
out-		**out**sell, **out**play
semi-		**semi**-skimmed, **semi**colon
sub-		**sub**title, **sub**way
super-		**super**natural, **super**power

LESSON 4.1 CRIME COLLOCATIONS

1 A Complete the sentences with a preposition.

1 The men were released from prison and put _____ probation.

2 Hundreds of young fans went _____ the rampage through downtown.

3 A new law, introduced to reduce vandalism, comes _____ force next month.

4 He was given points on his license _____ speeding.

5 We agreed to help the police _____ their inquiries.

6 An investigation is being held _____ the causes of the accident.

7 The gang was arrested and held _____ custody.

8 Two teenagers were identified and charged _____ assault.

9 The man was described as a hardened criminal who posed a serious threat _____ the public.

10 Police fired tear gas _____ the protesters in an attempt to disperse the crowd.

B Underline phrases in Exercise 1A which match meanings a)–j) below.

a) comes into effect

b) asked to report to a probation officer at regular intervals rather than being sent to prison

c) may cause a risk to others

d) received a penalty which involves putting numbers on your driving license — when you reach a certain number, your licence is taken away from you for a period of time

e) took part in a class of violent, frenzied behavior

f) assist in a police investigation

g) officially accused by a court of deliberately causing harm to another person

h) legally confined by the police

i) released CS gas in a crowd (often used during riots)

j) the police are trying to discover what caused something

LESSON 4.2 SOCIAL ISSUES

1 A Match the social issues with pictures A–H.

1 white-collar crime

2 illiteracy

3 poverty

4 gender inequality

5 censorship

6 ageism

7 organized crime

8 antisocial behaviour

B Complete the sentences using the words/phrases above.

a) A definition of _____ is when people don't have enough money for their basic needs.

b) Due to _____, women often get paid less than men for doing the same job.

c) _____ is harmful to other people and shows that you do not care about other people.

d) _____ is a term for illegal activities, such as scams and fraud, carried out by businesspeople.

e) Because of _____, people are often prevented from speaking and writing the truth.

f) _____ means people cannot read or write, often because they could not get an education.

g) _____ refers to a coordinated group of criminals who engage in illegal activities to make money and gain power.

h) _____ comes from negative stereotypes about older people.

LESSON 5.1 IDIOMS: SECRETS

1 A Match the phrases in bold in sentences 1–5 with similar phrases in a)–e) below.

1 This is **classified information**.   *c*

2 She **divulged** a secret.

3 What I said is **between you and me**.

4 It's a **covert** operation.

5 She's behaving as if she **has something to hide**.

a) She **looks furtive**.

b) It's **hush-hush**, so don't tell anyone.

c) ~~These documents are~~ **confidential**.

d) She **blurted out** the secret.

e) This action is **top secret**.

B Match the phrases from Exercise 1A with pictures A–E.

C Which phrases in Exercise 1A are usually used in formal situations, e.g. government and business discussions/documents?

LESSON 5.2 MULTI-WORD VERBS

1 A Complete the sentences using the particles in the box.

on back over away around off up down

1 If you have a problem with your husband, you should talk it _____.

2 Things are looking _____: sales have improved and we've got some excellent new products.

3 Even though he was exhausted, he soldiered _____ and reached the top of the hill.

4 They killed _____ my proposal because it was too expensive.

5 Those children are too excited – they need to calm _____.

6 Please clean _____ your stuff – it's all over the floor!

7 She was well behaved for a few days but now she's slipped _____ to her old ways.

8 Those boys are always lounging _____ doing nothing!

B Think of ways to rephrase the ideas in the multi-word verbs above.

1 We can use 'discuss it' instead of 'talk it over'.

LESSON 6.1 PREPOSITIONAL PHRASES

1 A Match the prepositional phrases in bold with phrases a), b) or c).

1 The ship was hit by the typhoon and blown **off course**. Now it's lost.	**a)** too slow to keep up
2 I started the race OK, but soon realized I was **off the pace** and had to give up.	**b)** away from a scheduled path
3 You can't get power into a golf shot if you're **off balance**.	**c)** in an unsteady position

4 We are not investigating the president. He's **above suspicion**.	**a)** the most important thing is
5 We never do anything illegal. Everything is **above board**.	**b)** assumed to be innocent
6 The planes are fast and comfortable, but **above all** they're safe.	**c)** legal

7 The manager said that, aged sixty-five, I was **over the hill** so he fired me.	**a)** too much
8 When I won first prize I was **over the moon**. I celebrated a lot.	**b)** past my best (too old now)
9 Her celebrations were excessive. They were **over the top**.	**c)** extremely happy

10 I didn't go to work because I was feeling **under the weather**.	**a)** thinking (probably wrongly)
11 Oh, do I have to cook dinner? I was **under the impression** you'd do it!	**b)** obliged by the law to tell the truth in court
12 When you testify in court, remember you are **under oath** and cannot lie.	**c)** a little bit sick

B How could speaker B respond to what speaker A says? Write down your ideas.

1 **A:** I was feeling under the weather yesterday.
 B: _____

2 **A:** I'm absolutely over the moon!
 B: _____

3 **A:** I was under the impression you were happy at work.
 B: _____

4 **A:** Do you think I'm over the hill? I'm only thirty-five.
 B: _____

5 **A:** I hear you resigned. Isn't that a bit over the top?
 B: _____

6 **A:** I'm above suspicion in this investigation, aren't I?
 B: _____

LESSON 6.2 LANGUAGE

1 A Complete the idioms in bold with the words in the box.

good	get	least	catch	cross	
tail	run	stick	word	shop	

1 Marisa was talking so fast I just **couldn't get a _____ in edgeways.**

2 Come on! Try to **_____ to the point.**

3 After ten minutes we realized that we were **talking at _____ purposes.**

4 I'm sorry. **I didn't _____ what you said.**

5 That kind of behavior is not acceptable. It sounds to me like she **needs a _____ talking to.**

6 I'm sorry. We've been **talking _____** all night. Let's stop talking about work now.

7 Could you **_____ that by me one more time?**

8 **I couldn't make head or _____** of what she was saying.

9 That's **an understatement to say the _____.**

10 Unfortunately, I think he **got the wrong end of the _____.**

B Which idioms in Exercise 1A would you use in situations a)—j)?

a) Someone has completely misunderstood what you have said (so they do something different).

b) You can't understand anything that someone is trying to say.

c) You can't hear what the other person is saying.

d) Someone is talking so much it's hard for you to say anything.

e) Somebody needs to be reprimanded for something.

f) You need someone to repeat what they said.

g) There has been a misunderstanding on both sides.

h) Someone should say what they want to say (instead of talking around the subject).

i) You think a situation is more serious than someone else suggested.

j) Someone talks about their work.

LESSON 7.1 SUFFIXES

1 A Put the words in the box in the correct column of the table according to their suffix. One word can be used in **two** columns.

> censor**ship**   exorbit**ant**   national**ist**   gover**nor**   respons**ive**   sen**ility**   fabric**ate**
> likeli**hood**   person**able**   kindli**ness**   ident**ical**   repet**ition**   sarc**asm**   glor**ify**
> trouble**some**   clas**sy**   expert**ise**   remi**ssion**   anx**ious**   hero**ic**

Verb	Noun	Adjective

B Complete the sentences using the words in parenthesis and a suitable suffix.

1 I _____, but I really don't know how to help. (sympathy)

2 Heat therapy has been proven to be highly _____ in cases of this kind. (effect)

3 I know it's an _____, but could I possibly use your bathroom? (impose)

4 I'm not sure that such _____ helps the company's image much. (frivolous)

5 He was in the _____ position of not having to work for a living. (envy)

6 Gemma felt so nervous during the interview that her answers were a little _____. (hesitate)

7 A delay of two hours failed to dampen their _____. (enthusiastic)

8 I found his attitude really _____. (chauvinist)

LESSON 7.2 IDIOMS: RELAXING

1 A Match the idioms in bold with pictures A–F.

1 I'm exhausted: I've been **burning the candle at both ends**.

2 I'm going to **while away** my old age reading and swimming.

3 We're just **hanging out** together.

4 I'm going to **chill out** for a few weeks.

5 I've been **working all hours** to finish my castle.

6 We were **burning the midnight oil** to finish it on time.

B Answer the questions.

1 Which idiom means you've been doing too much late at night and early in the morning?

2 Which two idioms refer to relaxing?

3 Which idiom means 'stand or sit around while not doing anything'?

4 What do you think the other two idioms mean? Do they have a negative or positive connotation?

C Write short answers to questions 1–6.

1 Where are the best places to hang out in your town/city?

2 How do you plan to while away your old age?

3 When did you last chill out?

4 As a student, do/did you ever burn the candle at both ends?

5 When might you need to work all hours to get a job or task done?

6 When is the last time you burned the midnight oil? What were you doing?

LESSON 8.1 PROVERBS

1 A Match the phrases in bold in sentences 1–10 with meanings a)–j) below.

1 We were so poor that we accepted the offer to live there. **Beggars can't be choosers!**

2 Ah, here's the report — two weeks late! **Better late than never**, I suppose.

3 It looks as if our team is going to win, but **don't count your chickens**.

4 He wasn't sure about starting up the business, but I told him to **strike while the iron's hot.**

5 Do what the teachers tell you, son, and **keep your nose clean.**

6 Working late again? **No rest for the wicked.**

7 It doesn't matter if you aren't at the top of the class, but always **put your best foot forward.**

8 Give your little brother some of your drink! **Share and share alike.**

9 I start working at 5:00 a.m. My mother always told me that **the early bird catches the worm.**

10 The government was brought down by journalists and writers, not soldiers. **The pen is mightier than the sword.**

a) Do everything you can to be successful.

b) If you start (work) early, you will have more opportunities.

c) Take decisive action while the conditions are right.

d) Don't get too confident of something until you're absolutely sure it's going to happen.

e) Bad people have to work constantly and aren't allowed to stop and rest. (We say this as a joke to a busy/overworked person.)

f) If you don't have much (money, opportunity, etc.), be grateful for anything you're offered.

g) Be generous to other people with your things (food, possessions, etc.).

h) Good writing is more effective than violence. (It's better to use your intelligence rather than violence to beat an opponent.)

i) Be good and don't get into trouble.

j) Even if you can't do something on time, do it anyway. This is better than not doing it at all.

B Which of the proverbs and sayings have equivalents in your language?

C Think of situations in which you might use the proverbs and sayings above.

You might say 'share and share alike' to a young child if he/she isn't sharing.

You might say 'strike while the iron's hot' to a business associate if you see a good opportunity.

LESSON 8.2 MEMORIES

1 A Underline expressions in the conversations below which relate to memory or memories.

1 A: Is there anything else you can think of that would help?

 B: No, nothing springs to mind.

2 A: I traveled across South America on horseback.

 B: Wow, that's a once-in-a-lifetime experience.

3 A: I've had such a wonderful day.

 B: Yes, it's been a real day to remember.

4 A: Can you remember that woman's name?

 B: No, but it's on the tip of my tongue.

5 A: Where's your bag?

 B: I've left it somewhere, and I can't for the life of me remember where.

6 A: There you are! Why didn't you call me like I asked you to?

 B: I'm so sorry. I clean forgot.

7 A: Do you remember when we studied history together?

 B: That's going back.

8 A: Do you remember when we used to study together during vacation?

 B: Of course. I remember it like it was yesterday.

9 A: Sorry, I've had a complete memory lapse and I can't remember your name.

 B: It's Lisbeth. Elisabeth Alexander.

10 A: Can you remember her phone number?

 B: Yes, it's etched on my memory.

B Which expressions refer to remembering or forgetting? Which refer to past experiences?

C Find expressions in conversations 1–10 which relate to meanings a)–e) below. There may be more than one possible answer.

a) I remember it very well.

b) It was an experience worth remembering.

c) I can't quite remember at the moment.

d) I completely forgot.

e) It was a long time ago.

LESSON 9.1 THREE-PART MULTI-WORD VERBS

1 A Find the three-part multi-word verbs in headlines 1–10. Use them to complete definitions a)–j).

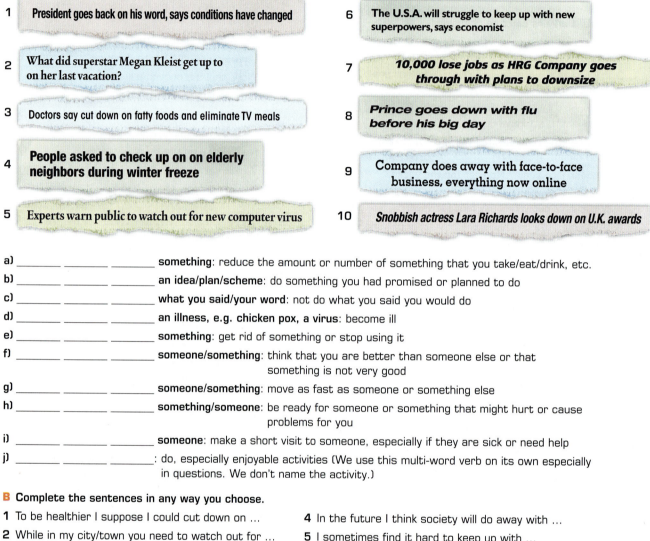

1 President goes back on his word, says conditions have changed

2 What did superstar Megan Kleist get up to on her last vacation?

3 Doctors say cut down on fatty foods and eliminate TV meals

4 People asked to check up on on elderly neighbors during winter freeze

5 Experts warn public to watch out for new computer virus

6 The U.S.A. will struggle to keep up with new superpowers, says economist

7 10,000 lose jobs as HRG Company goes through with plans to downsize

8 Prince goes down with flu before his big day

9 Company does away with face-to-face business, everything now online

10 Snobbish actress Lara Richards looks down on U.K. awards

a) _____ _____ _____ **something**: reduce the amount or number of something that you take/eat/drink, etc.

b) _____ _____ _____ **an idea/plan/scheme**: do something you had promised or planned to do

c) _____ _____ _____ **what you said/your word**: not do what you said you would do

d) _____ _____ _____ **an illness, e.g. chicken pox, a virus**: become ill

e) _____ _____ _____ **something**: get rid of something or stop using it

f) _____ _____ _____ **someone/something**: think that you are better than someone else or that something is not very good

g) _____ _____ _____ **someone/something**: move as fast as someone or something else

h) _____ _____ _____ **something/someone**: be ready for someone or something that might hurt or cause problems for you

i) _____ _____ _____ **someone**: make a short visit to someone, especially if they are sick or need help

j) _____ _____ _____ : do, especially enjoyable activities (We use this multi-word verb on its own especially in questions. We don't name the activity.)

B Complete the sentences in any way you choose.

1 To be healthier I suppose I could cut down on …

2 While in my city/town you need to watch out for …

3 I would never look down on …

4 In the future I think society will do away with …

5 I sometimes find it hard to keep up with …

6 Someone who started to do something interesting recently is …

LESSON 9.2 COLLOCATIONS WITH IDEAS

1 Look at the phrases and definitions below. Use phrases a)–f) to complete sentences 1–6.

a) **get the wrong idea about something**: misunderstand a situation

b) **(not) have the faintest idea about something**: have no understanding of something

c) **(be) full of bright ideas**: have a lot of good ideas

d) **(be) someone's idea of a joke**: someone thinks this is funny

e) **have an idea of/about something**: be fairly certain about something, but not completely certain

f) **have a clear idea about something**: have a good understanding of what you want

1 I think I _____ who took the money, but I can't prove it.

2 You mustn't _____ about Dan and Helen — they're just friends.

3 Is this _____? Because I don't think it's very funny!

4 They seem a bit confused. They don't seem to have _____ of what they want.

5 The children were _____ for how they could spend the afternoon.

6 I'm sorry but I _____ what you're talking about.

LESSON 10.1 SYNONYMS

1 A Circle the word in each list that is not a possible synonym.

1 impure / unadulterated / natural / genuine

2 shun / ignore / ostracize / welcome

3 guess / estimate / assume / hypothetical

4 argue / squabble / admit / dispute

5 run / stroll / meander / saunter

6 lightweight / cumbersome / awkward / heavy

7 considerable / extensive / minimal / substantial

8 sincere / dishonest / straightforward / unambiguous

B Choose the correct alternatives.

1 I have to *admit/dispute* I was very surprised by the results.

2 We took a *stroll/meander* through the deserted streets of the old town.

3 The porter carried my bags, which were rather *cumbersome/awkward*.

4 I trusted him immediately. His manner was very *straightforward/dishonest* .

5 We decided that the best policy would be to *ostracize/ignore* what was happening altogether.

6 We have to *estimate/assume* that they reviewed all the information available.

LESSON 10.2 AMBITION

1 A Look at the cartoon story. Use the words in the box to complete the captions.

lifetime   big   off   heart   stroke   desire   hogging   wonder

Jodie **had a burning** _____ to be famous.

From a very young age, she **set her** _____ **on** becoming a singer.

At school she was constantly _____ **the limelight.**

She practiced every day, and everyone knew she would eventually **hit the** _____ **time**.

One day she had **a** _____ **of luck:** a talent agent came to her town and saw her perform.

When he signed her up, it looked as if all her hard work had **paid** _____ .

She was an instant success but, not wanting to be **a one-hit** _____ , she kept developing.

Now she's **a legend in her** _____ , but she still goes home to visit her friends and family.

B Cover the captions and retell the story. Try to use the completed phrases in bold.

LESSON 1.2

7 B Check your profile. Do you agree with the description?

MBTI PROFILES		
ESTJ	**The Overseer**	responsible, logical, norm-following hard workers. You enjoy being the person in charge and often make good supervisors.
ESTP	**The Persuader**	action-loving, "here and now" realists with excellent people skills. You don't always agree with rules and regulations, but are good at solving problems.
ESFJ	**The Supporter**	social butterflies that value relationships, supporting and nurturing others. You are dutiful and have a deep concern for others. You often end up as caretakers.
ESFP	**The Entertainer**	cooperative, "here and now" people-persons that enjoy excitement and love new adventures. You like to be the center of attention and hate being alone.
ESTJ	**The Chief**	strategic, organized natural leaders. You are able to understand complicated organizational situations and are quick to develop intelligent solutions.
ENTP	**The Originator**	logical, innovative, curious and inventive. You can always find ways to improve things and are good fun to be with.
ENFJ	**The Mentor**	warm, supportive and encouraging. You tend to focus on others and have excellent people skills. Good at language skills, you do well in leadership roles.
ENFP	**The Advocate**	introspective, values-oriented, inspiring, social and extremely expressive. You are natural advocates for things you feel to be important.
ISTJ	**The Examiner**	responsible, loyal and hardworking. You have an acute sense of right and wrong and work hard at preserving established norms and traditions.
ISTP	**The Craftsman**	adventurous and independent. You like to figure out how things work and have great mechanical and technical skills. You are adaptable and spontaneous, and thrive on new and exciting situations.
INTJ	**The Strategist**	introspective, analytical, determined people with natural leadership ability. You are a perfectionist, expecting a lot from both yourself and others.
INFJ	**The Confidant**	introspective, caring, sensitive, gentle and complex people that strive for peace and derive satisfaction from helping others.
ISFJ	**The Defender**	traditional, loyal, quiet and kind. You are sensitive to other people's needs because you are very observant and pay attention to detail. You do not seek positions of authority.
ISFP	**The Artist**	artistic, creative, loyal, independent and sensitive. You have a keen appreciation of beauty, and are easy to get along with.
INTP	**The Engineer**	logical, individualistic, reserved and very curious individuals. You focus on ideas, theories and the explanation of how things work.
INFP	**The Dreamer**	introspective, private, creative and highly idealistic individuals that want to do good in the world. You often have a talent for language and writing.

LESSON 1.3

7 A Work in pairs. Describe and discuss the portraits below. Use the following questions to help you.

- What can you say about the person's job or personality from the picture?
- How do you think he/she is feeling? Why do you think this might be?

LESSON 2.1

Student B

9 A Read the paragraph below and underline four metaphors related to time and money. Match them with meanings 1–4.

"Stuck in a stressful job, I was living on borrowed time. I ate badly and was constantly sick. Whenever I tried to relax, I found myself thinking about work. Even on weekends, I felt as if my boss was tapping me on the shoulder, saying, "You're wasting precious time!" One Sunday, I visited my grandfather. I said, "I know I should put aside some time for myself, but I just can't afford to spend time relaxing. I'll lose my job." He said, "No. You can't afford not to. If you go on like this, you'll lose your mind. Which is worse?"

1 keep time free

2 using time badly (not doing anything with your time)

3 don't have time to do something

4 survive after you would expect to be dead

B Read your paragraph to your partner twice. Which metaphors did he/she notice? Explain the meaning of the four metaphors to your partner.

LESSON 2.3

7 C Read the text to find out what really happened. Do you think the bosses did the right thing?

Case 1 The boss organized a day of training in the new management system for all assistants. The event was held in a nice hotel, with a gourmet dinner and free drinks afterwards. The CEO explained to all assistants the importance of the new system and how it would make everyone's lives easier eventually.

Case 2 The boss collected all of the negative comments online and printed them out. Then she had a meeting with the employee, inviting him to air his complaints and suggest solutions. The man was so embarrassed and surprised that his boss took his complaints seriously and really listened (she even made a procedural change suggested by him) that he stopped posting criticism and abandoned his blog.

Case 3 The boss wrote a memo to all employees, saying exactly what was and was not allowed to be charged as expenses. Without naming the woman, he included many of the items that she had been charging the company for (clothes, tickets to the theater, etc.). He knew the employee would recognize that she had been caught. The boss also explained that any corporate entertaining needed to be cleared with him before it happened.

LESSON 5.1

9 A This is how the story continued.

It was a small wooden box, which her mother had kept hidden in the back of her closet. Madge lifted the lid gently and peered inside. The moment she saw them, she recognized his handwriting. At the bottom of the box, lying unopened after all those years, were dozens of letters from the man she had wanted to marry.

LESSON 6.2

8 A Student B

The English Village

At the Happy English Village in Taoyuan, Taiwan, children arrive at the end of their normal school day to spend time speaking English and having fun. The village has themed rooms (a store, restaurant, airport, coffee shop, cookery room and dance studio). Children work in groups of twelve with volunteer foreign teachers.

LESSON 10.3

8 B Read your role. Think about your answers to questions 1–3 below.

Group A

You are the school administrators.

- Your budget is $800 (for renting movies, buying food and paying staff for overtime).
- You think students should pay $5 per day (two movies).
- You want to serve snacks only.
- You think the festival should last three days.
- You think the school administrators should choose the movies because you need to make sure they are appropriate.
- You want the student Film Festival Committee to develop a web page about the festival to go on the school's website. You think this will attract students to the school.
- You want the festival to take place next semester so there is time to arrange it properly.

1 What is your main objective in this negotiation?

2 What do you think the other team's objective is?

3 What are your other objectives? Which of these are quite important? Which are not so important?

LESSON 5.2

1 B Read the myths below and answer the questions.

1 What is the myth?
2 Which myths were disproved by experiments?
3 What is the truth about the myth?

5 Pick up your food within five seconds of dropping it and it'll be safe to eat

Microbiologists at Clemson University, South Carolina, tested this. They found that bacteria, like salmonella, can survive for weeks on carpet, wood and tiles, and contaminates food within seconds of contact.

6 Driving is safe with a hands-free device

This would seem to be intuitively true. Surely using a hands-free device is just like having a conversation with someone in the car? Research tells a different story. It's even worse for your concentration than alcohol, according to the Transportation Research Laboratory. They tested drivers with or without alcohol, as well as with cell phones and hands-free devices. Afterwards, the drivers answered the experimenter's questions. Driving performance under the influence of alcohol was significantly worse than normal driving, yet better than driving with a phone – even one with a hands-free kit.

7 Goldfish have short memories

A fifteen-year-old schoolboy has debunked this myth. Rory Stokes placed a piece of Lego (a small, plastic, colored block) in the water of a fish tank at feeding time. Thirty seconds after placing it, he sprinkled food around it, so that the fish would start to associate it with eating. At the beginning of Stokes' experiment, it took the fish over a minute to swim over to the Lego. After three weeks, it took under five seconds. In the second part of the experiment, Rory removed the Lego from the feeding process and then reintroduced it after six days. It took the fish just 4.4 seconds to associate it with food again.

8 Owls have the ability to rotate their heads through 360 degrees

A bit of simple science allows us to disprove this myth. An owl's neck has fourteen vertebrae, which is twice as many as humans. Consequently, an owl can turn its head up to 270 degrees. In other words, they could start by facing 12 o'clock and turn their heads in a clockwise direction until facing roughly 9 o'clock. – impressive, but not 360 degrees.

LESSON 5.2

5 A You are going to debunk a myth of your choice. It can be about a person, a profession, a country or a belief. Here are three ideas. Complete the title and notes on page 60.

1 We only use ten percent of our brains

This myth is often cited by people who want us to believe that we can learn to master paranormal activities such as telepathy. Brain imaging techniques, e.g. PET scans, disprove this myth. They clearly show us using the whole brain on a daily basis.

2 Sushi means raw fish

It does not mean raw fish. The name refers to the rice used in the dish. Sushi is rice made with rice vinegar, salt and sugar dressing. Traditionally, it's topped with fish, fish eggs, or a variety of vegetables.

3 Bulls are angered by the color red

Bulls do not get angry because of the color red. Professional matadors traditionally use a red cape, but it wouldn't make any difference if the cape was a different color because cattle are color-blind. It is the movement of the cape that angers the bull, not the color.

LESSON 7.1

1 D Read part two of the story and check your answers to Exercise 1C on page 80.

An investigation was immediately launched into his disappearance. Five days later, John Darwin was arrested on suspicion of fraud and deception. A photograph, published in a tabloid newspaper, revealed that Mr. and Mrs. Darwin had been seen together in Panama and had bought a house there together.

It turned out that Mr. Darwin had planned the whole disappearance from the beginning after finding himself in financial difficulty. On the day of the 'disappearance', Mr. Darwin had in fact pushed his kayak out to sea and later returned home to his wife. What he did then was spend the next few years hiding inside the house and rarely leaving. When visitors came, Mr. Darwin supposedly hid in the neighboring house, escaping though a hole he had made in the wall of an upstairs bedroom. He changed his appearance, spent a lot of time on the internet and applied for a passport under a false name.

Mr. and Mrs. Darwin traveled to Greece and then to Panama, looking for opportunities to start a new life together, while Mrs. Darwin kept up the pretence that her husband was dead to her friends, colleagues and two sons. When Mrs. Darwin received the life insurance money taken out in her husband's name, Mr. Darwin moved to Panama, where he bought an apartment and waited for his wife to join him. When she finally managed to emigrate, they bought a $250,000 tropical estate and planned to start a hotel business selling canoe trips. John Darwin finally returned to the U.K. claiming that he was missing his sons and was fed up with living the deception.

In the meantime, in the U.K. several people had become suspicious. It was a colleague of Anne Darwin's who eventually put the pieces of the puzzle together. She had overheard a conversation which Anne Darwin had had with her husband on the telephone before leaving for Panama. She then typed the names 'Anne+John+Darwin+Panama' into Google images and found the photograph, which she later sent to the media and to the police.

John and Anne Darwin were both sentenced and served time in prison for fraud and deception. Their ill-gained assets (money and property) were taken from them and their sons refused to talk to either of them, claiming that they had been victims of the scam and they no longer wished to have any contact with their parents.

John and Anne Darwin were both released from prison, and later divorced. It is thought that Anne felt betrayed by her husband, and has since tried to rebuild her life in secret, without him.

LESSON 4.4

7 Student B: read the notes about a famous forger.

WHO: Tom Keating, art restorer and painter (1917–1984)

WHAT: Painted technically amazing forgeries. Used a London art dealer to sell the works in U.K. auction houses in the late 1950s and 1960s.

WHY: Art critics didn't appreciate his work. He hated the system – it enriched art dealers and left painters poor.

HOW HE WAS CAUGHT: In the 1970s, a set of works 'by Samuel Palmer' aroused suspicion. Auctioneers were uncertain of the paintings' provenance. Keating admitted he'd forged them. He claimed to have made over 2,000 forgeries by 100 painters.

LESSON 10.3

8 B Read your role. Think about your answers to questions 1–3 below.

Group B

You are the student Film Festival Committee.

- You think the event will cost $1,500 (for renting films and buying food).
- You think students should pay $10 and be allowed to attend all the movies (two per day).
- You want to serve international food to match the films (e.g. during a Brazilian film, you will serve Brazilian food).
- You think the festival should last five days (Monday–Friday).
- You think the student Film Festival Committee should choose the movies because you know what students like.
- You want to create a promotional leaflet to hand out to all students.
- You want the festival to take place this term because everyone is enthusiastic about it.

1 What is your main objective in this negotiation?

2 What do you think the other team's objective is?

3 What are your other objectives? Which of these are quite important? Which are not so important?

LESSON 3.5

4 B

1 lead in a pencil

2 a chick in an egg

3 Are you asleep?

4 a hole

LESSON 6.2

8 A Student C

Mobile English

With the Millee Language Program, children in rural areas in India are learning English on their cell phones. In remote villages, good English teachers are hard to come by, but cell phones are reasonably cheap. The children learn vocabulary by playing games on their phones. They can then take the phones wherever they go, so that even the fields where they work can become a classroom.

LESSON 8.1

9 A When would you use the proverbs below? Match proverbs 7–12 with situations g)–l). Do you have equivalents in your language?

7 There's no place like home.

8 Nothing ventured, nothing gained.

9 Don't judge a book by its cover.

10 Actions speak louder than words.

11 Practice makes perfect.

12 Absence makes the heart grow fonder.

g) I love to travel but I feel happier when I return.

h) I haven't seen Miroslav for six months and I really miss him!

i) He looks ordinary but actually, he's a genius!

j) She's a great tennis player because she works at it six hours a day.

k) He doesn't talk much but he gets the job done.

l) If you don't take any risks, you'll never know what you can achieve.

LESSON 8.2

7 A Student B: listen to Student A's sentences and choose the correct responses a)–e).

a) It's a Cajun dish with shrimp. Try some!

b) Yes, I have. I went there to see my brother who was living in Beijing.

c) Neither do I. Why don't you let Johnnie have a look? He's good with technology.

d) Do you? I can't stand them.

e) I think so. They've just got one more thing to do.

B Look at your sentences. Delete any words you can leave out due to ellipsis. Read your sentences to Student A. Student A will choose a response.

1 Have you been in the job for long?

2 Are you sure she's coming today?

3 Someone called you earlier and left a message.

4 Do you want tea or coffee?

5 Did you see the movie last night?

LESSON 4.4

Tom Keating: Part 2

WHAT HAPPENED NEXT: Keating admitted his guilt and went to court. The trial stopped as Keating was ill, and he avoided a prison sentence.

HOW GUILT WAS PROVED: Keating left 'time bombs' (evidence) in the paintings. For example, he wrote in white paint on the canvas before painting the picture, so the writing could be detected under x-ray. He sometimes added anachronisms to paintings or put a layer of glycerine under the paint; when the painting was cleaned, the cleaning chemicals interacted with the glycerine to destroy the work.

CONSEQUENCES: Keating later recovered and hosted a TV program, *Tom Keating on Painters*. In the program he revealed the techniques of the old masters like Rembrandt and van Gogh.

VALUE OF WORK: After Keating's death in 1984, the value of his work rose to $12,000-$15,000.

LESSON 6.4

8 Group B

Growth of cloning. Cloning is already with us, but it isn't just for rich folks who want clones of their favorite pets. Cloning will provide one solution as we seek to protect endangered animals from extinction. To ensure that these animals never die out, we will develop special labs to preserve species.

Hi-tech fitness clothing. Exercise clothing will contain monitors that give you real-time information about your state of health. This information will include your heart rate, the number of steps you take, your running speed, and how much liquid you are losing when you sweat. The clothes will automatically transfer data to your other exercise gear of the same brand.

Smart virtual personal assistants. A smart app will monitor your email, calendar and texting behavior and make suggestions. So if you are planning to meet a friend, the app geolocates you both and provides a display of cafés and restaurants in the area and even helps you reserve a table.

LESSON 9.1

9 A You are an art dealer. Read about your clients and look at the sculptures below. Decide which sculpture to recommend to each company.

1 Icontech.biz is an internet start-up run by twenty-one-year-old twins. There is no one over thirty in the company and everyone wears jeans and shorts. The company recently relocated to a stylish one-story office. The owners want a dramatic sculpture for the roof. It must fit their company motto: Live for Now.

2 Daniels & Stone is a conservative, traditional law firm. The new boss wants a more exciting image for the firm, but doesn't want to offend old clients. He is looking for a sculpture to go outside the main entrance of the building.

3 Green Tuesdays Ltd. is a company that sells organic food. It is run by fifteen ex-hippies who live in a multi-colored bus. In two years, the company has expanded by 180 percent and now has a stunning new office building surrounded by trees and hills. The owners want a striking sculpture to go in reception.

LESSON 10.2

7 C Check your answers for Exercise 7B on page 120.

1 a scrap (of attention) (n) → a very small amount
2 dazzled (adj) → amazed
3 ascension (n) → rise
4 clamor (n) → continuous loud noise
5 geriatric (adj) → old (person)
6 a beacon (of hope) (n) → a shining light

LESSON 4.4

7 Student A: read the notes about a famous forger.

WHO: Han van Meegeren, Dutch painter (1889–1947)

WHAT: Painted forgeries. Studied old masters' techniques, mixed own paints using old formulas, even used badger hair paintbrushes, common in the 17th century.

WHY: Art critics said his work was unoriginal. He rebelled against the system.

HOW HE WAS CAUGHT: In 1945, after World War II, a Vermeer painting was discovered among enemy possessions. It was traced back to van Meegeren. He was charged with treason for selling Dutch property to an enemy official, and faced a possible death penalty. On trial, van Meegeren said he had painted the 'Vermeer' himself.

LESSON 8.2

7 A Student A: look at your sentences. Delete any words you can leave out due to ellipsis. Read your sentences to Student B. Student B will choose a response.

1 Have you ever been to China?
2 I don't know why I can't get this camera to work.
3 I love olives.
4 Have they nearly finished?
5 What's that? It looks wonderful.

B Listen to Student B's sentences and choose the correct responses a)–e).

a) Yes, she said she'd be at the airport at 2p.m.
b) No, I wanted to but I fell asleep!
c) No, I haven't. I've only recently started.
d) Did they? Do you know who it was?
e) No thanks. I've just had one.

LESSON 9.1

10 B

preposition	meaning	examples
up	*increase or improve*	speed up, brighten up, jazz up
on	*continue*	go on, carry on, keen on
off	*remove, cancel or end something*	pension off, cry off, call off, switch off
out	*be in the open*	find out, speak out, stand out, call ot
down	*decrease or reduce*	slow down, narrow down, crack down,
away	*removal or disposal*	put away, blow away, take away
back	*return (to the past)*	brink back, think back, look back, cast (your mind) back
around	*with no direction or aim*	mess around, stand around, hang around
over	*think or talk about*	mull over, pore over, look over, think over

)) COMMUNICATION BANK

LESSON 4.4

Han van Meegeren: Part 2

WHAT HAPPENED NEXT: The court made him do another forgery while he was in prison. He painted *Jesus among the Doctors*. The court asked a group of international art experts to study van Meegeren's work.

HOW GUILT WAS PROVED: Experts noticed the chemical Albertol in the paint. Albertol – only produced in 20th century – was unavailable in Vermeer's time.

CONSEQUENCES: The court dropped the charges of treason and sentenced van Meegeren to a year in prison for producing forgeries. He died of a heart attack before he could serve his time.

VALUE OF WORK: The value of van Meegeren's own paintings rose to $30,000 after he was exposed as a forger.

LESSON 6.4

8 Group A

Smart washing machines. No more manual settings necessary! Smart washing machines will not only be able to recognize the textiles and fabrics you put in there; they will also have sensors to detect the amount and type of dirt on the clothes. They will then program themselves to do the washing.

Home 3D printing. 3D printers are already being developed for medical procedures such as manufacturing new body parts, but now they are making their way into our everyday lives. They will be used to make copies of household objects such as kitchen utensils, vases, even artwork.

Growth of eco-homes. Rainwater harvesting, sewage recycling, green roofs, renewable energy ... these are all features of eco-homes that will revolutionize domestic life. Eco-homes will become the norm in many countries, combining high- and low-tech solutions to help save the planet one house at a time.

LESSON 9.2

12 Exhibit notes

First impression: nice ideas, but not very dramatic visually

Simple layout – fifteen recent British inventions laid around the gallery with short information boards on each

Some of the ideas are interesting, e.g. a hypersonic alarm which only teenagers can hear (called a mosquito) – used to stop teenagers loitering where they aren't wanted

Some not so interesting or original, e.g. electric bicycle, baby bottle with automatic warmer

Information about the story behind the invention – OK – interesting to note that some ideas have been inspired by young people (one child was just eight when he suggested the idea to his father)

Overall – disappointed – it only takes about ten minutes to go around the whole exhibit – feeling a little flat, rather than inspired

Highlight – section where people have written their own ideas of problems which could be solved with new ideas/solutions – some really funny, new ideas

LESSON 7.1

7 A Read the rules of the game.

THE RULES

Where are you?

You're on one of the Admiralty Islands, a group of small islands off the north coast of Papua New Guinea in the Pacific Ocean. You were able to swim there, with a few belongings, after your plane crashed en route to a conference in Australia.

What do you have with you?

A penknife, a pen and some paper, a small mirror, a bottle of alcohol and water-resistant tape. Plus, up to five items of your own choice. None of them would, in themselves, allow you to escape (so no inflatable boats, sadly). But used together, and perhaps with a few items from the island, you can hatch an escape plan.

What have you tried so far?

Building a raft, but you quickly realized it would not get you to safety on Papua New Guinea 300 kilometers away before you ran out of the fruit you'd stashed for the journey. Shining a mirror towards the boats that pass on the horizon has failed, too.

Unit 1 Recording S1.1

1 John's not in the office. He might be having lunch.
2 I'm fed up. We've been waiting for an hour!
3 She owns a small house by the river.
4 Can you be quiet? I'm trying to work.
5 The letter arrived today. She'd been expecting the news since Monday.
6 That chicken dish tasted great.
7 Who do these keys belong to?
8 By next September, we'll have been living here for twenty-five years.
9 I'm working on a project at the moment.
10 My partner was making dinner when I got home so I helped.

Unit 1 Recording S1.3

1 He'll spend hours on the computer.
2 They would complain all the time.
3 She'll disagree with everything you say.

Unit 1 Recording S1.6

M = Mariella   J = John

M: For any of you who work surrounded by other people, you'll know that one of the biggest stressors in the world of work is not the work itself, it's the people we work with. There are the people who need to be noisy when you're trying to be quiet, there are the ones who "shush" you when you're telling a really good story, there are the sweeping generalizers, and the detail-obsessed nit-pickers, the obsessive planners, and the last-minute deadline junkies. You, of course, are perfect. These days there are tests for just about everything, and personality is no exception. If you've ever been intrigued to define your type, or sat down and completed a questionnaire at work, then it's likely you'll have come across the Myers-Briggs Type Indicator, known to its fans as the MBTI. Myers-Briggs is the world's most widely used personality questionnaire. From Beijing to Boston to Bournemouth, office workers, college students, and people who are simply curious to find out more about themselves, answer a series of questions to determine which of sixteen different personality types they fall into.

J: How did you feel completing the questionnaire that you completed, just yesterday I think?

M: Em, I found it not particularly challenging. Maybe I didn't think about it as much as one ought to.

...

M: The preferences are split into four sections, so prepare yourself for the psychological part. The first category determines whether you are an extrovert or an introvert. The second tells you whether you prefer to sense or intuit information. The third deals with decision-making: thinking or feeling. And the fourth, our approach to actions: judging and perceiving. Ultimately, you end up with a four-letter acronym like ENFP, or ISFJ, which describes your personality type.

J: How do you prefer to, if you like, recharge your batteries at the end of a tiring day?

M: Well, most of the time, I prefer to go home and be quiet and read or slow down ... put my children to bed and so on.

J: Typically, when we ask people this sort of question. Typically, introverts are more likely to talk about spending quiet time, time on their own, reading, etc. Extroverts are more likely to talk about spending time with people. ... I don't know if you ever had the opportunity to put together any ready-to-assemble furniture or anything like that. How did you go about doing it?

M: Well, you know, I'd lose the screws, and then the directions would be underneath the box, and then I'd lose another part of it, and it would take quite a long time and be quite an infuriating process.

J: OK. Typically when we ask that question, people with a preference for sensing will like to follow the instructions. People who have a preference for intuition, it's not that they disregard instructions, but they're a little bit more of a guide ...
If you imagine perhaps a friend of yours gives you a call, and says "I've just been robbed." What would you, what would your reaction be, what would you do?

M: Do you know, it's so difficult, because I think it depends on the person, you know ...

J: In some ... matter ... to me it's a matter of what you do first because both people with a preference for thinking, (and both people with a preference for feeling) ... will do both things. They'll do the practical things. "Have you called the police?" "Is the person still there?" "Have you, you know, called the insurance?", etc., etc. And they'll then go on to, "And how are you?"

M: Well, in that instance I would definitely fall into the thinking category, I think.

J: How do you go about doing the grocery shopping?

M: Uh, I, I'm in love with online food ordering, um so I do that, and then all the things that I've forgotten, 'cause I don't do it with any great system, I spend the rest of the week running out and picking up things.

J: OK. Typically, people with a preference for judging will be quite organized about those sorts of things. People with a preference for perceiving may also make lists, but those lists have a more aspirational quality.

M: Random feel, let's say?

J: Yeah, they are things that they might buy or they might not buy. If they see something more interesting when they get to the supermarket, they'll get that instead.

M: At the end of my conversation with John, I got my personality type, which I'll tell you about later.

Unit 1 Recording S1.7

M = Man   W1 = Woman 1
W2 = Woman 2

M: So, er, looking at this photo of the girl in the blue apron ...
W1: Yeah.
M: I'd say she's around thirty years old.
W1: Yeah. She looks nice, actually.
W2: I imagine maybe mid-thirties.
M: Oh, really?
W2: Or something like that, yeah.
W1: If I had to make a guess, I'd say actually thirty-two.

M: I wouldn't say that old.
W1: There's something about her, isn't there?
W2: Yes.
M: She looks friendly.
W2: Well, there's something in her eyes, actually, that makes me think she's about to laugh or something.
M: Have you noticed her apron's got some sort of white marks on it, kind of uh. ...
W1: Yeah, she's obviously been baking bread, right?
M: Yes.
W1: She looks quite serene, though.
W2: She does, yeah. She's — she — she looks like you'd get along with her.
W1: Yes, I suppose you would, yeah.
W2: Yeah.
M: What about where she's working? What would you say?
W1: Well ...
W2: That's bread, isn't it? Oh, is it? Is it bread? I think it's ...
M: Wasn't — is it cheese in the background?
W1: Don't think ...
W2: I think that's bread.
M: OK.
W2: It could be a bakery, you know, as there's like bread and stuff in the background.
W1: Yeah, she's got a bit of flour down there as well.
W2: Oh, yeah. Yeah, she must have been ...
W1: So ...
M: One of those fancy delis, don't you think?
W1: Probably. Should we go to the next — yeah, picture?
M: Yes, let's have a look.
W1: Have you got — the — this lady, the older lady, yeah?
W2: The older lady, yeah.
M: Oh, yeah, yeah, I've got her.
W1: Yeah, there she is.
W2: What do we think about her?
W1: Oh, she looks very dignified, doesn't she?
M: Definitely.
W1: Um ...
M: She looks, I would say, she looks intellectual, maybe that's because of her age, but ...
W2: Yeah.
W1: Yeah.
M: Something about her face that just makes me think she's seen a lot.
W2: Yeah, she gives the impression of being very intellectual.
M: Yeah.
W2: I might guess she's a professor at a college or ...
M: Yeah.
W2: Um, something really brainy like that.
W1: It seems to me she's very pretty as well.
W2: She is, yeah.
W1: She could have been a model or something like that.
W2: Oh, you think?
W1: Yeah.
M: The outfit's quite sort of snazzy, isn't it? You know. She could have been something like that in a — in her heyday.
W1: She looks — well she's done her makeup nicely, hasn't she?
M: And that — that necklace might suggest that she has got something to do with fashion.

W1: Yeah. Yeah.
M: Let's look at the next one.
W1: Yeah, what's the …
M: Ah, right.
W2: This young guy.
M: He looks happy.
W2: He looks pretty cool, actually.
M: Big smile.
W2: Yeah.
W1: Nice bright T-shirt.
M: Uh, I wonder what his job is.
W1: I'm pretty sure he's a creative type of some sort.
W2: I'd guess it's something to do with computers because he's, you know, he's surrounded by them, so maybe graphic design, something cool.
M: There's something about him that says sort of creative, doesn't it? You know, with the — with the bags around.
W1: Yeah, uh, what do you think about all those bags in the background?
W2: Oh, yeah. I hadn't noticed those.
W1: I wonder what those are for.
M: They might suggest that he designs the bags perhaps. I don't know.
W1: Yeah, maybe. Maybe he's like a creative type or something, or marketing or something that involves computers, like you said.
M: What's that in the window, right through the back? It looks like a lot of bikes, is it?
W2: It makes me think he's in a gym, which is really strange, isn't it? 'Cause he doesn't look …
W1: Yeah, a gym.
M: Maybe he's the receptionist at a gym. No.
W1: I'm pretty sure …
W2: What, with bags out everywhere and computers?
M: OK, no.
W1: Yeah.
W2: I don't know though.
W1: I'm pretty sure he's a lot of fun though. He looks like he's fun, doesn't he?
M: What about — how old would you put him?
W1: Oh, um …
W2: I'd guess he's about twenty-something. Or, do you think he's older?
M: Oh, definitely older. Yeah, I'd guess he's about forty-ish.
W1: No way. Really?
W2: Do you think so?
W1: I like his hair. I think it's really cool.
M: Yeah, he just looks kind of happy.

Unit 1 Recording S1.8

1 I'll be there soon. I just have a couple of things to do.
2 Why don't we meet at about eight-ish?
3 I left a lot of stuff at the hotel, but I can pick it up later.
4 Don't worry. We've got plenty of time.
5 We've sort of finished the accounts.
6 There'll be about forty or so people attending.

Unit 1 Recording S1.10

My treasured possession is a very old carpet that has been in my family for four generations. My great grandfather was a salesman. He sold carpets in Calcutta. During the 1950s he went bankrupt and went to South Africa to find his fortune. Legend has it that he took nothing but the clothes he was wearing and this carpet. I'm not sure that this is true, but that's the story. Anyway, he made his fortune in South Africa, and the carpet remained in the family. When he died, my grandmother inherited it, and instead of putting it on the floor of her house in Durban, she hung it on the wall. Even as a young child I remember it. It's brightly colored: reds, white, green and gold, with these beautiful patterns that look like leaves, and I just remember it hanging on the wall of the dining room and always wondering why a carpet was on the wall. Anyway, eventually it was bequeathed to me, and um, it's now on my wall. It's a little bit old and frayed now. I suppose I should repair it. Some of the weaving is falling apart, but it still looks OK. When I die, my children will have it, and then their children, so it will always be in the family.

Unit 2 Recording S2.1

1

He would've
He'd've
He'd've helped her.

2

wouldn't
wouldn't've
This conference wouldn't've happened.

3

We would've
We'd've
We'd've seen the sunrise.

4

I would've
I'd've
I'd've come sooner.

Unit 2 Recording S2.2

P = Presenter   A = Alex   S = Sarah

P: Now, you might think of a library as a dusty old place full of books that nobody uses anymore. But in a "living library", the books are real people. People who can share a significant personal experience or a particular perspective on life. Today we've got two people here to tell us about their "living book" experiences. Alex Fuller, who was a book at his living library event in Orlando, and Sarah Charles, who was a reader at an event in Atlanta. First of all Alex, hi …
A: Hello.
P: Alex, can you tell us a little bit about the experience? What kind of book were you? And what was it like?
A: Uh, yeah … Well, the event was organized by the college and was meant to tackle prejudices. I arrived in a bit of a hurry, and … uh … quickly checked through the catalogue to see what kind of "books" were available, and to, uh, sign myself in as "a student".
P: A student. OK. And what sort of prejudices were you expecting?
A: Yeah, well, uh, I wasn't sure what to expect really, but when you read the catalogue, against each "book" there are a few of the typical prejudices and preconceptions that people might associate with your "title". So, next to "student" people had written things like "lazy", "politically apathetic", "study useless degrees". And also "waste taxpayers' money", "can't cook" and "spends all his money on beer". Well, thinking back to the previous night, I wasn't sure how I was going to tackle any of those accusations.
P: I see. So what did you do?
A: Well, first we just had to go and sit in the waiting room. And I was beginning to have second thoughts, to be honest. I was quite uneasy about it all. But anyway, then the public started coming in. It was like sitting on a shelf, waiting and hoping that someone would choose you, and hoping that you would be able to find something to say when they did.
P: Uh, right. And presumably someone did choose you.
A: Yeah … an older man, with gray hair and a suit, came to collect me. And as we were walking over to our corner, I was planning my responses to the expected accusations. But, in fact, as we started talking over coffee, we compared our experiences — you know, student life in the 1960s, with its riots and protests, wild music, and all the ambitions they had of changing the world. And student life now.
P: OK … and what did you discover? Anything interesting?
A: Actually, we found that we shared a lot of the same ideologies, and that many things haven't really changed.
P: Ahh … that's interesting. So, do you think there was any point in the session? Did it change your opinions at all?
A: I think the directness of the experience was eye-opening really. It forces you to have a very candid discussion, so people have to keep an open mind about things, and that has to be good.
P: Thank you. And Sarah … how was your experience? Was it similar? Did you enjoy the "living book" experience?
S: Hi. Thank you. Yes, I really enjoyed the experience. Um, I went to a three-hour session in Atlanta, and I was really surprised at how much I learned. It gives you a chance to really talk to people who may be from a different religion, or culture — uh, people who you don't normally get to talk to in your everyday life.
P: Great. So, who did you talk to?
S: I met all kinds of people, some wonderful people. One of them was a lady named Carrie, a blind woman. Carrie is visually impaired, having lost her sight due to illness when she was a child. The first thing that struck me about Carrie is that she's fiercely independent. She doesn't like other people doing things for her, so you can imagine that can be a bit difficult.
P: Absolutely. So, what did you learn from Carrie?
S: OK, her mission was to tackle the stigma that people attach to blind people, that they're helpless. So, she wants to challenge the stereotype that just because a person can't see, they can't do anything for themselves.
P: And, how does she do that?
S: Well, uh, Carrie lives a perfectly normal life, uh, she goes to work, goes out socially — and does all the things that the rest of us do. Well, she

can't drive, but that was really one of her few limitations. She told me about other successful blind people around the world who have had a great impact on society — uh, people who've been successfully employed, or studied degrees, published books, even participated in Olympic events. These are the people that have been Carrie's inspiration.

P: That's wonderful. Tell me, did you ask Carrie about her other senses? You know, people often say that people who are blind use their other senses because these are quite well developed.

S: That's right. Carrie feels that she's quite a good judge of character, because she's able to "see" people for who they really are, on the inside, rather than just how they want to present themselves, or how you may judge them because of the clothes they're wearing. As she put it, she's able to "see with her heart" rather than her eyes.

P: OK … how interesting. So, did the conversation change your views on disability?

S: Yes, it did, definitely. My conversation with Carrie gave me a whole new perspective. It taught me not to be narrow-minded about disability, and I thank her for that.

Unit 2 Recording S2.4

M1 = Man 1   M2 = Man 2
W1 = Woman 1   W2 = Woman 2

M1: As far as I'm concerned, we cannot trust the news we read these days.

W1: Mmm.

M2: Why not?

M1: Because journalists have an axe to grind.

M2: What? That's debatable.

M1: I think it's very rare to get a truly impartial journalist. I don't think it's within human nature to be impartial. You side on one side or the other.

M2: Why, why would a journalist want to be partial? Why would a journalist not want to be impartial? Surely that's the job of a journalist.

W2: Oooh, I don't know about that.

M1: It, it is … why?

W2: No, I, I'm agreeing with you. I'm just saying I think there are some journalists who cannot be trusted. They have an agenda … they, they aren't there to tell the truth, they're there to sell newspapers … or they have an axe to grind.

M1: Yeah, it's a job, they're being paid, and, uh, effectively they're the mouthpiece for whoever is paying them.

M2: But isn't the job of a journalist to be, to be rigorous? I mean, if somebody comes up with a piece of nonsense, or just whatever, er, you know a piece of received information that they're spouting, isn't the job of a journalist to get to the bottom of that and say "What do you really mean by that, have you got proof of it, who, you know, what are your sources?" That's their job, right?

W1: Exactly. You know they're going in there asking "Where's the evidence for what you're saying?" They're not just going to say, you know — "Oh, you tell me every sheep in Wales is blue" and they're not going to go, "Oh, right. I'll just write down every sheep in Wales is blue." They're going to say, "Okay, well, show

me photographs, take me and show me these sheep."

M1: But, but the bigger issue here, if you ask me, is that they're there to sell newspapers and newspaper owners have political agendas.

W2: Quite frankly, it's a business as well, right?

M1: It's a political business.

M2: From what I can gather about the nature of … of the dispassionate idea of being a journalist, what a journalist is after is the truth. If that journalist then goes to work for a particular paper that's got a particular angle … a particular axe to grind, then certainly that journalist may err towards one side of the political spectrum or the other. But only a bit, I would say. I would say they are still after truth at its heart.

W1: Exactly. Surely any journalist worth his or her salt is going to make the case for both sides. Anybody just arguing one side in a totally biased way is not going to be taken seriously.

M1: Why? Why are there so many libel trials then if we can trust everything journalists write?

W2: Um, from what I can gather, people and journalists included don't even know that they're biased, and they'll write, you know, something trying to be impartial and they, they won't realize that they actually have a slant on it. You can't help it.

W1: I find that highly unlikely. I mean, they're not stupid people, are they?

M1: Some of them are, for some newspapers, the way they write, incredibly stupid.

W2: But I'm sure the people being libeled are just people who didn't like what was said about them?

M2: Could we … do you think we could agree that the basic honesty of journalists is probably not to be questioned, but that there are a few bad apples in the cart?

W2: Yeah.

M2: And that there are journalists who give other, you know, who are bad journalists, who are partisan and who are arguing a particular political slant who give other journalists a bad name.

M1: Well, I'd say that there are a few bad carts rather than a few bad apples!

Unit 2 Recording S2.5

1

A: Journalists have an axe to grind.

B: What? That's debatable.

2

A: Why would a journalist not want to be impartial?

B: Oooh … I don't know about that.

3

A: Journalists don't even know that they're biased.

B: I find that highly unlikely.

Unit 2 Recording S2.6

1 I really don't know about that.

2 I'm really not sure about that.

3 That's highly debatable.

4 I find that highly unlikely.

Unit 2 Recording S2.7

C = Chairperson   Q = Questioner
S = Speaker

S: OK, I'm going to talk about the influence of nature versus nurture. And I'd like to begin by stating that, as I see it, by far the strongest influence has to be "nurture". The reason I think this is that I believe the way we're brought up will have a much stronger influence on how we behave than anything that's in our genes. I mean, some people will argue that our abilities are determined pretty much exclusively by our genes, so if your father was a great scientist with a natural ability for mathematics, then there's a pretty good chance that you might inherit that same ability. Personally, I think it's ridiculous to suggest this. I think that when a parent has a particular strength, or interest, or achieves something wonderful in a particular field, then the chances are that when they have children, they will try to instill in the children the same kind of interest. They will pass on their knowledge, their passion for the subject. They are quite likely to engage the child in activities related to that field, perhaps for quite a lot of the child's time. And it's as a result of this that the child may also develop strengths or abilities in the same field. I absolutely reject the idea that nature endows us with these inborn abilities. I mean, you can be born with the best natural musical ability in the universe, but if you don't practice the piano, then nothing will come of it. On the other hand, I think you can teach people to do just about anything so long as you dedicate time and give the child the right kind of encouragement or put them in the right situation. So, to conclude, I would have to argue that nurture plays a much stronger role in the development of who you are and the talents that you develop than nature does.

C: OK. Thank you. And now, let's open the discussion up and take questions from the floor. Does anyone have a question for one of the speakers?

Q: Yes, I'd like to ask a question to the last speaker. I think it is quite obvious, if you look around you, that people often very much resemble their parents in terms of their physical appearance and even their personalities. Why then do you not think that it is equally possible that a child will inherit its parents' ability or intelligence?

S: That's a good question because yes, we can see that we do inherit physical characteristics from our parents. However, the point I'm trying to make is that we cannot rely on something we are assumed to be born with. For me, the influence of nurture is far stronger. I believe that everyone has the same potential. They just need to be given the right conditions to nurture and develop that potential. Thank you for the question.

C: Thank you. Are there any other questions?

Unit 3 Recording S3.1

1 cave houses

2 fingerprint

3 cotton candy

4 movie set

5 long-tail boat

6 nine-year-old girl

Unit 3 Recording S3.2

M = Man   W = Woman

W: Where did this interest in homes come from? You obviously had your own, but then what?

M: Well, I trained as an architect and as a young man I traveled a lot, and my two interests eventually connected. But I had a real awakening when I traveled in Africa and parts of Asia. In Indonesia I saw these enormous tree houses built high in the sky, made with the wood from banyan trees, and it just took my breath away, these houses fifty feet in the air.

W: Why did they build them so high?

M: Well, it's a refuge from wild animals and mosquitoes, and also, in their culture, they believe in evil spirits, and these spirits are earthbound. So, it's really for protection. You're safe if you're higher up.

W: And you've also written about houses on stilts in your book.

M: Yes. All along the Amazon Rainforest you can find fishermen living in these houses built on wooden stilts. I was fortunate enough to stay in a fishing community there for a month and see first-hand how it works, and it's pretty interesting …

W: And on the other side of the world, igloos, too.

M: I stayed in an igloo in Greenland for three weeks.

W: And you survived to tell the tale.

M: I did. Actually, they're far more comfortable than they look. They're pretty cozy inside. The packed ice and snow acts as an insulator.

W: So if we take the average sort of Westernized home — maybe bricks and cement, a bit of wood — how do they compare to so-called primitive dwellings without toilets and running water, that kind of thing? Is there any comparison?

M: Well, we have to understand what we mean by primitive housing. The original home was a cave, and when we talk about a caveman we think of someone extremely primitive, with no culture. But the funny thing is that caves are pretty good places to live. They're cool in the summer and warm in the winter, they give superb protection in that they'll never blow over in the wind, and in fact they're well made for decoration.

W: In what sense?

M: Well, the so-called primitive caveman made paintings on the walls which survived thousands of years. And y'know, um, any place you find caves, whether it's France, Spain, the United States, uh, China, people have lived in them and decorated them and adorned them with figurines and artwork. But we have to recognize that these houses are built in accordance with the habitat and the surroundings. Y'know, igloos keep out the cold and snow; tree houses provide safety. Then there are yurts, which are portable houses made of a wooden frame and animal skins — you can carry them around with you. Well, a yurt is built so that the nomads in Central Asia can move as the season and the weather changes. So you see, houses can be beautiful but in most cultures they're built to be purely functional, above all.

Unit 3 Recording S3.4

environment environmental
regenerate regeneration
drama dramatic
clarify clarification
object objective

Unit 3 Recording S3.5

Just to give you a bit of background information, Harrogate council has announced the creation of cycle hubs as, uh, part of its cycling strategy for the next five years. Now, the aim of this project is to set up cycle hubs. What are hubs? Hubs are areas where innovative ideas for cycling can be piloted and where resources can be targeted to, uh, increase cycling. So, what we plan to do is, uh, to introduce these new hubs in downtown of Harrogate, located in areas with a high concentration of cyclists. Uh, this solution will help us create, um, a safer environment for the cyclist. Cycling is an incredibly efficient mode of transportation. It's fast, it's environmentally friendly, and, uh, it's cheap — with of course the added bonus of keeping you fit. So basically, what we're proposing to do is to get everybody around the table to discuss the merits and demerits of, uh, whether or not the idea of a cycling hub in downtown Harrogate is a good or a bad idea basically. So, um, does anyone have any questions?

Unit 3 Recording S3.6

W1 = Woman 1   W2 = Woman 2

W1: Uh, Canada has one of the highest standards of living in the world and, you know, long life expectancy … um and it's one of the world's wealthiest nations, so it's really quite a nice — nice place to live. Um, and on the downside, I suppose there's um — in a lot of areas you have to deal with bad winter weather, so um, not — not in all places but in a lot of places we get a lot of snow and um, really cold temperatures in the winter, um, and that can be quite difficult to deal with, although you do get used to it.

I would describe Canada as, uh, geographically massive. Um, I think it's kind of difficult to explain how — just how big the country is. It's the second largest country in the world apart from Russia, or next to Russia, um, and yeah, so it's just really, really, really big and very, very diverse.

Every province is different, um, and, you know, to visit Canada you really have to go far and go for a long time to — to really appreciate the the vastness of the country. Um, what um, if I was making a documentary I'd probably focus on things like, you know, we're very, very lucky in Canada to have a huge range of fresh water, um, great lakes, rivers everywhere, literally. Um, we have three coasts: the Pacific coast, the Atlantic and the Arctic, and we actually have the longest coastline in the world. So you get incredible um, diversity, um, everything from wildlife to bird life, um, and also diversity in climate so, you know, we have temperate rain forests and we have deserts, we have, um, arctic uh, prairies, we have volcanoes, mountains, um, you know, almost half of Canada is covered in forests.

Uh, some similarities um, between the United States and Canada, um, that I can think of is that um, we both have a strong history and a long standing history of aboriginal peoples, um, and we share the longest border in the world.

W2: Well, undoubtedly one of the best things about Argentina is um, the values, um, people and, and their values, how they view life and they — we tend to attribute quite a lot of um, um, sort of value to our, our family. We care a lot about our families and and our gatherings, and we kind of gather on Sundays and we have a big barbecue, and everybody comes and we all talk about our weeks and what we've been up to and it's a good chance to catch up. Um, we also care a great deal about our friends, um, we celebrate Friend's Day, which is a big celebration and we have a lot of fun, and we give each other cards and thank each other for our friendship. Um, so I think that's kind of the best thing about Argentina: people are very warm, very caring, and there's a — we've got a great sense of solidarity.

Um, I guess if you — a lot of people think that Latin America is just Latin America and that all the countries are the same and, you know, like Brazil and Argentina are the same thing, but we're very different um, with our — we we've got like I, I guess if you could put it in into words, Brazilians are very upbeat and very happy, and Argentinians we're … we've got a sense of longing for, for the old world, and this, uh, melancholic view of the of the world and so we … the outlooks are very different, and hence the culture is, is very different.

An interesting way of seeing Argentina would be um, if you were to film a documentary, it would be through following one person like through a day or through a couple of days because then you start getting a sense for all the things that, um, go on in the country, and like, you know, for instance when I used to teach there, it was like I used to start my day not knowing what my day would be about because there's always a strike, there's always a picket line, there's always all these difficulties you have to overcome through, throughout a day, and … but at the same time you can see how resourceful people are when dealing with difficulties and how, um, relaxed and laid back they are about them, in a way. So it's, it's an interesting way of living. Um, it's a constant struggle but at the same time keeping your smile.

Unit 4 Recording S4.3

1 civil liberties
2 human rights
3 free trade
4 freedom of speech
5 religious freedom
6 illegal immigration
7 intellectual property
8 gun control
9 environmental awareness
10 capital punishment
11 economic development
12 child labor

Unit 4 Recording S4.4

1

I really admire Malala Yousafzai. Her story is astonishing. She was a BBC blogger at the age of eleven, and in that role she revealed the state of schooling for girls in Pakistan. Basically, girls were being prevented from getting an education, and she campaigned against this and shed light on what was going on in the country. And, of course, this got her into all sorts of trouble with the Taliban, and a few years later she was shot point blank in an assassination attempt. Miraculously, she survived, but for me the amazing thing is that instead of being scared she continued to advocate for children's rights. I think she spoke to the United Nations and various presidents. And, of course, people with that kind of courage and determination are one in a million, and so a few years ago she was awarded the Nobel Peace Prize. She was the youngest person ever to win it, at just seventeen years old.

2

Rigoberta Menchu is my hero, without a doubt. She's an extraordinary woman and someone I really look up to. She's an indigenous woman from a poor background in Guatemala, and she's fought for human rights all her life. Several members of her family were murdered when Rigoberta was still young, and she was exiled to Mexico for her own protection. But the interesting thing is, this didn't deter her at all. She just carried on campaigning against the human rights violations and the atrocities perpetrated by the military. So obviously she's a very, very brave person. But I think what kind of propelled her into the world's consciousness was the book she published about her life, called I, Rigoberta Menchu. This kind of alerted people to the wider struggles and made her a household name, a beacon for justice, certainly in the world of human rights advocacy. And she's such a humble person – she's a stellar figure in Guatemala, but you wouldn't know it from her manner and her appearance and the way she carries herself.

3

Someone I admire is Cornel West, an American intellectual. He speaks out about all kinds of issues, like civil rights, particularly for African Americans and for the poor. What stands out is his charisma and that he's an amazing, electrifying speaker. You can see him on YouTube or acting in two of the Matrix films. He's kind of like a crazy preacher, but really funny and sharp, and, OK, he has a PhD from Princeton, but he has a really good grasp of pop culture, and when he speaks he uses all these academic references but also references to TV and rap music. Also, he's completely fearless. He criticized President Bush but also President Obama, and I think he was arrested at one point for civil disobedience in New York. He's just a tower of strength and eloquence.

Unit 4 Recording S4.5

M = Man   W = Woman

M: So did you see that thing on the news about that uh, seventy-year-old grandmother who um, who stopped the jewel thieves?
W: Oh, the the one yeah, who knocked one of them off their bike, off their motorcycle?
M: Yeah.
W: That was amazing.
M: Wasn't it extraordinary? And they were robbing this jewelry store and smashing the windows.
W: Yeah, yeah, yeah, and she just came up and completely …
M: And nobody was doing anything about it.
W: … hit them straight over the head with her great, massive handbag.
M: With her shopping bag.
W: Shopping bag or something.
M: Full of, I don't know, beans or something.
W: Cans of beans, yeah!
M: But, I mean, would you do that, in that situation?
W: Oh I, I, if it was up to me, I think I would probably be too cowardly and I'd end up just calling the police, I have to admit.
M: I know, it's interesting, isn't it? I mean, you know, if, if I ever found myself in that situation, I would like to think that I would be, you know, an ordinary hero as well, but come, you know, push come to shove, whether or not you actually do it or not is another question, isn't it?
W: Yeah, yeah, I mean.
M: I mean the fact is that it's dangerous.
W: How many … were there six of them she took on?
M: Something like that, yeah.
W: That really is …
M: And she knocked one of them off their motorcycle, and then … and it was only then that all the other passers-by came and, you know, landed on him, yeah.
W: Oh yeah, jumped on the bandwagon, yes.
M: But she'd done, done the whole thing.
W: No, you have to … I completely take my my hat off … hat off to her for that because that is truly heroic to just charge in there, but no way would I do that. I just can't see my, uh, yes I, I own up to cowardice. I would be calling someone.
M: Well, a friend of mine said that he thought it was absolutely, you know, completely stupid, totally wrong thing to do. I said no, I thought that if more people, you know, were like that, you'd have a better society.
W: Yeah. The thing is, as you said before, I don't know, I think it has to be one of those instantaneous reactions. You either don't think about the consequences, and you, you jump in and you, you do what you can, or it's, I mean, as soon as you hesitate I think you're lost really.
M: Yeah.
W: And uh …
M: I think to be absolutely honest, if it was up to me, in the same situation, I'd probably run away.
W: Really? Yes, well I, I think I'd probably do my part by calling the police.

Unit 4 Recording S4.7

M = Man   W = Woman

M: So what do you think? How were they caught?
W: Well, it's usually some detail in the artwork, right? Like the forger uses the wrong kind of paint or the canvas is made of the wrong type of material or something like that. It's usually human error, right?
M: I think so. And in this case it was human error, but not quite what you're saying.
W: Could it be something to do with the family? I mean it's quite unusual to have a whole family involved. I think art forgers are usually lone wolves, aren't they? Maybe it was the elderly parents. Maybe they let something slip. Or perhaps they said something that gave the game away somehow.
M: Nope. Good guess, though. The mistake was made by the forger, Shaun. And it wasn't a painting. It was an Assyrian relief, kind of like a flat sculpture, from six hundred BCE.
W: Six hundred BCE? Oh, so maybe he used the wrong type of stone or plaster. Or could it be that the design didn't match up to designs from six hundred BCE? Maybe it was too modern?
M: You're on the right track. The relief included horses and the horses' reins. The ones in the forgery were apparently "inconsistent with other reliefs of that period". But also – you'll like this – there was a spelling mistake on the inscription!
W: No way!
M: This mistake was "considered very unlikely on a piece that was supposedly made for a king". And then George panicked …
W: George is the father, who sold the art, right?
M: Yes. George panicked and said he'd sell the piece for a very low price.
W: Aha. So it's connected to the elderly parents, too.
M: Yeah, it all seemed too suspicious, so the police got involved and eighteen months later they arrested the whole family.
W: Wow. That's some story.
M: Yeah, but the interesting thing is that the family didn't seem to do it for the money. They lived in a small, messy house, and Shaun made all his forgeries in the garden shed. Anyway, in the end, Shaun was sentenced to four years in jail, and the family had to pay back $500,000. The parents were spared prison sentences because of their age.

Unit 5 Recording S5.1

J = Jenni Murray   A = Ailish Kavanagh
E = Eva Rice   G = Girl   W1 = Woman 1
W2 = Woman 2

J: Now, if I'd ever told anybody how much my dad earned, he'd have been absolutely furious. I'm not sure that I ever really knew. We were raised in an atmosphere where families kept to themselves and you told nobody your business. And then it all changed as we became more knowledgeable about the kind of dangerous secrets that might be held behind closed doors, and the damage they could do. We were encouraged as a society to tell these tales and let it all hang out. So, can we still keep a secret?

G: One of my friends told me to keep a secret about how she was going out with this other girl's boyfriend. And I kind of went up to the girl and told her by accident. It just fell out. She got really, really annoyed and it was – oh, it was horrible. It was like I thought she was actually going to slap me. It was so bad. Oh, my god. We made up like two hours later, but it was just the initial, you know, … I should never have told her secret though. So, it was my fault.

A: Have you ever given away anyone's secret by accident?

W1: Probably, just Christmas presents. Maybe, accidentally telling someone what their Christmas present was. My husband nearly did that yesterday, actually. He took an afternoon off work to go and uh, go and get something for my … for Christmas for me. He wouldn't tell me for days where he was going, and almost let it slip where he was. I, really, really wish he had given it away.

A: What's the hardest secret that you've ever had to keep?

W2: I revealed a secret of a, of a romance that I had with an older man … that I revealed to my husband because I decided that I had to tell him … uh, so that … because I couldn't live with this secret. If I had to live in honesty with my husband, I had to reveal to him this secret and face the consequences. And, as you can see, this is the consequence – we've grown closer together as a result of that.

A: So the consequences were quite good then, it seems?

W2: They were. Here he is, still at my side, and I'm at his side. So that was a very big secret that I kept, but I did reveal it.

J: Ailish Kavanagh talking to people in Croydon. So when do you spill the beans and be honest, and when is it better to stay mum? Eva Rice is the author of a novel called *The Lost Art of Keeping Secrets*. Do you really think we have lost the art of keeping a secret?

E: I, I certainly do. I think that nowadays everyone's so encouraged to say everything at all times, and express the way they feel, um, at the drop of a hat. And, I think that the point of my book was to get across the fact that sometimes keeping a secret isn't always a bad thing. It can be something that, um … can bring a more positive outcome than always, always telling everyone how you feel.

J: So, what kind of secret would you keep?

E: I think, in, well, like the characters in my book, if you're keeping a secret that is, in some way, going to protect somebody from something. Obviously, I don't want to give away too much of the plot. But if you're protecting somebody in a way that isn't going to damage them when they do ultimately find out, um, I think that in that case a secret is a very good thing to keep. But nowadays, it's something that is frowned upon, and something that is considered wrong. And you're supposed to tell everyone the way you feel twenty-four hours a day, and so it's something that you shouldn't do is keep a secret.

Unit 5 Recording S5.6

M = Man   MA = Mark   W = Woman

W: What do you think about organizations like WikiLeaks?

M: Well, to be honest, I think they should be stopped. And the reason why I say that is because they are responsible for leaking all kinds of confidential information, some of which is highly sensitive information about people who work in government, or military strategy, and they release this kind of information in a way which is, which is quite honestly … completely reckless. They seem to have no regard for the ethics of what they're doing, and um, I think they should be stopped. They've exposed people who they say are informants, and now the lives of those people and their families are now in danger.

W: Hold on a minute. Can you be sure about that? Is there any evidence to prove that?

M: Well, no, probably not, not absolute proof. But, that's not the point. The only way to prove it'll be if something terrible happens to those people as a result of the information that has been disclosed. The, the point is that governments and, you know, certain organizations simply have to be able to keep some information private. It doesn't make sense for everybody to have access to all the information that they want. Let me put it this way. It's like saying you need to give everybody your bank details, because we all have the right to know, but you don't. You don't have the right, and it's simply ridiculous to think that you do. If you think about it, it's just irresponsible, and it's dangerous.

W: I don't see how you can say that. Don't you think that there are cases when it's right for the public to know what's happening? Mark, where do you stand on this?

MA: Well, yeah, absolutely. I agree. It's not something I've thought much about before, but in fact, I think that WikiLeaks is one of the best things to happen in the last few years. It's opened up access to information, and it means that big companies, and governments will need to be much more careful about how they deal with things in the future because they can no longer hide behind secrets. And, that's how it should be. After all, if you think about it, you can't give people the protection to do whatever they want without fear of being discovered. Whether it's companies using spies to find out what rival companies are planning, or governments holding people illegally, or using illegal practices to get information. I think freedom of information can only be a good thing, and it's like a wake-up call to all those who previously thought that they could get away with wrongdoing by just keeping it quiet. That just doesn't work anymore.

M: But, that doesn't take into account the fact that some information, like um, military information, is highly sensitive, and shouldn't be allowed to spread around the internet where simply anybody can get hold of it and use it for whatever purposes they wish.

MA: I think you'll find that actually information has always been leaked. It's just the medium that has changed now, so that with the internet it's that bit easier, but there've always been whistle-blowers, and there will continue to be.

It's no different. The point I'm trying to make is that if the chances of you being discovered are increased, the likelihood of you being exposed, then it'll make you think twice about the actions you're taking, whether you're in government or in a big corporation. I think you'll find that people will be more careful in the future, and in my opinion, that can only be a good thing.

Unit 5 Recording S5.8

OK, so I'm going to tell you about some secret places to go in my city. Well, I live in Edinburgh and the first place I'm going to talk about is … I think the Japanese Kyoto Friendship Gardens. If you look around the grounds of the Lauriston Castle in Cramond, which is a lovely castle, then secluded away you'll find the Japanese gardens. Uh, they were opened to celebrate the twinning of Edinburgh with Kyoto, and they are just a wonderful place to sit and relax, look at the blossom on the trees, and enjoy the serenity of the place. It's very, you know, very Zen … and you would never believe it's there. Next, this is a place you could easily walk past, unless you knew about it. Most people have never heard about it. It's number two Wellington Place, in Leith. It's just a normal-looking Edinburgh door. There's no plaque outside or anything like that. But, the Scottish author Irvine Welsh wrote his debut novel, *Trainspotting*, in the top-floor apartment of this house. So, that's a secret I always point out to people when we walk past. Insider information. Um … next I think I should tell you about the rooftop terrace on top of the National Museum of Scotland. It's not what you'd call a big secret, but this place is really hidden away and can seem quite difficult to get to. But, it's so worth it when you get there because you can get these fantastic views of the city and the castle. It's amazing, especially on a clear day. And, there's a really nice café up there, too.

Unit 6 Recording S6.2

S = Stephen Fry   D = David Crystal

S: Professor David Crystal says that the migratory patterns of our language as it continues to move across the globe, gives us a whole range of Englishes, and that process is becoming ever more intense.

D: So, just as once upon a time there was British English and American English, and then there came Australian English and South African English, and then Indian English and then Caribbean English. Now, it's down to the level of Nigerian English, Ghanaian English, Singaporean English, and so on. And, these are the new Englishes of the world. What happens is this: that when a country adopts English as its language, it then immediately adapts it to suit its own circumstances. I mean, why have a language? You have to express what you want to say which is your culture, your people, your identity. And when you think of everything that makes up an identity — all the plants and animals that you have, the food and drink, the myths, the legends, the history of your culture, the politics of it, the folk tales, the music, everything has to be talked about in language. And that means your local language, local words to do with the way you are and different from the way everybody else is. And so the result has been, as English has been taken up by, well over seventy countries in the world as an important medium of their local communication. But, they have developed their own local brand of English.

S: How many people spoke the language we are now conversing in say 600 years ago?

D: Ahh, well, certainly we know around about 1500, 1600, there were four million speakers of English in England.

S: And, now in the early part of the twenty-first century, how many … ?

D: Well, if you distinguish between, first language speakers and foreign language speakers, there's about 400 million or so first language speakers, English as a mother tongue — or father tongue, depending on your point of view — around the world, and about five times as many who speak English as a second or a foreign language, so we're talking about two billion people, you know, a third of the world's population, really. The important point to notice is that for every one native speaker of English, there are now four or five non-native speakers of English, so the center of gravity of the language has shifted, with interesting consequences.

Unit 6 Recording S6.4

Speaker 1

It's a trend that started in the States and spread certainly in Europe. And, it's when guys wear their jeans halfway down their hips so you can see their underwear. Apparently, it all started in the prison system in the States. What happened was that prisoners aren't allowed to wear belts 'cause these can be used as a weapon. And the prison uniforms were often too big for the inmates. So you'd have a little guy wearing a huge baggy pair of prison-issue trousers, and so the prisoners ended up with these trousers halfway down their legs. So, the trend has its roots in the prison system, but somehow it spread beyond those walls, so rappers like Ice T started wearing their trousers like this, and it led to widespread adoption of the style. It's known in some parts as a kind of gangster look because, obviously, it originated in prison, but actually it's pretty common now among young people, so basically, it's crossed over into the mainstream. And, I guess this is how fashions start and spread 'cause they kind of come from nowhere, out of the blue, and then early adopters, I think they're called, help to make them fashionable and suddenly you've got a trend.

Speaker 2

As a TV producer, I've obviously looked at the trend of reality TV. It all started to take off in the nineties with the emergence of programs like Big Brother and Pop Idol. But, actually, I'd say it originated from earlier programs, stuff that was done in the seventies and eighties. I think the popularity of these shows has caused a big shift in how programs are made. Production values are quite low, and the emphasis is now on making something cheap and quick. Because of this, TV companies make bigger profits, and it's this that resulted in these shows spreading around the world. So,

what I'm really saying is we'll keep making these programs now until the, um, the public tires of them. And it's because of the public's taste for knowing about real people and real lives.

Unit 6 Recording S6.5

1 People now expect to download music for free, and CD sales are at their lowest ebb. Basically, the music industry has had to completely change its business model.

2 We saw some great presentations at the conference. The hotel was wonderful and we loved the food! So, overall, it was really worth it.

3 Bloggers take news from reporters and write comments. They don't do much reporting. So, what I'm really saying is that without real reporters, there's no news.

4 Sales of the game soared in May, jumped again in July, and rose dramatically in December. To sum it up, we've had an incredible year.

5 The report says young people believe in openness. They like sharing their private lives online. In conclusion, young people don't value their privacy as much as older generations do.

6 We had developed a great product, so logically it should have been a success. However, we had technical problems. Then a competitor stole the idea. All in all, it was a complete disaster.

Unit 6 Recording S6.7

M = Man   W = Woman

M: So, the gadget is called Midomo, and it's a type of water carrier on wheels, but it also works as a filter. According to the description here, it was invented because in some parts of Africa, people need to walk several miles to fetch water. And, also, of course, contaminated water accounts for so many illnesses and deaths in sub-Saharan Africa.

W: So, it's like a container for water, but it also cleans the water?

M: Yeah, it's a bit like a wheelbarrow. You collect the water in this container, and then while you're walking, as the wheels turn, the filter system starts working to clean the water.

W: So, it solves two problems at once. It could save millions of lives because it filters dirty water, and it also makes it easier to transport the water.

M: It's an amazing invention. And I think one of the biggest benefits is that it's relatively cheap.

W: Oh, OK. What kind of prices are we talking about?

M: It'll go on the market for around about a hundred and twenty dollars. I guess the question is whether to fund it or not. Can we see any drawbacks?

W: I can't really see any negatives. You'd have to ask how durable it is. Is it likely to break? What materials is it made from? How easy is it to manufacture and export? But, overall, it seems like a great investment.

M: Yeah, not just for financial reasons, but also it's going to save lives.

W: And, is it a big company that's making it available?

M: No. It's a start-up called Red Button Design. They're based in the U.K.

W: OK. My initial reaction is that it's worth investing in this, but obviously we'd need more details about the product.

M: I agree. I think it has a lot of potential.

Unit 7 Recording S7.2

1 OK, run around the field one more time, then you can have a breather.

2 Just go to the party and let your hair down.

3 She's going to take time out from work to finish her PhD dissertation.

4 I went traveling in order to take my mind off the tragedy.

5 It's hard to switch off on weekends.

6 If I've been working a sixteen-hour shift, I usually go to the bar to unwind.

Unit 7 Recording S7.3

Speaker 1

The way I switch off is by going hiking. We have excellent trails near where I live in Canada, where you can walk for a couple of hours. Some days when I'm out there I literally don't see another person. For me, it's a good way to take time out from my routine. The actual hiking's challenging because we're at high altitude and going up hills and across some rocky terrain, but that's fine because it means you're so focused on the walk you can't think about anything else. The only dangerous moment was about a year ago when I saw a mountain lion on the trail about twenty yards away. It stopped, looked up at me, had a little sniff, and decided it didn't want me for dinner.

Speaker 2

If I want to unwind, I play the piano. I don't think anyone would confuse me with Beethoven — I'm really not very good — but I just find it relaxing. It's like doodling or something. You just let your fingers wander and go with the flow. I play all kinds of music, even some of my own compositions, which, as I say, are nothing special. My friends say my stuff sounds like elevator music — the kind of thing you hear in the elevator of a sleepy hotel. I think they're probably right.

Speaker 3

Any team sports do it for me. I can be having the most stressful day, but then I meet up with my friends for a game of football or Ultimate Frisbee and all my problems melt away, at least temporarily. I think it's that idea of just running around in the open air, getting sweaty. Maybe it's a remnant of childhood or something, when you had nothing to worry about, so you just ran around all day. It works for me.

Unit 7 Recording S7.4

M = Man   W = Woman

M: Did you read that article recently about, um, uh, I can't remember her name, a New York journalist who …

W: Oh, the one about the nine-year-old child?

M: Yeah, who left her son, uh, in central New York and left him to come back on his own, to make his own way back at the age of nine.

W: Amazing!

M: Amazing?

W: Yes!

M: Oh, come on! You must be joking.

W: I'm absolutely serious.

M: Well, in what way amazing? I mean he could have gotten lost, he could have been attacked, he could have been mugged, he could have …

W: That's absolutely right, and we have …

M: What, and that's good?

W: Look, we have to, as parents, now take a stand against all this coddling nonsense. I was allowed to do a lot at a very young age, and it helped me make the right decisions about how to protect myself and learn to be streetwise. These kids don't know anything these days.

M: Well, I agree with you up to a point, but I mean, you can't think that a nine-year-old should be left alone to kind of grow up in the course of two hours.

W: I'm sure you don't think that he should never make his own way home then and never learn?

M: Of course not, but not at the age of nine!

W: Right, well that goes against my better judgement because I actually think it's, it's more responsible as a parent to show them by chucking them in at the deep end.

M: Right. So it's, you think it's more responsible to abandon your child, you can't really think that?

W: She didn't abandon the child.

M: Well, effectively she did.

W: The, you know he lives in New York, and anyway …

M: What, so who, well that's one of the most dangerous places in the world!

W: How can you say that? There are far worse places in the world. It's all relative.

M: Of course it's all relative, but if you look at the muggings and the crime rate in New York, it's horrendous, and a nine-year-old wouldn't have a clue how to deal with all of that. It's, it just doesn't make sense to me.

W: It wasn't, from what I know, at two o'clock in the morning so, you know, you have to take it with a grain of salt a bit.

M: Right.

W: Right, so …

M: Because all crime happens at two o'clock in the morning?

W: I'm sure you don't think then that it's terribly dangerous to leave a child in a, in a city in the middle of the morning, that they know and they're not four …

M: I do at the age of nine. He didn't even have a cell phone!

W: He's probably a nine-year-old that's really got a lot going on, you know. That's the whole point, I think, to take the child as an individual.

M: I understand the wanting the empowerment. I just think we're in a hurry to, to push our kids to grow, grow up too soon …

W: Oh, come on!

M: … these days, I don't understand it.

W: Oh, please!

M: What's the hurry?

W: You know everybody feels that, if everybody feels like that, we're never going to get anybody that stands up for themselves.

M: Oh, that's ridiculous! We're talking about a nine-year-old!

W: Well, that's absolutely right.

Unit 7 Recording S7.6

M = Man   W = Woman

W: I think there are two ways to look at it. Freedom, to me, means letting your hair down and being able to relax completely.

M: Right. I know what you mean.

W: But, we should also bear in mind political freedoms.

M: Well, exactly. That's what I was going to say. When I think of freedom, I immediately think of its opposite, of persecution and all the oppression going on around the world.

W: So, the lack of freedom …

M: Not only lack of freedom but actual oppression, people being denied human rights, such as the right to vote.

W: To be part of a functioning democracy.

M: Also, freedom to worship, freedom of religion.

W: And, maybe you could add to that the freedom to access information without it being blocked or censored. This seems to have been in the news a lot lately.

M: That's right. The issue of governments trying to control what the population can and can't see or hear or read. I think people would be horrified if they knew just how widespread censorship is, and how much their freedoms are being eroded. And, I'm not only talking about developing countries. It's in many developed countries, too.

W: While we're on the subject of censorship, do you think freedom of speech is still a big problem?

M: Yes. In general, I'd say that one of the biggest issues is the freedom to express yourself, so it's freedom of speech and freedom to wear what you like. As I see it, those are all essential freedoms.

W: And, perhaps the biggest issue of all in recent years, bearing in mind the various refugee crises, is freedom to travel. Open borders.

M: Yes, definitely. There must be … what … hundreds of thousands of people trying to escape their countries because of poverty or persecution, to make better lives for their families, and these people are labelled "illegal" because perhaps they don't have the right documents. But the question is: who has the right to stop other people from seeking a better life elsewhere? If your country has been half-destroyed by war or sanctions, who wouldn't want to leave to give their kids a better future? For me, the freedom to travel is a basic human right.

Unit 8 Recording S8.2

G = Geoff Watts   M1 = Man 1   M2 = Man 2
C = Claudia Hammond   S = Simon Chu
L = Louise   J = John Aggleton

G: Hello. We're looking back quite a bit in this week's program, back to childhood for a start. Now, ever had that feeling of being suddenly carried back in time by a particular odor? You probably have because it's a common experience. The smell of coal does it for me, and even stronger mint sauce. One whiff of that, and it's back to Sunday lunch in the house where I was born. There is, it seems, something special about smells when it comes to evoking memories. Now, as Claudia Hammond reports, psychologists think they may be getting to the root of it.

M1: The smell that always really takes me back in time is the smell of disinfectant, and kind of cedary wood. And, for some bizarre reason it reminds me of being at school when I was about seven.

M2: Whenever I smell privet, walk past a hedge or something, it takes me instantly back to my kindergarten, to the rather smelly passage through from the garden to the school restaurant, where we had our lunches. It takes me straight back there.

C: For some reason, the memories evoked by smells seem to be stronger than memories that come back to you, say, from looking at a photo. In the field of psychology, they call it the Proust phenomenon, after the famous incident with the madeleines in *Remembrance of Things Past*. One of the people studying the Proust effect is Doctor Simon Chu, a lecturer in psychology at Liverpool University. The link between smell and memory has hardly been touched by researchers, because until recently, it's been very difficult to prove in the lab. Using familiar smells, like vinegar and talcum powder, Simon Chu tries to trigger autobiographical memories. So, what have you got here? You've got about eight little plastic boxes.

S: Here we've got things like raw mixed herbs, we've got, um, some cigarette ash, some vinegar, ketchup, got some paint. What I'm going to do is I'm going to give you a word, and I'm going to ask you to tell me as much as you can about a particular experience that the word reminds you of.

C: First, he gives his volunteer Louise a word, like "cigarette". And she has to come up with an event from her past linked to the word. Once she's remembered everything she can, he lets her sniff the real thing from one of his special boxes.

S: I'd like you to sniff gently at this and tell me anything else you can remember about that particular experience.

L: Oooh, um, stale cigarette smoke … that's a horrible smell. I can still smell it from here. I just remember … just the smell of it and the fact that it, you can still smell it on yourself ages later. And, then when you go home, you suddenly realize that your parents are probably going to be able to smell it on you as well. And, then you get that fear inside you that they're going to know that you were smoking, and you know there were mints, and the perfume and that kind of thing — desperately trying to cover up the smell, so that your parents don't know what you've been up to.

C: Confronted by the actual smell of cigarettes, Louise remembers far more about the event than she did when she was simply given the word "cigarette". In particular, she remembered the fear that her parents would find out she'd been having a sneaky cigarette. It seems that smell is very good at bringing back the emotional details like this.

S: There is something quite unusual and special about the relationship between smells and memory.

J: For me, the most evocative smell is that smell you get when candles have just been snuffed out. And it takes me back to my childhood when I was a singer in a church choir, in a village in Berkshire. And, towards the end of the service, one of the servers used to come out and extinguish the big candles up by the altar. And, if I just smell that smell, of candles being snuffed out, I'm instantly back at that time, and the memories are of the music of my boyhood, the church music of the time.

G: Odors that prompt the memories of times past.

Unit 8 Recording S8.4

Conversation 1
A: You coming to the party?
B: Yes, I think so.

Conversation 2
A: Did you just delete the file?
B: Hope not.

Conversation 3
A: Want to try this perfume?
B: No, but I'll try that one.

Conversation 4
A: You think we'll have enough time to discuss this later?
B: We'll have a little.

Conversation 5
A: You going away on vacation this year?
B: No. Ann Marie doesn't have enough money, and neither do I.

Conversation 6
A: You sure you've got enough copies for everyone?
B: Yes, lots.

Unit 8 Recording S8.5

S = Stephanie   J = John

S: John, you're a time management consultant. What exactly do you do?
J: Hello, Stephanie. I advise individuals and companies on how to maximize their time. It involves looking at the processes they use to accomplish tasks, looking at how deadlines are set and met, and examining people's working habits to see if there are any shortcuts or more efficient ways to do things.
S: Right, OK. So, what type of companies do you work with?
J: All kinds, really. Everything from very traditional manufacturing firms to internet start-ups. Every company wastes time at some point and every company wants to save time. Having said that, I'd say some companies are more efficient than others.

S: Can you go into more detail? So, let's say I want to restructure my day to get more work done. How would you approach it?
J: Well, the first thing I do is observe your routine. What's your normal day like?
S: Sure.
J: As a journalist, you probably have deadlines.
S: Definitely.
J: You're probably under pressure. But, looking at it another way, you may have a lot of freedom about where and how you work and what time of day. You don't have the constraints of, say, the traditional office worker.
S: I never thought of that. But, yes, it's true.
J: So, you need to work quickly, but on the other hand, you probably have great resources: people who can help you, contacts, archives. And, these are the tools you use to accomplish the task.
S: Right.
J: OK, so then we'd look at your typical day, starting from the moment you sit down at your desk. What's the first thing you do? Probably, if you're like everybody else, you check your emails. Maybe you read the news, go on a couple of social media sites, and respond to a few messages. But, I'm looking at how long this takes you and how much time is spent off-task. I'm also looking at what you're looking at. Do you have a calendar? Do you use to-do lists, prioritized tasks that you need to finish at certain times of the day? Some people have lists next to their lists. They write down the names of contacts and other information that they use in order to achieve the task.
S: That's a good idea. Can you think of anything else you might look at?
J: How much media is around you? By which I really mean, how many distractions are there? If you have text messaging, Facebook, the TV, the phone, the cell phone, all within reach, then what are your chances of working uninterrupted for more than ten minutes?
S: I know what you mean. Alternatively, those might be the sources of my information.
J: Yes and no. You need them, but at some point you have to work without them if you're going to write something original.
S: Right. So, you obviously go into a lot of detail looking at what people do every day. Any other suggestions for how I might save time?
J: Loads! One other thing you can do is …

Unit 8 Recording S8.7

When I was about eleven or twelve, and everybody uh, from elementary school was moving up to middle school, my parents gave me the option to go to a specialized performing arts school or a regular school. And um, it was very important, 'cause I remember them sitting me down and showing me brochures of everything, and there was no pressure either way. And, at that young age, I made the decision to go to a performing arts school. And, luckily for me, I, I, it's panned out, and I've had a career in that, um, that line of work. But, I then found myself faced with another decision, because we were moving, and, uh, we had to leave school, and did we want to continue with performing arts school or did we want to go to a normal school? And, at that point, I was about fourteen, and I decided that I want to get an education and

leave the theatrical world at that point, still very, very young to make those decisions. And, I did, I left and went to a regular school and got a, uh, you know, high school degree behind me and everything, and my sister didn't she carried on at the performing arts school, and she went straight into work, very early, and was really successful. I've always wondered if perhaps I should have chosen the other option, 'cause it was a longer road for me, and I'm still very much on it. And, um, and I suppose that the next major decision, the final decision was whether to have children or not or take this huge job that was offered to me, and I chose my children, in that case. So, I'm very grateful I've got two wonderful boys, um, and I've still got my career but I just, um, kind of wonder what would have happened if …

UNIT 9 Recording S9.2

Speaker 1

People always ask me that, and it's a very difficult question to answer. One thing is that it's no good just sitting around waiting for an idea to come. If I'm stuck for an idea, I have to switch off and do something else for a while. Doing the dishes is pretty good, doing something mundane, that you don't have to think too hard about. So, I like to invite lots of people over for dinner, so that in the morning there are lots of plates to wash, and that gets me thinking. When you free the mind, it helps spark creative connections. So, you're doing the dishes, or taking a shower, and suddenly an idea might come to you. You actually have to take your mind off the writing, off the task in hand. And, that's when you think of something creative. It's funny how our brains work. Sometimes, I'll go out into the garden, or go for a run to clear my head. When I get back to my desk, the ideas flow a lot more easily.

Speaker 2

Inspiration? Goodness. Inspiration is everywhere, I guess. I'm inspired by people. The people around me, by people who achieve great things, or live through terrible hardships. The world around us is full of stories, and people doing things differently. And, when you work in advertising, you're always looking for something new. A new way of conveying your message. Ahh … nature. Nature is another great inspiration. Going somewhere beautiful is a really good way to get new ideas. Or playing an outdoor sport. Sometimes, I'll go skiing or snowboarding, and there's something about it, the fresh air and the outdoors, perhaps it's the sky and the mountains. I don't know. But, while I'm there, I'll have lots of ideas for things I can do when I get back to work.

Speaker 3

Um, books mainly, old recipe books … like Margaret Costa, a classic. I'll look through old recipes and then try to recreate the same idea but with a modern, more contemporary twist. Yes, old tomes. Larousse is another one, with plenty of ideas, or sometimes I'll go to the Michelin guides, you know the restaurants with stars — they have books, so I look there, too. Unfortunately, I rarely eat out myself, so I don't get ideas that way, but books are a great inspiration. And, there's something about having big, heavy books in the kitchen that have been with you a long time. They inherit your personality a little, and hold in them so many memories of enjoyable meals.

Speaker 4

This is going to sound a bit odd, but something that has really inspired me in life has been the people who didn't believe in me. You know, I wasn't the smartest kid in school. In fact, I left school as soon as I could. But at school, there was this one teacher, who I'd never really gotten along with. And, he told me I that I would never get anywhere, that I would never achieve anything really worthwhile. And, I remember thinking, through the loathing, that I would prove him wrong. I felt this huge sense of determination. Um, and I've carried that with me, you know, at times when things aren't going well, and I'm not sure if I can make a success of something. I'll think about that. And, it really inspires me to put in that extra bit of effort to prove to myself that he was wrong. For an entrepreneur, that determination to succeed is really important.

Unit 9 Recording S9.3

1 some, coming, company
2 took, book, looking, good
3 on, novel, cottage
4 coin, toying
5 actor, original, ridiculous
6 shoot, to, whose, who
7 mouth, out
8 door, brainstorm
9 show, going

Unit 9 Recording S9.4

Speaker 1

If there's one thing I cannot stand it's getting off a car on the London subway and lots of people on the platform trying to get on the car before I have gotten off. Honestly, it drives me up a wall! Don't they understand that if I can't get off, then they can't get on, so they need to let me off. And, I have in the past actually raised my voice at tourists.

Speaker 2

The last time we went to Cornwall, we went to the lovely little town of Fowey, and I discovered what I could describe for me as paradise. It's a tearoom that somebody could describe in a book, and it still wouldn't be as good as, as the actual experience when you go in — beautifully decorated. It's got those little, um, cake plates with, piled up with the most beautiful sumptuous cupcakes. And, then in the back part, they've got a lovely Rayburn, and if you decided you wanted sardines on toast or scrambled egg or something, they'll just whip it up for you. Every single thing you could imagine on your dream menu. I could have sat there for a week and worked my way through the menu. It was the most wonderful, delicious and, and, the people were so friendly. And, they'd gone to such trouble to make this gorgeous place to eat. And, um, I'd definitely go back there again.

Speaker 3

The other night I saw the best show ever, it was a show called *Dirty Dancing*. It's on in the West End, absolutely fantastic. The acting was amazing, the dancing was amazing, the songs were terrific! I mean uniformly they were absolutely terrific. And, I don't know who played the mother, but she was especially good, honestly, really the best show ever, you must see it!

Speaker 4

I cannot recommend highly enough a trip to one of the beautiful islands of Thailand. I went there last year, and there is absolutely nothing better than finding yourself on a private beach with a cool drink in hand and having a dip in tropical warm waters. And, I saw one of the most spectacular sunsets I've ever seen. And, honestly, I couldn't believe my luck when I saw turtles in the water. I've always wanted to see turtles. It was idyllic.

Speaker 5

The worst meal I ever had was quite recently. It was absolutely horrendous. The restaurant was grossly overpriced. Honestly, it was a total waste of money. But, it's also, you know, minutes of my life that I won't get back. Um, the service was appalling, and the waiter just seemed like he'd rather be doing anything else. Clearly, it's hard to cook for a lot of people, I understand that, at the same time. But, you know, meals were coming out at all different times. We had appetizers arriving and then the main course and then nothing for about an hour. It was horrendous.

Speaker 6

I bought the "one-touch can opener", and it has changed my life, seriously, and I'm not even overstating how amazing it is. It's an all-time classic of products, you have to get one, and I couldn't believe my luck when it arrived in the mail, just for me, and it does exactly what it says it will. You touch it once, and you leave it alone. It's incredible! It's the most incredible thing. You don't have to, you can do something else if you want. It's one of the most spectacular life-changing products you can buy, because all of that mess and effort taken away um. So, if you're ever thinking about it, just do it. It's awesome, seriously, the best product.

Unit 9 Recording S9.7

OK, the person I want to nominate is not famous. He isn't a celebrity and has never been on TV. Um, he's one of those people who goes under the radar because he's so humble. I'm nominating him because he's made a huge difference to people's lives. His name is Tomasso Beltrini, though everyone calls him Tom, and he's 63 years old. Tom is a factory worker, but in his spare time for the last 30 years, he's worked tirelessly with immigrants and refugees who are new to Australia and helped them with the language and with forms and documents. He helps them find apartments and jobs, and he, um, provides moral support and sometimes even financial support. He's based in a small town near Perth, which has a high number of immigrants and refugees. So, uh, sometimes these are people who come to the country quite traumatized by their experiences back home. Maybe they're escaping war or persecution, and what they need is a new start in life and a friendly face and someone to pick them up and help them to integrate into society. Well, Tom's been doing that as a volunteer at our Refugee Center for three decades. He's an example to us all. He must have helped thousands of people, and he's done it with incredible dignity and kindness. Uh, I don't think we'll ever know how much good he's done, but I know this: he'd be a worthy winner of this award because no one deserves it more.

Unit 10 Recording S10.1

1 They set off on an epic journey
2 After 26 years on the road
3 A trial run of the trip in Africa
4 It was a valuable learning experience
5 Spend a couple of years touring the continent
6 After quitting his job
7 The couple headed straight for the Sahara desert
8 Traveling off the beaten path

Unit 10 Recording S10.2

1 My life would be considerably better if I had a normal job.
2 Being a celebrity is nothing as glamorous as it seems.
3 One good thing about fame is that it's far easier to book a table in a restaurant.
4 Even for a celebrity, it's every bit as difficult to enjoy life.

Unit 10 Recording S10.4

When I taught in New York City high schools for 30 years, no one but my students paid me a scrap of attention. In the world outside the school, I was invisible. Then, I wrote a book about my childhood and became mick of the moment. I hoped the book would explain family history to McCourt children and grandchildren. I hoped it might sell a few hundred copies and I might be invited to have discussions with book clubs. Instead, it jumped on the best-seller list and was translated into 30 languages, and I was dazzled. The book was my second act. In the world of books, I'm a late bloomer, a johnny-come-lately, new kid on the block. My first book, *Angela's Ashes*, was published in 1996 when I was 66, the second, *'Tis*, in 1999 when I was 69. At that age, it's a wonder I was able to lift the pen at all. New friends of mine (recently acquired because of my ascension to the best-seller lists) had published books in their twenties. Striplings. So, what took you so long? I was teaching. That's what took me so long. Not in college or university, where you have all the time in the world for writing and other diversions, but in four different New York City public high schools. (I have read novels about the lives of university professors where they seemed to be so busy with adultery and academic in-fighting you wonder where they found time to squeeze in a little teaching.) When you teach five high school classes a day, five days a week, you're not inclined to go home to clear your head and fashion deathless prose. After a day of five classes your head is filled with the clamor of the classroom.

I never expected *Angela's Ashes* to attract any attention, but when it hit the best-seller lists, I became a media darling. I had my picture taken hundreds of times. I was a geriatric novelty with an Irish accent. I was interviewed for dozens of publications. I met governors, mayors, actors. I met the first President Bush and his son, the governor of Texas. I met President Clinton and Hillary Rodham Clinton. I met Gregory Peck. I met the Pope and kissed his ring. Sarah, Duchess of York, interviewed me. She said I was her first Pulitzer Prize winner. I said she was my first duchess. She said, "Ooh," and asked the cameraman, Did you get that? Did you get that? I was nominated for a Grammy for the spoken word and nearly met Elton John. People looked at me in a different way. They said, "Oh, you wrote that book. This way, please, Mr. McCourt", or "Is there anything you'd like, anything?" A woman in a coffee shop squinted and said, "I seen you on TV. You must be important. Who are you? Could I have your autograph?" I was listened to. I was asked for my opinion on Ireland, conjunctivitis, drinking, teeth, education, religion, adolescent angst, William Butler Yeats, literature in general. What books are you reading this summer? What books have you read this year? Catholicism, writing, hunger. I spoke to gatherings of dentists, lawyers, ophthalmologists and, of course, teachers. I traveled the world being Irish, being a teacher, an authority on misery of all kinds, a beacon of hope to senior citizens everywhere who always wanted to tell their stories. They made a movie of *Angela's Ashes*. No matter what you write in America, there is always talk of The Movie. You could write the Manhattan telephone directory, and they'd say, "So, when is the movie?"

Unit 10 Recording S10.5

S = Serena   D = David

S: So, David, tell us a little more about negotiating. Is it all about the words you use?
D: Much of negotiating is in body language and gesture, but it's also vital that you use the right words.
S: OK, so I'm at the beginning of some kind of negotiation. How do I start? What's my opening gambit?
D: The first thing you want to do is name your objectives.
S: OK.
D: So, you can use a phrase such as "We want to sort this out as soon as possible". This makes it clear what you want from the discussion. Another thing you need to do is explore positions.
S: What does that mean exactly? Can you give an example?

D: It means asking questions like "Can you tell me more about this?" "What do you have in mind?" Exploring positions is all about asking what the other guy wants and then really listening.
S: I see. So, we're trying to establish common goals.
D: Yeah, then you need to make an offer.
S: And, this is where the real negotiating starts.
D: Exactly, and the "if" word becomes so important because your offer is going to be conditional on certain terms being met, concessions and compromises being made. So, you might say, "If you do this for me, I'll do this for you." "What if we gave you access to this?" "What if we supported your idea?"
S: I see. So, it seems in negotiating, the word "if" is the biggest word in the language.
D: That's right.
S: What about negotiating meaning? Like checking that you understand the conditions on offer?
D: Essential. Negotiations can be long and tiring, but you cannot switch off for a moment. If you missed something, don't bluff. Ask about it. Go over the points more than once. Be sure. Ask, "Do I have this right?", "Are you saying this or that?"
S: OK. And what about the endgame? Let's say the haggling is over. It's decision time and you need to refuse or accept the deal.
D: Well, refusing is always delicate. You really don't want to close off all further discussion, so you need to be tactful. You never just say no. Instead, you give reasons and explanations. You might say, "That's more than I can offer". "That would be difficult for me because of my situation". "I'm not sure I can do that because I promised something else".
S: In other words, you refuse without saying no.
D: Yeah. It's at this stage you might want to stall for time, or defer the decision, or if you're in business, consult a more senior colleague. The next stage is when you've reached agreement. You say something like, "Good. That sounds acceptable to me." Or "Great. We've got a deal." But that's not it.
S: It isn't over?
D: You need to follow up the deal. Be polite and civil. Say something like, "We can talk about it again and review the situation in a few months." If it's a more formal deal, we can say "Let me know if you have any questions." The thing is to follow up the deal. Always keep the conversation open.

Unit 10 Recording S10.7

I guess my dream job would have to be a filmmaker. Making short films, well, making full-length films, too — that would be wonderful. The kind of films I'm interested in are those realistic animation films. What appeals to me is that it's wonderfully creative. There's so much you can do. You can do anything. I'd relish having the opportunity to work in an environment like that. I'm fairly qualified in that, well I'm doing a degree in time-based art and digital film at college so we do a lot of work on film, image, sound and performance. I've made a series of short films, using various different techniques, so I've got a bit of experience behind me. And, I'd like to think I'm a fairly creative individual. I have lots of ideas about how to do things, and I'm not afraid to try out new ideas, to experiment. I'd say I've got quite a good eye for things that are going to work, like an instinct. I can sense if something is working or not visually, or if we need to change it. I think it's essential to be open-minded and forward-thinking. There are a lot of people now doing fantastically creative things, and making movies, so it's quite hard to be able to stand out from the crowd. So, you need good business sense too, to make sure your movie is successful. It's not just about having the ideas. You need to be a good organizer, so you can manage a project. And, you have to be flexible. As for moving towards getting my dream job, as I said, I'm still studying at the moment, but I try to do as much creative work as I can in my spare time. I'm also getting some work experience with an advertising company, looking at how we can use short films in advertising. I'm hoping that this experience will help me to find a job when I graduate.

Catalogue Publication Data

Authors: Antonia Clare, JJ Wilson
American Speakout Advanced Student Book with DVD-ROM and MP3 Audio CD
First published
Pearson Educación de México, S.A. de C.V., 2017
ISBN: 978-607-32-4064-2
American Speakout Advanced Student Book with DVD-ROM and MP3 Audio CD & MEL Access Code
ISBN MEL: 978-607-32-4029-1
Area: ELT
Format: 21 x 29.7 cm   Page count: 184

Managing Director: Sergio Fonseca ■ **Innovation & Learning Delivery Director:** Alan David Palau ■ **Regional Content Manager - English:** Andrew Starling ■ **Publisher:** A. Leticia Alvarez ■ **Content Support:** Canda Machado ■ **Editorial Services Manager:** Asbel Ramírez ■ **Art and Design Coordinator:** Juan Manuel Santamaria ■ **Design Process Supervisor:** Aristeo Redondo ■ **Layout:** Lourdes Madrigal ■ **Cover Design:** Ana Elena García ■ **Photo Research:** Beatriz Monsiváis ■ **Photo Credits:** Pearson Asset Library (PAL)

Contact: soporte@pearson.com
This adaptation is published by arrangement with Pearson Education Limited

Pearson Education Limited
Edinburgh Gate
Harlow
Essex CM20 2JE
England
and Associated Companies throughout the world.

First published, 2017

ISBN PRINT BOOK: 978-607-32-4064-2
ISBN PRINT BOOK MEL: 978-607-32-4029-1

Impreso en México. *Printed in Mexico.*

1 2 3 4 5 6 7 8 9 0 - 20 19 18 17

Esta obra se terminó de imprimir en marzo de 2018, en Editorial Impresora Apolo, S.A. de C.V., Centeno 150-6, Col. Granjas Esmeralda, C.P. 09810, México, Ciudad de México.

D.R. © 2017 por Pearson Educación de México, S.A. de C.V.
Avenida Antonio Dovalí Jaime #70
Torre B, Piso 6, Colonia Zedec Ed. Plaza Santa Fe
Delegación Álvaro Obregón, México, Ciudad de México, C. P. 01210

www.PearsonELT.com

Pearson Hispanoamérica
Argentina ■ Belice ■ Bolivia ■ Chile ■ Colombia ■ Costa Rica ■ Cuba ■ República Dominicana ■ Ecuador ■ El Salvador ■ Guatemala ■ Honduras ■ México ■ Nicaragua ■ Panamá ■ Paraguay ■ Perú ■ Uruguay ■ Venezuela

Acknowledgments

The Publisher and authors would like to thank the following people and institutions for their feedback and comments during the development of the material: **Brazil:** Vanessa Munford; **Czech Republic:** Matthew Smith; **Poland:** Konrad Dejko; **Portugal:** David Petrie; **Turkey:** John Thompson; **UK:** Sally Fryer, John Barron, David Byrne.

We are grateful to the following for permission to reproduce copyright material:

Book Covers

Book Covers 10.2 from Angela's Ashes, Tis and Teacher Man by Frank McCourt, copyright © 2005, 2006, Harper Perennial. Reprinted by permission of HarperCollins Publishers Ltd.

Figures

Figure 6.2 from 'Top Ten Languages in the Internet 2010', www.internetworldstats.com, Internet World Stats, copyright © 2000-2015, Miniwatts Marketing Group.

Tables

Table 6.2 from 'Growth in Internet (2000-2010)', www. internetworldstats.com, Internet World Stats, copyright © 2000-2015, Miniwatts Marketing Group.

Text

Extract 1.1 adapted from 'First Name Terms' by Giles Morris, The Guardian, 24/09/2007, copyright © Guardian News & Media Ltd 2007; Extract 1.2 from 'How MyersBriggs Conquered the Office' BBC Radio 4, and Extract 1.3 from 'Getting the Picture: The camera has attitudes' by Tim Marlowe interviewing David Bailey, May 2014, copyright © The BBC; Extract 2.1 from 'The 101 best pieces of advice ever received' by Olivia Parker, Anna Tyzack and Celia Walden, The Telegraph, 29/12/2012, copyright © Telegraph Media Group Limited; Extracts 3.1 from 'Postcards: Where You've Been and What You've Seen' by Alistair McDonald, Anthony McEvoy and Greg Jackson, Lonely Planet Magazine, Issue 15, pp.11-18, March 2010. Reproduced with kind permission of the authors; Extract 3.1 from 'Rediscover Lisbon: Let them Eat Cake' by Matt Bolton, Lonely Planet, Issue 19, p.94, July 2010, copyright © The BBC; Extract 3.1 adapted from 'Introducing Lisbon', Lonely Planet, Reproduced with permission from the Lonely Planet website www. lonelyplanet. com, copyright © 2015 Lonely Planet; Extract 3.3 adapted from 'Welcome to The Perfect City' by Frank Swain, BBC Focus, Issue 210, pp.70-75, Dec 2009, copyright © Frank Swain. Reproduced with kind permission; Extract 5.1 adapted from 'When and how should you reveal a secret?' BBC Radio 4, 23/11/2005, copyright © The BBC; Extract 5.2 adapted from 'Myths Buster' by Jo Carlowe, Jo Minihanel and Caroline Green, BBC Focus Magazine, Issue 213, pp.34-39, March 2010, copyright © Immediate Media Company Bristol Ltd; Extract 6.1 adapted from 'Timeline of the Far Future', 6 January 2014 and Extract 6.2 from 'Fry's English Delight', Series 3, episode 4: Future Conditional, CD2 Track 10: Predictions, September 2010, copyright © The BBC; Extract 7.1 from 'get me out of here!' BBC Focus magazine, Issue 211, p.54, January 2010, copyright © Immediate Media Company

Bristol Ltd; Extract 8.2 from 'Leading Edge', BBC Radio 4, 2003, copyright © The BBC; Extract 9.2 from 'How to Find the Next Big Idea' by Steven Johnson, Psychologies Magazine, p.104, December 2010, copyright © Kelsey Publishing Ltd; Extract in Language Bank, unit 9 adapted from 'The £40 Art Collection', 2010, www.ed.ac.uk. Reproduced with permission of the Talbot Rice Gallery, The University of Edinburgh; Extract 10.1 adapted from 'Gunther, Christine and Otto: How a man met a woman and they set off on an epic journey across six continents in one amazing unbreakable car', copyright © The BBC; and Extract 10.2 from Teacher Man: A Memoir by Frank McCourt, pp.3-4, 2005, copyright © 2005 Frank McCourt. Reprinted by permission of HarperCollins Publishers Ltd and The Friedrich Agency.

Media credits

The publisher would like to thank the following for their kind permission to reproduce their media:

Audio

BBC Worldwide Learning: BBC R4 Leading Edge, BBC R4 program, BBC R4 Womans Hour, BBC series 3, ep.4: Future Conditional

2005 Frank McCourt and Green Peril Corp. By permission of HarperCollins Publishers Ltd: Teacher Man, Harpercollins (Frank McCourt)

All other media © Pearson Education

Illustration acknowledgements: Fred Blunt 18, 22, 51, 57, 148, 149, 151, 152, 154, 157; In house 13; Mark Willey 119.

Photo acknowledgements

The Publisher would like to thank the following for their kind permission to reproduce their photographs:

(Key: b-bottom; c-centre; l-left; r-right; t-top)

123RF.com: Andrei Shumskiy 7b (icon), 11t, 19b (icon), Andres Rodriguez 26r, 31br (icon), 43b (icon), 55b (icon), Tom Wang 56t; 67b (icon), 79b (icon), forsterfoto 84, Rido 94 (n), Karin Lau 95, 103b (Icon), Foodandmore 111c, 115b (icon), **Alamy Images:** De pictz 7cl, National Geographic Image Collection 7bl, 8, Moodboard 19r, Dmitriy Shironosov 19cl, Dmitriy Shironosov 23, Moodboard 28-29, Alex Segre 39tl, Peter Kneffel 43r, Robert Harding Picture Library Ltd 47r, WENN Ltd 48l; Peter Kneffel 52, Ryan McGinnis 67cl, Ryan McGinnis 71tl, Peter Noyce FRA 71tr, PYMCA 75r, James Copeland 76b, BestPix 85, FourT4 91l, Steve Cavalier / Alamy 91l, Steve Cavalier / Alamy 93t, Phil Talbot 94 (f), VintageCorner 94 (h), Simon Turner 103l, 104t, Alan Gallery 104b, Nic Hamilton Photographic 104c, Blue Jean Images 115t, Arctic Images 117t, Chris Rout 160tc, **Alistair McDonald:** 32; **Anthony McEvoy:** 31l, 33/C; **BBC Worldwide Ltd:** 16 (inset), 28 (inset), 31r, 40 (inset), 52 (inset), 64 (inset), 67r, 76 (inset), 88 (inset), 100 (inset), 112 (inset), 124 (inset); **Corbis:** Hulton-Deutsch Collection 19t, Stuart Freedman / In Pictures 77; Bettmann 93b, **Fotolia.com:** lapas77 7r, Debu55y 11b, lapas77 16-17, MegWallacePhoto 25t, Tilo Grellmann 31cr, Phil_Good 34, deserttrends 35l, Tilo

Grellmann 38, rabbit75_fot 40-41, Tamas Zsebok 55t; Monkey Business 59b, Mr Doomits 67cr (scooter), hperry 69r, Erin Cadigan 74bl, clivewa 74-75t, Mr Doomits 74cr, jool-yan 79r, jool-yan 88-89, digitalstock 91cr, Bookworm32 94 (b), cobaltstock 94 (m), cs333 94 (c), dmitryabaza 94 (j), J and S Photography 94 (a), Mario Savoia 94 (d), monticelllo 94 (i), Pioneer111 94 (k), razihusin 94 (g), stringerphoto 94 (e), arthurhidden 98, Vasakna 98-99, digitalstock 99tr, Jasminko Ibrakovic 99tl, Mirexon 99 (b), Maxim Pavlov 99 (a), clivewa 111cr, berc 115cr, berc 123tl, Aleš Nowák 150 (c), Celso Pupo 150 (d), MasterLu 150 (b), Razvan Stroie 150 (a), **Getty Images:** Nick Dolding 7cr, ByeByeTokyo 10t, David M Benett 12, Cultura / Nancy Honey 14, Nick Dolding 15r, Ray Tamarra 20tl, STR / Stringer 43cl, Marco Di Lauro / Stringer 47tl, STR / Stringer 47bl, amriphoto 55r, James Lauritz 55cr, George Marks 55l, George Marks 58, Sue Flood 60tr, James Lauritz 62, amriphoto 64-65, Arquiplay77 67cr, Andrea Pistolesi 67t, Anadolu Agency 70t, Spencer Platt 71tc, AFP 72, Arquiplay77 74-75, Cultura RM / Liam Norris 74l, All rights reserved by Oscar Wong 79cr (a), All rights reserved by Oscar Wong 87, moodboard 91cl, moodboard 97, Peter Cade 103cl, Peter Cade 107, Loop Images / Contributor 109, Ulf Andersen 115cl, Raquel Maria Carbonell Pagola 117r, Tuul 117b; Ulf Andersen 120tl, Hill Street Studios 122t, Tooga 158bl, Martin Poole 160t, Brian Doben 163tr, Chris Mellor 163bl, Craig Roberts 163tl, **Greg Jackson:** 33/B; **Mercedes/Gunther Holtorf:** 115l, 116-117; **PhotoDisc:** Geostock 79l, 80tl, Ryan McVay. Getty 79cl, Ryan McVay. Getty 83r; **Pearson Asset Library:** Andresr 13(t), CandyBox Images 22(t), Alsu 23(t), Alexander Raths 26(t), 123rf.com 27(t), James Steidl 29(t), Rob Judges. Pearson Education Ltd. 44(t), Mark Bassett. Pearson Education Ltd. 45(t), Ostill 56(t), michaeljung 59(t), Jörg Cartensen. Pearson Education Ltd 61(t), Jan Kranendonk 66(t), 123rf.com 70(t), SNEHIT 88(t), Khamidulin 95(t), 123rf.com 97(t), Sizov 98(t); **Plainpicture Ltd:** Cultura / Daniel Allan 15l, Johner 158br; **Rex Features:** Nick Harvey 19l, Shutterstock 20tr, Nick Harvey 21, Novastock / Stock Connection 36, Dan Callister 37, imageBROKER 39tr, Sipa Press 48c; Mark Large / Associated Newspaper 50tr, Rex Shutter stock 80br; **Shutterstock. com:** Sofarina79 7t, Amir Ridhwan 8(t), Rawpixel.com 10(t), vvoe 11(t), LanKS 11c, Amir Ridhwan 12(t), meatbull 14(t), Elzbieta Sekowska 15(t), Petr Jilek 16(t), Dja65 17(t), PT Images 19cr, Iakov Filimonov 20(t), Matej Kastelic 21(t), alphaspirit 22, baranq 24(t), bikeriderlondon 26tc, PT Images 26tl, racorn 29(t), javarman 31t, Marteric 31cl, My Good Images 32(t), Monkey Business Images 33(t), yvon52 34(t), bepsy 35(t), Marteric 35r, velvetweb 36(t), Pavel Svoboda Photography 36(t), Funny Solution Studio 38(t), Claudio Divizia 40(t), Mark52 41(t), Amble Design 43cr, ER_09 43t, Gunnar Pippel 43l, 44b, Bignai 47(t), Jstone 48r, Sergey Sukhorukov 49(t), andrey_l 50(t), Stephen VanHorn 50l; ckeyes888 51(t), Paolo Bona 52(t), Popova Valeriya 53(t), Nito 55cl, Ivan Mateev 57(t), Neirfy 58(t), Nito 59t, Jarno Gonzalez Zarraonandia 60l, Tupungato 60c, Gil C 62(t), Claudio Divizia 63(t), Ppictures 64(t), Shutterstock 67l, Phil McDonald 68(t), Palette7 68-69, Mark Herreid 69(t), ChameleonsEye 72(t), Gil C 73(t), Ryby 74t,